Language and Globalization

Series Editors: **Sue Wright**, University of Portsmouth, UK and **Helen Kelly-Holmes**, University of Limerick, Ireland.

In the context of current political and social developments, where the national group is not so clearly defined and delineated, the state language not so clearly dominant in every domain, and cross-border flows and transfers affect more than a small elite, new patterns of language use will develop. The series aims to provide a framework for reporting on and analysing the linguistic outcomes of globalization and localization.

Titles include:

David Block
MULTILINGUAL IDENTITIES IN A GLOBAL CITY
London Stories

Jenny Carl and Patrick Stevenson (*editors*)
LANGUAGE, DISCOURSE AND IDENTITY IN CENTRAL EUROPE
The German Language in a Multilingual Space

Diarmait Mac Giolla Chrióst
LANGUAGE AND THE CITY

Julian Edge (*editor*)
(RE)LOCATING TESOL IN AN AGE OF EMPIRE

Roxy Harris
NEW ETHNICITIES AND LANGUAGE USE

Clare Mar-Molinero and Patrick Stevenson (*editors*)
LANGUAGE IDEOLOGIES, POLICIES AND PRACTICES
Language and the Future of Europe

Clare Mar-Molinero and Miranda Stewart (*editors*)
GLOBALIZATION AND LANGUAGE IN THE SPANISH-SPEAKING WORLD
Macro and Micro Perspectives

Ulrike Hanna Meinhof and Dariusz Galasinski
THE LANGUAGE OF BELONGING

Leigh Oakes and Jane Warren
LANGUAGE, CITIZENSHIP AND IDENTITY IN QUEBEC

Colin Williams
LINGUISTIC MINORITIES IN DEMOCRATIC CONTEXT

Forthcoming titles:

John Edwards
LANGUAGE AND SOCIAL LIFE

Alexandra Galasinska and Michael Krzyzanowski (*editors*)
DISCOURSES OF TRANSFORMATION IN CENTRAL AND EASTERN EUROPE

Language and Globalization
Series Standing Order
ISBN 978–1–4039–9731–9 Hardback
978–1–4039–9732–6 Paperback
(*outside North America only*)

You can receive future titles in this series as they are published by placing a standing order. Please contact your bookseller or, in case of difficulty, write to us at the address below with your name and address, the title of the series and the ISBN quoted above.

Customer Services Department, Macmillan Distribution Ltd, Houndmills, Basingstoke, Hampshire RG21 6XS, England

Language, Discourse and Identity in Central Europe

The German Language in a Multilingual Space

Edited by

Jenny Carl and Patrick Stevenson
University of Southampton

palgrave
macmillan

First published 2009 by
PALGRAVE MACMILLAN

Palgrave Macmillan in the UK is an imprint of Macmillan Publishers Limited,
registered in England, company number 785998, of Houndmills, Basingstoke,
Hampshire RG21 6XS.

Palgrave Macmillan in the US is a division of St Martin's Press LLC,
175 Fifth Avenue, New York, NY 10010.

Palgrave Macmillan is the global academic imprint of the above companies
and has companies and representatives throughout the world.

Palgrave® and Macmillan® are registered trademarks in the United States,
the United Kingdom, Europe and other countries.

ISBN-13: 978–0–230–22435–3 hardback
ISBN-10: 0–230–22435–0 hardback

This book is printed on paper suitable for recycling and made from fully
managed and sustained forest sources. Logging, pulping and manufacturing
processes are expected to conform to the environmental regulations of the
country of origin.

A catalogue record for this book is available from the British Library.

A catalog record for this book is available from the Library of Congress.

10   9   8   7   6   5   4   3   2   1
18   17   16   15   14   13   12   11   10   09

Printed and bound in Great Britain by
CPI Antony Rowe, Chippenham and Eastbourne

Contents

List of Tables

List of Figures

Tamah Sherman is a postdoctoral researcher in the Department of General Linguistics at Charles University, Prague. Her research focuses on the numerous forms of contact between Czech and English in the Czech Republic after 1989. She is a member of the EU Network of Excellence LINEE, in which she leads the team of researchers dealing with communication in multinational companies in Central Europe. Together with Jiří Nekvapil, she is the co-editor of the volume *Language Management in Contact Situations: Perspectives from Three Continents* (forthcoming). Her publications include articles in *Osnabrücker Beiträge zur Sprachtheorie (OBST)* and *Current Issues in Language Planning*.

Patrick Stevenson is Professor of German and Linguistic Studies at the University of Southampton. His current research interests include the politics of language, multilingualism, language and migration, and language biographies. He has published widely in the field of German sociolinguistics and his recent book publications include: *Language and German Disunity: A Sociolinguistic History of East and West 1945–2000*, and the edited volumes *Language Ideologies, Policies and Practices: Language and the Future of Europe* (with Clare Mar-Molinero) and *Discourses on Language and Integration: Critical Perspectives on Language Testing Regimes in Europe* (with Gabrielle Hogan-Brun and Clare Mar-Molinero, 2009).

Jane Wilkinson is Lecturer in German at the University of Leeds. Her main research interest is in the cultural production of borderlands and she is currently working on a project entitled 'Cultural Encounters at Germany's Eastern Border'. She is also interested in the relationship between culture and locality more broadly and is author of *Performing the Local and the Global: The Theatre Festivals of Lake Constance* and of articles in *Language and Intercultural Communication, Tourism and Cultural Change, Third Text* and *Seminar*.

Péter Maitz is an Assistant Professor in the German Department of the University of Debrecen, Hungary. His research interests include sociolinguistic theory and methodology, bilingualism, language ideologies and the relationship between language and identity. His doctoral thesis was on language conflict, language choice and language use in the Hungarian part of the Habsburg Empire in the nineteenth century. He has recently held a research fellowship at the University of Augsburg and is currently working on a monograph on the unity and diversity of historical linguistics.

Jiří Nekvapil is an Associate Professor of Linguistics in the Department of General Linguistics at Charles University, Prague, where he teaches sociolinguistics, discourse analysis and general linguistics, and he has published extensively in these areas. His current research interests lie in issues of language interaction and focuses on Language Management Theory. He is a member of the EU Network of Excellence LINEE. His main recent publications include *Small and Large Slavic Languages in Contact* (co-edited with R. Marti) and *Media, Wars and Identities* (co-edited with B. Dupret and I. Leudar).

Klára Sándor is Professor of Linguistics at the University of Szeged. She is also a member of the Hungarian National Assembly. Her research interests include language change, conversation analysis, language and politics, gender studies and the sociology of language. She is currently working on research projects on communication in the twenty-first century and the cognitive embeddedness of linguistic value judgements. Her main recent publications include chapters in edited volumes on gender in Hungary, mobile communication and Hungarian as a minority language.

Britta Schneider is a research assistant in the Department of Linguistics at the University of Frankfurt, Germany. She is currently working on a binational dissertation at Frankfurt University and at Macquarie University Sydney, Australia, on national and historical discourses about language and transnational language ideologies in Salsa scenes. Her main research interests include language in transnational contexts, language ideology and the discursive construction of language. She is the author of *Linguistic Human Rights and Migrant Languages. A Comparative Analysis of Migrant Language Education in Great Britain and Germany*.

Kristine Horner is a Lecturer in German and Sociolinguistics in the School of Modern Languages and Cultures at the University of Leeds. Her research focuses on the interrelationship between language, identity and power and the construction of linguistic and social boundaries. She has written on language and national identity, linguistic purism and language-in-education ideologies in Luxembourg and is currently writing a monograph on language testing and the discourses of endangerment, integration and citizenship.

Sylvia Jaworska is a Language Studies Coordinator in German at Queen Mary College, University of London. Her main research interest is in the field of language policies, language planning and language teaching with special reference to German as a foreign language. She is also interested in discourse analysis and corpus linguistics, particularly in the investigation of discursive constructions of gender.

Michał Krzyżanowski is a Senior Research Fellow in the Department of Linguistics, Lancaster University and Assistant Professor in the School of English, Adam Mickiewicz University, Poznań. He has researched extensively on critical text and discourse analysis, approaches to media discourse, European studies, multilingualism and linguistic diversity. His recent book publications include *(Un)Doing Europe: Discourses and Practices of Negotiating the EU Constitution* (with F. Oberhuber), *Qualitative Discourse Analysis in the Social Sciences* (with R. Wodak), *The Politics of Exclusion: Debating Migration in Austria* (with R. Wodak), *Discourse and Transformation in Central and Eastern Europe* (with A. Galasińska) and *European Public Sphere and the Media: Europe in Crisis* (with A. Triandafyllidou and R. Wodak).

Grit Liebscher is an Associate Professor of German at the University of Waterloo in Canada, and she is a sociolinguist with a focus on interactional sociolinguistics and conversation analysis. Her research interests include language use among German-Canadians and language and migration in post-unification Germany. Major recent publications include several book chapters as well as articles in the *Modern Language Journal*, the *International Journal of Bilingualism*, the *Canadian Modern Language Review* and the *Zeitschrift für angewandte Linguistik*. She has also co-edited (with a team of scholars from the University of Waterloo) a book on Germans in the North American diaspora.

Notes on the Contributors

Jenny Carl completed her doctorate on representations of European identities in parliamentary discourses in Scotland, Wales and Northern Ireland at the University of Osnabrück, Germany. She is currently a postdoctoral researcher at the University of Southampton, working on German and Austrian foreign language policy and German language practices in Central Europe, and in the EU Network of Excellence LINEE (Languages in a Network of European Excellence). She is writing a monograph (with Patrick Stevenson) on *Language and Social Change in Central Europe: Discourses on Policy, Identity and the German Language*.

Kateřina Černá is a doctoral candidate in the Department of General Linguistics in the Faculty of Philosophy and Arts at the Charles University, Prague. Her research interests are in the field of discourse analysis, conversation analysis and bilingual education. Her dissertation involves dialogue dynamics and structure. Her most recent publication relates to school discourse and discursive practices in political interviews.

Thomas Cooper completed a dual-doctorate in Comparative Literature and Central Eurasian Studies at Indiana University and then taught Central European literature in the Department of Slavic Languages and Literatures at the University of North Carolina. He has held research fellowships at the University of Vienna and at Columbia University. Following a year's research at the Collegium Budapest Institute for Advanced Studies in Hungary he is currently teaching as Associate Professor at the Károly Eszterházy University.

Jennifer Dailey-O'Cain is an Associate Professor of German applied linguistics at the University of Alberta in Edmonton, Canada. Her research includes work in language, migration and identity in both Germany and German-speaking Canada and language attitudes in post-unification Germany. Major recent publications include several book chapters as well as articles in the *Modern Language Journal*, the *International Journal of Bilingualism*, the *Canadian Modern Language Review* and the *Zeitschrift für angewandte Linguistik*. Her forthcoming book, *First Language Use in Second and Foreign Language Learning*, co-edited with Miles Turnbull, will be published by Multilingual Matters.

Contemporary European Studies (UACES), which provided funding for the conference which enabled us to subsidize a number of participants who would otherwise not have been able to take part.

Jenny Carl and Patrick Stevenson
Southampton, September 2008

Acknowledgements

This volume was inspired by a conference with the same title that was held in July 2007 at the Centre for Transnational Studies, the University of Southampton. Most of the chapters are based on papers given at the conference, and all of them have benefited from the discussions at this event and subsequently from extensive dialogues between the authors and with the editors. As with all such undertakings, this has been a time-intensive but also a stimulating and rewarding experience, and we would like to take this opportunity to thank all the contributors for their enthusiastic cooperation and for their uncomplaining willingness to meet sometimes very tight deadlines. At the same time, we would like to thank those participants in the conference whose work is not directly represented here for their own contributions in terms of discussion and debate.

For invaluable assistance with the preparation of the conference we are indebted to Nicky Robbins, and we also owe our thanks to Livia Schanze and her team of students who gave so generously of their time to help during the event and make it a success: Jianying Du, Michal Jirout, Petra Kasparkova, Nikki Puckey and Paulina Tomasik.

We are very grateful to our commissioning editor Priyanka Pathak, for her encouragement, guidance and support, and to Helen Kelly-Holmes and Sue Wright for agreeing to accept this volume in their series on Language and Globalization. In the final stages of the preparation of the volume, the meticulous help of David Fleming in checking the typescript was invaluable, and we hope this did not distract him too much from his dissertation.

Finally, we would like to record our gratitude to our colleagues in Southampton, especially as ever Clare Mar-Molinero, for their constant support and encouragement, and to two organizations whose sponsorship we greatly appreciate: the UK Arts and Humanities Research Council, which awarded us a large research grant for the project on The German Language and the Future of Europe (www.glipp.soton.ac.uk) of which the conference was a part, and the University Association for

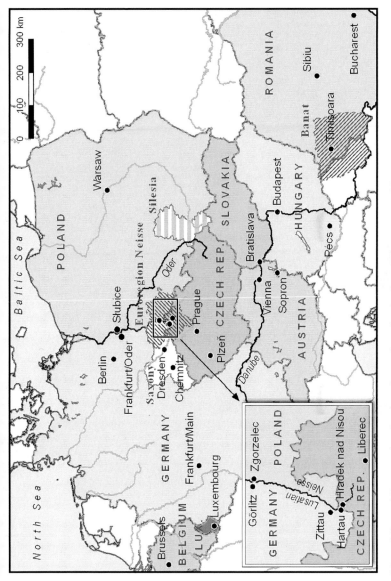

Map of Central Europe, showing locations referred to in the studies presented here

1
Introduction: Central Europe as a Multilingual Space

Patrick Stevenson and Jenny Carl

Where *is* Central Europe? Or indeed, where is the centre of Europe? These are rather different questions, but they are equally problematic. Posing either question presupposes the possibility and availability of an answer, but this in turn suggests the existence of discrete spaces and places that can be identified, demarcated and designated. Stanisław Mucha's documentary film *Die Mitte* (2004), in which he travels the length and breadth of Europe in search of an answer to the second of these questions, shows at one level the futility of such a quest – not because he finds no answers, but because he finds so many. Eschewing attempts to determine a cartographically measurable centre, and ignoring the dictates of cultural traditions that would point to the metropolis of Vienna or Berlin, Prague or Budapest, he unearths claimants in unlikely locations scattered across six countries: from Hessen, the Teutoburger Wald, Cölbe and Tirschenreuth in Germany through Braunau am Inn in Austria, Krahula in Slovakia, Suchowola, Kutno and Piątek in Poland, Purnuškes and the Mountain of Crosses in Lithuania to Rachiv in Ukraine. However, the journey also opens up perspectives on the meaning of such concepts as 'the centre of Europe' or 'Central Europe' as deriving from discourses that are always both *of* (or *on/about*) and *in* (or *from*) particular places (Blommaert 2005: 223).

The first question – where is Central Europe? – is not about identifying a location at all, but rather about drawing boundaries. A better question might therefore be 'where does Central Europe stop?' Furthermore, this question can be asked independently of the second one, since Central Europe may or may not focus on (or emanate from) a centre. It is a plastic, flexible construct that is not tied to physical, political or historical frontiers, and may not even be a single continuous, uninterrupted space; on the contrary, it is almost endlessly polysemic. Yet its physical

1

extent is determinable, if at all, in political and historical terms as well as in relation to cultural traditions and human (social and individual) experiences. 'Central' here is apparently to be defined not in opposition to 'peripheral', but to east/west and/or north/south. However, these again are only secondarily geographical dimensions: they are primarily categories that have evolved historically and are conditioned in terms of sedimentations of political, economic and cultural allegiances and conflicts.

These sedimentations arise from a multiplicity of cultural traditions and languages in a space where borders have constantly been changing. During the course of the nineteenth and twentieth centuries, nation-states emerged and vanished, they were partitioned, usually as a consequence of war, and were caught between allegiances to the various different and competing, often multinational and multilingual, powers of Prussia, the Habsburg, Russian and Napoleonic empires and later the Soviet Union and – relatively briefly – Nazi Germany. All these powers represented particular linguistic and religious hegemonies as well as patterns of administrative, legal and economic organization, and they demanded to varying degrees allegiance to 'their' values from the countries and people they ruled. Their values, or ideologies, were not originally representative of 'east' or 'west' respectively, but after the end of the Second World War certain patterns became associated with either 'side', so that one way of conceiving of Central Europe, at least until 1989, was the space in which these spheres of influence confronted each other.

As the spheres of influence of these empires shifted, so did administrative and legal borders, but this fluidity – and often contingency – was mostly triggered and accompanied by ideological conflict and often war. The nation-states of Poland, the then Czechoslovakia, Hungary and Romania (as well as the Baltic and Balkan states, for that matter) emerged from nineteenth-century opposition to those hegemonic powers, and reached independence after the First World War, although for Hungary this 'resettlement' meant that it lost about two thirds of its territory and significant parts of its population in the 1920 Treaty of Trianon.

This period, however, lasted only approximately 20 years until the eve of the Second World War, when Hitler and Stalin rearranged this geographic territory, including the area of what is now western Ukraine. As a consequence of their pact, they abolished the Polish state and divided it between the Soviet and Nazi empires; at the same time Czechoslovakia was annexed by Germany. The Hungarian and

Romanian states, by contrast, remained formally independent and this distinction has proved to be significant for bilateral relations with Germany until the present day. Territorially, formally, these states in Central Europe achieved lasting independence only after 1945, but they then fell under Soviet ideological and military hegemony which lasted until the transformations of 1989. The aftermath of those transformations, however, also signified the end of the 'territorial lid' on Central Europe, which reignited tensions between the Czech and Slovak populations in Czechoslovakia, and 1993 saw the creation of two independent republics, which represents one of the most recent changes to the borders in Central Europe.[1]

Moreover, the end of the Cold War meant not only that people in Central Europe embraced the freedoms and promises of western liberal democracies and market economies, but they also abandoned the formerly compulsory learning of Russian in favour of the formerly restricted German and English. Their appeal did not only derive from the fact that English had by then become the world lingua franca of science, economy and entertainment (most notably popular music and film) and that German had a long history of regional cultural and economic ties, but it was also a statement of opposition to the imposed language ideology of 'Russian only' under the communist regimes (see Földes 2002: 341). The influence of and opposition to language ideologies, however, is not a new phenomenon of the post-1989 period; on the contrary, it has played a crucial role in the social, cultural and political development of the region over the last two centuries. This question has been particularly relevant in relation to the position of the German language, and the following chapters all deal with this in some way, either in terms of its present status and contact with other languages or in terms of the legacy of its past. If we consider the historical footprint of the German language, it is clear that it was for a long time the language of power in Central Europe, culminating in the nineteenth century, when it was not only the language of the political elites in the Prussian and Habsburg empires but also the language of trade, advances in science and cultural innovation across the region (see Rindler Schjerve 2003). Speaking German – even without having an ethnic German family background – was considered to be a sign of 'good breeding', whereas the 'native' languages did not possess as much symbolic capital. However, the Herderian ideology of linguistic homogeneity, according to which 'languages' and 'nations' are mutually defining and coterminous and which fuelled nineteenth-century German nationalism (Gardt 2000; Stevenson 2002: 15–24; Gal 2006),

was also enthusiastically embraced by consistent opposition movements in most Central European countries (see Barbour and Carmichael
2000). The linguistic dimension was important for these emerging
nationalisms in the struggle against monarchic hegemony, and with
growing administrative emancipation laws were passed in several countries which increasingly marginalized German for public purposes (see
Maitz and Sándor, this volume) and subsequently changed patterns of
language education and transmission to younger generations. None the
less, the German language did retain a foothold in the region, even during the communist era when it was the language of one of the sister
states (the GDR) and thus a legitimate foreign language that could be
learnt at school.

On another level, however, it was also the language of national
minorities across Central Europe (see Eichinger et al. 2008). As a result
of the frequent shifting of borders linguistic communities and cultural traditions came to straddle nation-states in the form of residual
national minorities that were either 'left behind' by the moving borders
or displaced or migrated into other, sometimes neighbouring territories.
The sizeable Magyar minorities in countries adjacent to the modern
Hungarian state are one such case, but the most widely dispersed
were the German minorities whose ancestors had migrated within the
Holy Roman Empire and the Habsburg Empire from German lands to
Bohemia, Silesia and Hungary among other places from the Middle Ages
onwards. When the Central European territories were resettled in the
early part of the twentieth century, these residual German populations
stayed in their host countries. However, their language was highly concentrated in the domestic and rural spheres, and sometimes also in other
sectors such as mining, and was able to survive in these niches even
during the twentieth century because it did not pose a challenge to the
newly dominant linguistic nationalisms. But then in the aftermath of
the Second World War the numbers of members of German minorities
in Central European countries were significantly reduced, since people were expelled from Poland, Czechoslovakia, Hungary and Romania
because of their nationality and their real or alleged association with the
Nazi regime. Furthermore, for several years after 1945 it was not oppor-
tune, in some places even illegal, to speak German in public. Yet, the
language survived in enough places to foster the re-emergence of the
demand for learning it after 1989, and many efforts were made (more
or less successfully) to rekindle historic cultural ties and linguistic traditions. Very recently, the demand for German has declined, mostly in
favour of English, but whereas English is the dominant global language

and as such unrivalled in this area, German is still a significant regional language for economic and cultural relationships (StADaF 2006: 5).

But while the recent enlargements of the European Union, incorporating most of Central Europe, and the deepening of integration in the areas of border control and the movement of people have fostered hopes that intra-European borders would diminish in importance, there is apparently no getting away from national and/or state-oriented conceptions of space in Europe, since even activities and practices that transcend the boundaries of nations or states are defined and categorized precisely in terms of their border-crossing particularity (Meinhof and Galasiński 2005). For this reason, the studies in this book are all in some sense 'located' either within the political, historical and cultural frames constituted by individual states or in the marginal, liminal spaces between them. At the same time, however, it is this constraint that allows the authors of these studies to problematize and explore the apparent stability and fixity of these arbitrary limits.

This question of indeterminate or fuzzy boundaries separating what are conventionally (that is, by arbitrary consensus) perceived as discrete entities is well recognized in linguistics (for a recent critique of the 'invention' of languages, see Makoni and Pennycook 2007; and Horner, this volume). Here, a typical and indeed often asked question might be 'where does German stop?' (see, for example, Barbour and Stevenson 1998: 7-13). Linguistic answers to such questions can only ever be partially adequate and require confirmation through an appeal to the perceptions and interests of language users or to the claims of political authorities, but the answers may then be circular and contestable and therefore inconclusive: 'I speak German and she doesn't, because I'm a German-speaker and she isn't', or 'This land is German-speaking territory because we declare it to be so'. Furthermore, as such declarations suggest, identifying the limits of languages and their legitimate domains entails a presumption of authority based on beliefs about the salience and value of particular linguistic forms (Blommaert 2006: 243).

There is a long tradition of wrestling with these ultimately insoluble riddles, and although the search for answers has been shown to be worth while because of the very uncertainty of the outcome and thus the questioning of previously unchallenged ideas, it is not our intention here to tilt at these particular windmills. The authors contributing to this book work with the convenient fictions of the terms ('Central Europe/Mitteleuropa', 'the German language') that we have cast, in a precautionary way, into doubt. Our collective aim is not to revisit this well-travelled path of enquiry. Rather, we will suspend our disbelief in the adequacy of such concepts and categories and pursue a different set of questions.

In Central Europe, then, the German language has long played a key role in processes of identification. However, while the historical and contemporary footprint of German across this region underpins all the studies presented here, and is the principal focus of the chapters by Jaworska on Poland and by Maitz and Sándor on Hungary, the main aim of this book as a whole is not to evaluate the role or future prospects of this or any other language. These are issues that have already been extensively researched by many scholars.[2] Nor is it intended to be representative in its coverage of those parts of Europe where German is in common use: this would, at the very least, have demanded chapters on language use in Austria and Switzerland in addition to those relating to Germany. As the book's title indicates, our perspective is different. Our principal aim is to explore some of the many ways in which language(s) is (are) conscripted into discourses on identity in this region. There are two common strands, with different degrees of emphasis, running through all these discussions. The first is the tension between, on the one hand, the persistence of national – or rather state – frames of reference and concomitant monolingual ideologies in discourses on identity in Europe (Blommaert 2005, 2006), and, on the other hand, a growing pressure - especially at the level of the local politics of personal interaction, but also at the pan-European level of language and cultural policy – towards practices that subvert, challenge or transcend this obstinately anachronistic structure (Mar-Molinero and Stevenson 2006). The second is the encounter between German - whether as the dominant, officially legitimated language, as the minority language of migrations (past and present) or as a (potential) regional lingua franca occupying the middle ground between global English and 'national' languages – and other languages (or in one case between different varieties of German).

Thus, the focus on the German language is not an end in itself but a means of showing, by taking different perspectives on language use involving this and other languages in multilingual 'contact zones' (Pratt 1992), some of the ways in which language contributes to contemporary social change in this region, 20 years after it began to be reconfigured following the end of the Cold War. On a still wider level, the book aims to make a contribution to the growing literature on language and globalization (see, for example, Fairclough 2006; Pennycook 2007; Coupland forthcoming; as well as the other books in the *Language and Globalization* series) by demonstrating and investigating local effects of global processes such as migration, transnational cultural production and institutional communication, and changes in the political economy of regions. The kinds of question driving the studies in the book, therefore, are: What role is the relationship between (speakers of different) languages playing today in the reshaping of societies and communities in this region? How is this relationship articulated in discourses and narratives on language? How is it manifested in individual repertoires and social practices? How is it determined by social and cultural policies, and vice versa?

The more locally focused studies are framed by two chapters that explore issues arising from attempts to shore up and promote the formation of a European identity which remains only weakly articulated and has so far failed to take root in the public consciousness. While questions of economic, social and security policy dominate the political agenda of the EU, they have little purchase on the imagination of individual people, and the institutions charged with developing, debating and implementing policies appear remote and disengaged from the realities of EU citizens' daily lives. Aspirations to enhance social cohesion and integration are not best served through the introduction of a common currency or a shared constitution – on the contrary, the experience of recent years has shown the capacity of such measures to divide rather than unite Europeans – or by regulating the labelling of food or harmonizing the structures of higher education. And as the EU expands incrementally towards a point at which it could become synonymous with Europe, while migration across its external and internal boundaries increases, the challenges of social and cultural diversity inevitably grow. In this context, questions of communication and representation take on greater urgency: how can the institutional centre be brought closer to the people and how can the people be brought closer to each other?

Michał Krzyżanowski opens this discussion by analysing media coverage of the 2004 EU enlargement process from the perspective of the extent to which it included consideration of specific linguistic consequences in particular and of multilingualism within the EU in general. The inauguration in January 2007 of a new portfolio for multilingualism in the European Commission signalled a recognition at this level of the salience of linguistic diversity, and the first incumbent of the new post of Commissioner for Multilingualism, the Romanian Leonard Orban, declared in a speech on 27 April 2007 that multilingualism 'has been, from the very beginning, part of the genetic code of the European Union' (Orban 2007). He has also published a 'political agenda for multilingualism' with the key objective of 'providing access to online information services and EU legislation to citizens *in their own languages*' (our emphasis),[3] and a plethora of reports (most recently by the High Level Group on Multilingualism: see Commission 2007, as well as the Commission's 2008 Communication) has reiterated the strategic necessity of establishing individual multilingual competence as a core skill of European citizens (for a critical discussion, see Stevenson 2008). However, responsibility for developing the policies that would convert these strategies into practice lies with member states.

Krzyżanowski therefore focuses his investigation on the national media of two neighbouring member states with significant stakes in the development of language policy in the EU: Poland, the largest 'new' member in terms of population and of 'native speakers' of a 'national language' (Polish),[4] and Germany, itself recently transformed into the largest 'old' member whose 'national language', German, has the highest number of 'native speakers' in the EU as a whole (see Eurobarometer 2006). He argues that the EU should be seen as 'both a political organism and a communicative space' (p. 24) which should therefore create structures that ensure the democratic legitimacy of its institutions and create conditions that enable democratic debates in both national and supranational public spheres. The perception of EU institutions as representative and inclusive thus depends in part on how far they are seen to reflect the linguistic diversity of their constituents. However, his sample survey of national newspapers suggests that very little attention is paid to these issues in these influential public fora and that both multilingualism and specific language issues remain under-politicized at the national level. To the extent that these questions are debated at all, the media discourses analysed here tend to support the prevailing language ideologies of monolingualism in 'national languages' within member states and of what Krzyżanowski calls 'hegemonic multilingualism' – that is, the continued institutional dominance of English, French and German – at the supra-national level.

In the closing chapter of the book, Kristine Horner resumes Krzyżanowski's critique of the ways in which the development of a representative 'cultural space' is managed in the EU, focusing in this case on discourses on European cultural identities in the context of institutionalized attempts to construct symbolic links between the extreme margins of the EU: Luxembourg (and adjacent areas of Germany, France and Belgium, together forming the so-called 'Grande Région') in the north-west and the Transylvanian region of Romania in the southeast. Her point of departure is the decision to designate the Grande Région and Sibiu/Hermannstadt jointly the European Capital of Culture (ECC) for 2007, the year in which the most recent enlargement of the

EU took place with the accession of Romania and Bulgaria. Promotional materials produced to proclaim and celebrate this joint venture sought to rationalize this otherwise arbitrary coupling by giving prominence to somewhat tenuous linguistic connections in the form of different Germanic varieties. While Poland and Germany, with their long history of mutual antagonism, sit in more or less uncomfortable proximity on either side of the imagined meridian that divided (and, some would say, continues to divide) east from west in Europe – and that is therefore a linear contender for the location of the 'centre' – Luxembourg and Romania face each other across the vast expanse of Central Europe with apparently very little in common. As Horner argues, however, precisely this disjunction is discursively manoeuvred into a demonstration of the cohesive capacity of the EU, in which language plays a crucial role: 'This foregrounding of presupposed shared linguistic repertoires pre-dating the era of the nation-state serves to construct a continuity between historical patterns of migration and current transformations in Europe, as well as the unity or "integration" of the space traversing the north-western and south-eastern stretches of imagined European place' (p. 242). She also shows how such optimistically pan-European discourses counteract the ideology of (national) monolingualism by exploiting the blurring of linguistic boundaries, in conjunction with visual representations of European regions in which state boundaries are faint, to decentre the state as a unit of difference in favour of the border-transcending region with its primordial traditions and potential for cultural exchange.

The nine chapters that are embraced by these discussions of European discourses on language and identity are linked to them and to each other in many ways, but above all by their exploration of language contact in relation to the two complementary phenomena (of stasis and movement) that underlie and define the tensions between the local, the national and the supranational in contemporary Europe: borders and migration. Borders exist in order to separate and contain, but their categorical fixity creates, at least potentially, opportunities for negotiation, and Chapters 3–6 consider different ways in which the recent transformations in Central Europe have given new salience to language contact across historical state borders. Migration involves movement, across or within bounded space, and from one place to another, but rather than making place irrelevant it emphasizes its importance, together with time, for the structuring and (in the case of multiple or continuous migrations) punctuation of experience. It also entails cultural and linguistic contact and exchange, sometimes transient and ephemeral, sometimes with long-lasting consequences. Chapters 7–11 thus deal with ways in which discourses on language and linguistic practices are marked by contemporary migration processes and by traces of past migrations.

Sylvia Jaworska picks up Krzyżanowski's theme of multilingualism and language contact in the context of Poland and Germany as debated in Polish national media discourses, but she reverses the focus of attention from an outward gaze across Europe as a whole to relations between the two neighbouring states. Her discussion acknowledges statistical data that indicate the continuing importance of German in Poland in terms of the demand for it among learners as a language with high investment potential, as cultural capital. However, she offsets this optimistic account against the growing clamour of media discourses in which the resurgence of hostility towards the western neighbour is increasingly challenging the positive rhetoric of reconciliation that characterized the early post-Cold War years. Jaworska argues that increasing disillusionment and resentment at perceived inequalities in the new economic environment, in which restrictions on access to material resources and employment opportunities and discrimination against Polish migrants in Germany are contrasted with the relatively generous treatment of the German minority in Poland, have led to a shift in public attitudes towards Germany and a re-evaluation of the returns on investing in learning German. At its worst, the discourse of good-neighbourliness has been replaced by a 'dialogue of the deaf' and the River Oder/Odra, marking the border between the two countries and already laden with a heavy cargo of historical tensions, is recast as the mythological River Styx.

Jane Wilkinson's chapter investigates attempts to overcome these new or renewed social boundaries between Poles and Germans through the organization of cultural activities in border areas which explicitly thematize transborder interaction. Starting from the ambiguity of borders as both markers of separation and zones of contact, she explores the potential of the theatre in particular to act as a third space in which the very 'edginess' of life in geographically and politically marginal communities can take centre stage. One of the most sensitive issues facing cultural entrepreneurs in such contexts is the choice of language or languages to be used in the performance, and, as Jaworska shows, the use of both German and Polish in this region is deeply imbued with mistrust and resentment built up over centuries (see also Meinhof and Galasiński 2005). Wilkinson argues that the 're-imagining of borderland spaces' (p. 76) represents a major cultural challenge that is often more intractable than that posed by the need for closer economic and political relations between neighbouring states and communities since it depends less on structural harmonization than on the capacity and the desire of individuals and societies to 'commune' with each other. One of the problems she finds in this respect is a deep-seated asymmetry in the linguistic and therefore communicative repertoires of Germans and Poles in the region, weighted heavily in favour of German as the language with more widespread currency. The symbolic domination accruing from this unequal distribution of linguistic resources reinforces historically conditioned tensions, which optimistic initiatives in theatrical innovation – such as staging plays in Polish in German theatres, promoting bilingual productions or displacing language altogether through dance and street theatre – have so far failed to mitigate.

The Czech-German border is, of course, no less highly charged than the Polish-German border and, like Wilkinson, Kateřina Černá scrutinizes attempts to open up a social space in which linguistic resources can be pooled as a means of fostering relationships less encumbered by the baggage of historical antipathies. She too identifies asymmetries in linguistic competence as a major stumbling block in this process (see Holly et al. 2003), but in this case argues that institutionally driven policies, specifically in the form of cross-border educational programmes, have better prospects of achieving reciprocal competence in 'partner languages' among members of neighbouring speech communities. Focusing on interaction between Czech and German schoolchildren and their teachers on a collaborative bilingual project between primary schools in the borderland, Černá's study combines methods from the ethnography of communication and ethnomethodology to explore in detail the patterns of linguistic behaviour exhibited by both children and adults and to tease out ways in which the participants use their linguistic resources (and their perceptions of each other's language use) as elements in social identity formation. Using the framework of membership categorization analysis, she shows how different identities are made relevant and prioritized by individual speakers in conversational interaction and how the choice of particular linguistic forms and references to language function as contextualization cues (Gumperz 1982), that is, as indicators that reference particular social contexts within which meanings can be inferred. Her analysis suggests that ethnic categories are more salient than others (such as age or gender) in the interactions studied, that language competence plays a key role in constituting these categories, and that deep-seated attitudes towards the asymmetrical nature of competence in each other's language are fundamental to this categorization process. By the same token, however, there is evidence that the salience of ethnic categories may decrease when linguistic asymmetry is reduced.

The studies by Jaworska, Wilkinson and Černá emphasize, among other things, how differing degrees of reciprocal language competence can in themselves constitute borders between members of neighbouring societies, but formal encounters between such speakers are obviously not confined to geographically marginal territories. In their chapter, Jiří Nekvapil and Tamah Sherman again discuss ways of drawing on multilingual repertoires to develop communicative practices within a common endeavour, but in this case their focus is on the institutional setting of multinational businesses. Like most states in this region, the Czech Republic has attracted substantial inward investment from many other countries over the last 20 years and many large companies based elsewhere have established subsidiaries there. The efficient operation of a company with a multinational workforce whose members speak different languages clearly requires some form of corporate language policy, whether in the form of a company-wide lingua franca (as is the case in some major German firms in which English is stipulated for internal communication) or in the form of locally negotiated arrangements. Using the framework of Language Management Theory, Nekvapil and Sherman investigate ways in which linguistic practices involving three languages – Czech, German and English – are managed in the Czech subsidiary of a German company. As their analysis shows, although company policy specifies English as the 'official corporate language', in practice both German and Czech are used for various functions, often within the same setting. By comparing policy documents, interviews with senior managers and observations of actual language use in different contexts, they demonstrate how the distribution of the three languages can be accounted for in largely functional terms, in which communicative needs may conflict with symbolic, social, emotional or privacy functions. They argue, therefore, that effective management of language use in multinational businesses cannot be achieved by the top-down imposition of a monolingual policy, but rather requires an understanding and analysis of complex local needs.

The recent expansion of multinational companies in new member states of the EU has, then, of necessity increased the cross-border traffic not only of goods, services and capital but also of people. This is, of course, not an exclusively contemporary phenomenon; indeed, as we have shown earlier in this chapter, Central Europe has been characterized by multiple migrations over the centuries. The remaining chapters therefore explore some further effects of present migrations as well as various ways in which past migrations have left their trace on the sociolinguistic and sociocultural landscape of this region. Péter Maitz and Klára Sándor begin with an historical account of changing sociolinguistic constellations in Hungary, focusing on the roles of the German language in the context of migration processes dating back to the Middle Ages. Their wide-ranging discussion is grounded in the development of language ideologies, especially the ideology of linguistic nationalism, which led first to the dominance of German and subsequently to its subordination and marginalization. A crucial aspect of their argument is the importance of distinguishing between different groups or categories of German speakers and avoiding the tendency, still prevalent in many sociolinguistic accounts of multilingual societies, to construct a homogeneous speech community on the basis of a supposedly shared language. In the case of Hungary, Maitz and Sándor draw a fundamental distinction between two 'layers' of German-speaking populations that had formed by the end of the eighteenth century: on the one hand, urban, bourgeois populations, descendants of the earliest German settlers in Hungary, who were generally literate and therefore predominantly used standard forms of German; on the other hand, rural, peasant populations, descendants of more recent migrants, who were clustered largely in monolingual German-speaking villages and almost exclusively used non-standard varieties of spoken German. It was the first of these two layers that was most profoundly affected by the shifting language ideologies of the nineteenth century: the Germanization policies practised under the Habsburg Empire and the Austro-Hungarian Monarchy had led to the dominance of German but under the nascent Hungarian nationalism of the mid-nineteenth century it was cast as the language of oppression and an obstacle to aspirations of national unity. The discourses of linguistic purity and homogeneity that were mobilized at the same time in the interests of German nationalism (see, for example, Gardt 2000, 2004; Langer and Davies 2005; Durrell 2007) were therefore instrumental in the demise of standard German as a vehicle of power in Hungary. Maitz and Sándor go on to show how the political crises of the twentieth century contributed to the further decline of German, resulting, on the one hand, in a reconfiguration of relationships between Hungarian and the different varieties of German, and, on the other hand, a distinction between German as a mother tongue (that is, local traditional dialects), now the dwindling heritage language of the remaining Hungarian-German populations, and German as a foreign language (that is, the standard variety) taught and learned in formal education by Hungarian-Germans and members of other ethnic groups alike.

The theme of the legacies of past migrations and changing relationships between particular language varieties and their speakers is taken up again in our own chapter, where we analyse ways in which the experience of the loss of language forms traditionally associated with German ethnicity is articulated in the life-stories of German speakers in Hungary and the Czech Republic. While Maitz and Sándor demonstrate the historical forces that led to the decline of German as a dominant language in Hungary and the linguistic assimilation of the ethnic German population – and an even more advanced stage of this process has taken place in the Czech Republic (see Nekvapil and Neustupný 1998; Nekvapil 2007) – our aim is to focus on individual agency and reveal a more differentiated picture of language shift by investigating different ways in which people have responded to broadly similar conditions of social and political change. We argue that while all members of these German-speaking communities share a common experience of challenges to traditional ways of life and a devaluation of their traditional forms of self-expression, their individual trajectories and the ways they process their encounters with loss are far from uniform. So, while the fact of language shift is undeniable and the master-narrative of the inexorable effects of social change on linguistic practices seems unquestionable, what (the threat of) language loss represents in people's lives, how they respond to it and how they incorporate it into their personal accounts of their lives remains to be discovered. Our analysis of individual language biographies is therefore an attempt to show how people use their recollections of such experiences to construct a particular perspective on their lives and to create a sense of coherence through assembling thematically linked fragments of their remembered pasts. Thus, in formulating their stories, the narrators not only locate their experiences of loss in relation to key events and periods in their lives, but also use these chosen moments to form a conception of time (a particular temporality) through which they situate their past in their present.

The construction of individual life-stories is one opportunity to negotiate and develop a sense of self, and to this end language biographies can draw reflexively on individual linguistic repertoires as a narrative resource. A more common process of self- or identity formation through linguistic means can be observed in terms of linguistic practices in dialogic interactions such as conversations or interviews. In their chapter, Jennifer Dailey-O'Cain and Grit Liebscher also explore relationships between language, time and place, in this case in the context of the ways in which individuals position themselves (Davies and Harré 1999) in conversation through their selection of particular features of their linguistic repertoires. They too are interested in the constraints imposed on present identification processes by past political conditions, but the focus of their fine-grained analysis is on how people work within these constraints to achieve particular sociolinguistic effects. Unlike the other studies here, their research is concerned with linguistic practices of people migrating within a contemporary national boundary but across a social space that derives from past political divisions: western Germans now living in eastern Germany. By combining methods of variationist sociolinguistics and conversation analysis, Dailey-O'Cain and Liebscher investigate ways in which these western migrants exploit their newly acquired knowledge of local dialect features in Saxony, the area to which they have moved, together with the other components of their existing linguistic repertoires (typically standard German and dialects from their place of origin) to project different identities in relation to social categories that are relevant in their new environment. The Saxon dialect is still strongly associated for both western and eastern Germans with memories of the GDR, but also, among Saxons themselves, with a resilient sense of local loyalty. However, a crucial aspect of the analysis in this chapter is the conception of discursive identity, which is not tied in a fixed relationship to specific social categories, but rather is formulated and shaped in the context of interaction. The authors therefore aim to show how individuals overtly describe their personal affiliations and exploit the linguistic resources available to them in order to adopt or perform 'different ways of being German' (p. 186). Thus the participants variously position themselves, both by what they say and by how they speak, as identifying either with their place of origin or with their new location, or alternatively as shuttling from one to the other or occupying a 'third space' between the two.

Britta Schneider is also interested in the performance of identities through linguistic (inter)actions in a particular 'national' context (again, of Germany), but in her chapter she explores language use in relation to 'imported' cultural practices by observing linguistic and other forms of behaviour in German Salsa clubs. She characterizes this form of social organization as a transnational, multiethnic and multilingual 'community of practice' (see Meyerhoff 2004) in that it brings together individuals from different countries (from Germany and elsewhere) who aim to achieve a sense of community through their engagement in a common endeavour – learning a particular form of dance associated with Latin America. To the extent that the social space created by these activities is constituted in part through the use of Spanish alongside the 'national' language German, these communities conflict with and confront the dominant language ideology of monolingualism. Moreover, this linguistic behaviour can be seen as transgressive in that it is adopted not only by native speakers of Spanish but also by non-native speakers, especially Germans, and that it is part of a kind of 'cultural crossing': 'German Salsa aficionados – or better: Salsa aficionados in Germany – not only meet to dance in Salsa venues, they very often also perform a particular type of identity and lifestyle' (p. 206). However, it seems that this performance has less to do with achieving a sense of belonging in relation to a specific cultural milieu than with attaining a feeling of otherness, of being temporarily apart from a society in which competence in – and especially the use of – languages other than the sole officially sanctioned one is considered legitimate only in the form of what Schneider calls 'elite bilingualism'. Furthermore, while code-switching and especially code-mixing may be seen as deviant or even subversive practices in relation to the monolingual norm, in the Salsa club they are considered emblematic of a desirable cosmopolitan lifestyle. At the same time, class, ethnicity and gender interact in complex ways that preclude generalizations about the value attached to such linguistic practices and that are instrumental in developing discourses of inclusion and exclusion within the Salsa scene itself.

Schneider's ethnography of Salsa clubs is indicative of ways in which hybridity in cultural practices may challenge the notion of 'national cultures'. In his chapter, Thomas Cooper takes up this theme and discusses the concept of transnational literatures by exploring the role of German-language literary production in relation to Romanian and Hungarian literatures in the contact zones of Transylvania and Banat in Romania, another destination of historical German migrations. He argues that rather than seeking a measure of the significance or vitality of German solely in terms of its use in functional domains of public life, such as education or commerce, we should consider its local cultural influence in its contribution to developing and sustaining a multilingual literary environment. Conventional accounts of Central European literatures typically perpetuate rather than disrupt the 'national paradigm' (p. 225), but Cooper positions his discussion of Romanian literatures within more recent scholarship that 'challenges the chauvinism of national collective identity by exploring interstices and intersections, rather than articulating (and thereby reifying) borders' (p. 226). Refusing to subscribe to essentializing conceptions of 'national literatures' in 'national languages' and rejecting the notion of a discrete German-language literature in Romania, he proposes instead a perspective that foregrounds the interaction between forms of literary production in different languages in terms of thematic and stylistic affinities, translation and intertextuality.

Cooper's critique of the concept of 'national cultures' and its use in support of 'national identities' in the Romanian context is followed by Kristine Horner's critique of attempts to orchestrate European identities through the construction of cultural associations between Transylvania and the 'Grande Région' around Luxembourg that we have discussed above.

It would be beyond the bounds of any single book to attempt a comprehensive account of the issues outlined in the first part of this chapter, and our aim is more modest. We hope to offer illustrative studies on language, discourse and identity that span the scale from the big picture of discourses on language policy to the detail of narratives in individual language biographies and that draw on a wide range of scholarly and analytical approaches (including discourse analysis, conversation analysis, textual analysis, narrative analysis and ethnographic observation) and source material (such as media texts, personal interviews and conversations, theatrical productions, literary texts, business meetings and official documentation). In doing so, we hope both to make new contributions to research on individual topics and to make research on our theme accessible to those working in other, related areas, and thereby stimulate lines of enquiry in future research that either build on individual chapters or develop cross-disciplinary routes towards a better understanding of linguistic practices in Central Europe and elsewhere.[5]

Notes

1. We are limiting our necessarily brief discussion here to the historical context of the countries that are dealt with in later chapters, which means that the Baltic and Balkan states, for example, are not taken into account in this respect.
2. See, for example, among many others Ammon (1991, 1995, 1998), Barbour (2000), Busch and de Cillia (2003), Clyne (1995, 2007), De Cillia and Wodak (2006), Eichhoff-Cyrus and Hoberg (2000), Gardt and Hüppauf (2004), Hoberg (2002), Hoffmann (2000), Krumm and Portmann-Tselikas (2006), Lüdi and Werlen (2005), Muhr and Schrodt (1997) and Stevenson (2002).
3. See http://ec.europa.eu/commission_barroso/orban/policies/policies_en.htm. Accessed 11 October 2007.

4. Both 'native speaker' and 'national language' are problematic concepts, but we do not elaborate on these issues here. See, for example, Davies (2003) and Millar (2005) for critical discussions.
5. See also Galasińska and Krzyżanowski (2009) for further research on these topics.

References

Ammon, U. (1991) *Die internationale Stellung der deutschen Sprache* (Berlin, New York: de Gruyter).
Ammon, U. (1995) *Die deutsche Sprache in Deutschland, Österreich und der Schweiz* (Berlin, New York: de Gruyter).
Ammon, U. (1998) *Ist Deutsch noch internationale Wissenschaftssprache? Englisch auch für die Lehre an den deutschsprachigen Hochschulen* (Berlin and New York: de Gruyter).
Barbour, S. (2000) 'Germany, Austria, Switzerland, Luxembourg: The total coincidence of nations and speech communities?', in Barbour and Carmichael (2000), 151–67.
Barbour, S. and Carmichael, C. (eds) (2000) *Language and Nationalism in Europe* (Cambridge: Cambridge University Press).
Barbour, S. and Stevenson, P. (1998) *Variation im Deutschen: Soziolinguistische Perspektiven* (Berlin and New York: de Gruyter).
Blommaert, J. (2005) *Discourse: A Critical Introduction* (Cambridge: Cambridge University Press).
Blommaert, J. (2006) 'Language policy and national identity', in Ricento (2006), 238-54.
Busch, B. and de Cillia, R. (eds) (2003) *Sprachenpolitik in Österreich. Eine Bestandsaufnahme* (Frankfurt, Berlin and Bern: Peter Lang).
Chambers, J. K., Trudgill, P. and Schilling-Estes, N. (eds) (2004) *The Handbook of Language Variation and Change* (Oxford: Blackwell).
Clyne, M. (1995) *The German Language in a Changing Europe* (Cambridge: Cambridge University Press).
Clyne, M. (2007) 'Braucht Deutschland eine bewusstere, kohäsive Sprachenpolitik – Deutsch, Englisch als Lingua franca und Mehrsprachigkeit?' in Humboldt-Stiftung (2007), 4–28.
Commission of the European Communities (2007) *Final Report: High Level Group on Multilingualism* (Luxembourg: Office for Official Publications of the European Communities).
Commission of the European Communities (2008) *Multilingualism: An Asset for Europe and a Shared Commitment*, Communication to the European Parliament (Brussels).
Coupland, N. (ed.) (forthcoming) *The Handbook of Language and Globalization* (Oxford: Blackwell).
Davies, A. (2003) *The Native Speaker: Myth and Reality* (Clevedon: Multilingual Matters).
Davies, B. and R. Harré (1999) 'Positioning and personhood', in Harré and van Langenhove (1999), 32–52.

De Cillia, R. and Wodak, R. (2006) *Ist Österreich ein 'deutsches' Land? Sprachenpolitik und Identität in der Zweiten Republik* (Innsbruck, Vienna and Bolzano: Studienverlag).

Durrell, M. (2007) 'Language, nation and identity in the German-speaking countries', in Fandrych and Salverda (2007), 37–57.

Eichhoff-Cyrus, K. and Hoberg, R. (eds) (2000) *Die deutsche Sprache zur Jahrtausendwende: Sprachkultur oder Sprachverfall?* (Mannheim, Leipzig, Vienna and Zurich: Dudenverlag).

Eichinger, L. M., Plewnia, A. and Riehl, C. M. (eds.) (2008) *Handbuch der deutschen Sprachminderheiten in Mittel- und Osteuropa* (Tübingen: Narr).

Eurobarometer (2006) *Europeans and Their Languages. Special Eurobarometer 243* (Brussels: European Commission).

Fairclough, N. (2006) *Language and Globalization* (London: Routledge).

Fandrych, C. and Salverda, R. (eds) (2007) *Standard, Variation und Sprachwandel in germanischen Sprachen* (Tübingen: Narr).

Földes, C. (2002) 'Deutsch und Englisch: Ein Sprachnotstand? Befunde und Anmerkungen aus einer ostmitteleuropäischen Perspektive' in Hoberg (2002), 341–64.

Gal, S. (2006) 'Migration, minorities and multilingualism: language ideologies in Europe', in Mar-Molinero and Stevenson (2006), 13–27.

Galasińska, A. and Krzyżanowski, M. (eds) (2009) *Discourse and Transformation in Central and Eastern Europe* (Basingstoke: Palgrave Macmillan).

Gardt, A. (ed.) (2000) *Nation und Sprache. Die Diskussion ihres Verhältnisses in Geschichte und Gegenwart* (Berlin and New York: de Gruyter).

Gardt, A. (2004) 'Language and national identity', in Gardt and Hüppauf (2004), 197–211.

Gardt, A. and Hüppauf, B. (eds) (2004) *Globalization and the Future of German* (Berlin and New York: Mouton de Gruyter).

Gumperz, J. (1982) *Discourse Strategies* (Cambridge: Cambridge University Press).

Harré, R. and van Langenhove, L. (eds) (1999) *Positioning Theory: Moral Contexts of Intentional Action* (Oxford: Blackwell).

Hoberg, R. (ed.) (2002) *Deutsch-Englisch-Europäisch. Impulse für eine neue Sprachpolitik* (Mannheim, Leipzig, Vienna and Zurich: Dudenverlag).

Hoffmann, H. (ed.) (2000) *Deutsch global. Neue Medien – Herausforderungen für die deutsche Sprache* (Cologne: DuMont).

Holly, W., Nekvapil, J., Scherm, I. and Tišerová, P. (2003) 'Unequal neighbours: coping with asymmetries', *Journal of Ethnic and Migration Studies* 29(5), 819–34.

Humboldt-Stiftung (ed.) (2007) *Braucht Deutschland eine bewusstere, kohäsive Sprachenpolitik?* (Bonn: Alexander von Humboldt Stiftung).

Krumm, H-J. and Portmann-Tselikas, P. R. (eds) (2006) *Begegnungssprache Deutsch. Motivationen, Herausforderung, Perspektiven* (Innsbruck, Vienna and Bolzano: Studienverlag).

Langer, N. and Davies, W. (eds) (2005) *Linguistic Purism in the Germanic Languages* (Berlin and New York: de Gruyter).

Lüdi, G. and Werlen, I. (eds) (2005) *Sprachenlandschaft in der Schweiz* (Neuchâtel: Bundesamt für Statistik).

Makoni, S. and Pennycook, A. (eds) (2007) *Disinventing and Reconstituting Languages* (Clevedon: Multilingual Matters).

Mar-Molinero, C. and Stevenson, P. (eds) (2006) *Language Ideologies, Policies and Practices: Language and the future of Europe* (Basingstoke: Palgrave Macmillan).

Meinhof, U. and Galasiński, D. (2005) *The Language of Belonging* (Basingstoke: Palgrave).

Meyerhoff, M. (2004) 'Communities of practice', in Chambers et al. (2004), 526-48.

Millar, R. M. (2005) *Language, Nation and Power* (Basingstoke: Palgrave Macmillan).

Muhr, R. and Schrodt, R. (eds) (1997): *Österreichisches Deutsch und andere Varietäten plurizentrischer Sprachen in Europa* (Vienna: Hölder Pichler Tempsky).

Nekvapil, J. (2007) 'On the language situation in the Czech Republic: What has (not) happened after the accession of the country to the EU', *Sociolinguistica* 21, 36–54.

Nekvapil, J. and Neustupný, J. (1998) 'Linguistic communities in the Czech Republic', in Paulston and Peckham (1998), 116–34.

Orban, L. 'Can Language Diversity Help towards Creating a European Identity?' http://ec.europa.eu /commission_barroso /orban /news /docs /270407_Speech_ Osnabruck_public.pdf. Accessed 11 October 2007.

Paulston, C. B. and Peckham, D. (eds) (1998) *Linguistic Minorities in Central and Eastern Europe* (Clevedon: Multilingual Matters).

Pennycook, A. (2007) *Global Englishes and Transcultural Flows* (London: Routledge).

Pratt, M. L. (1992) *Imperial Eyes: Travel Writing and Transculturation* (London: Routledge).

Ricento, T. (ed.) (2006) *Language Policy: An Introduction to Language Policy Theory and Method* (Oxford: Blackwell).

Rindler Schjerve, R. (ed.) (2003) *Diglossia and Power: Language Policies and Practice in the 19th Century Habsburg Empire. Language, Power and Social Process* (Berlin and New York: Mouton de Gruyter).

StADaF Ständige Arbeitsgruppe Deutsch als Fremdsprache (2006) *Deutsch als Fremdsprache weltweit. Datenerhebung 2005* (Berlin, Bonn, Köln and München).

Stevenson, P. (2002) *Language and German Disunity: A Sociolinguistic History of East and West in Germany 1945–2000* (Oxford: Oxford University Press).

Stevenson, P. (2008) 'The German language and the future of Europe: towards a research agenda on the politics of language', in *German Life and Letters* 61(4), 483–96.

Part I

Language and European Identities: Centre and Periphery

2
Discourses about Enlarged and Multilingual Europe: Perspectives from German and Polish National Public Spheres

Michał Krzyżanowski

Introduction

This chapter[1] explores how the European Union's numerous recent policies on multilingualism have been received in the German and Polish national public spheres and whether, via the carriers of different language ideologies (see below), those public spheres arrived at a view that the EU's policies have improved the image of its institutions as linguistically diverse and multilingual. It is hypothesized that the perception of EU institutions as 'multilingual' and therefore inclusive is increasingly desirable if the citizens of the EU (including those in the post-transformation countries of Central and Eastern Europe) are to identify with the EU's institutions as their representatives and are to treat them as a reflection of the growing multiplicity and diversity of a broader European space. By the same token, it is argued that creating a multilingual image of the EU would be crucial in eradicating its widely disputed 'democratic deficit' in both 'old' and 'new' EU member states.

The present chapter analyses how supranational (European) issues are debated in the national public spheres of the two neighbouring post-transformation countries of Germany and Poland: it explores how the (national) media discuss the EU's (supranational) policies and examines whether and how such debates help construct a new, democratic image of the EU, while also stimulating a cross-national debate on European matters within a European public sphere (see also Trenz and Eder 2004; Langenbucher and Latzer 2006; Fossum and Schlesinger 2007; Triandafyllidou, Wodak and Krzyżanowski 2009). The national-supranational link is further established here by approaching the EU as both a political organism and a communicative space which, however, cannot be separated from its broader, socio-political contexts (*inter alia* of member states). Therefore, the communication taking place within the EU and its institutions is seen as connected to other communicative spaces located within Europe in general, and in the national public spaces of the EU member states in particular. I will therefore aim to show, as Wodak and Wright (2006: 254) argue, that

> the European polity is dependent on the constant and bi-directional flow of communication, the responsiveness to public concerns, and the establishment of a plurality of public spaces, where European problems can be discussed and a 'European consciousness' can be expressed.

From this perspective, language choice, language shift, language contact and language policies should be seen as playing an increasingly important role in the practices and regulations of the EU organizations as well as in the broader European public sphere constituted by national media and national public spaces (see also Wodak and Koller 2008).

This study focuses on the analysis of media discourse on the 1 May 2004 EU enlargement in liberal and conservative quality newspapers in Germany and Poland for the following reasons.[2] First, by looking at the qualitative features of how national media in selected European countries position issues of language(s) and/or multilingualism vis-à-vis the EU institutions, we can assess whether those issues were indeed problematized within the media and, if so, when and how. Second, this study seeks to discover whether, in the German and Polish public spheres, the importance of language(s) and/or multilingualism-related issues was indeed put into the context of the 2004 EU enlargement and transmitted to the respective national publics. Third, the study analyses different language ideologies which were constructed in the media in relation to the EU's enlargement in general and its institutions in particular.

Exploring language ideologies

Inspired by critical approaches to language policies and language planning (see e.g. Wright 2000, 2004; de Cillia, Krumm and Wodak 2003; Phillipson 2003; Spolsky 2004; Ricento 2005; Shohamy 2006), the present chapter draws extensively on different conceptions of language ideologies as elaborated in sociolinguistics and linguistic anthropology (cf. Silverstein 1998; Gal 1998, 2005; Blommaert 1999a;

Blackledge 2005; Mar-Molinero and Stevenson 2006; see also the chapters by Horner, Schneider and Wilkinson, this volume). Hence, while at the general level language ideologies are viewed here as 'cultural ideas, presumptions and presuppositions with which different social groups name, frame and evaluate linguistic practices' (Gal 2006: 13), they must also be conceived as (re-)constructed and negotiated in debates 'in which language is central as a topic, a motif, a target, and in which language ideologies are being articulated, formed, amended, enforced' (Blommaert 1999b: 1). Such ideological debates are taking place in both the public and semi-public spheres. Accordingly, language ideologies are 'produced in discourses, in news media, in politics, in narratives of national belonging, in advertising, in academic text, and in popular culture' (Blackledge 2005: 44).

The assumption underlying this study is that language ideologies debated in the German and Polish media oscillate between two poles: (a) monolingualism or selective or hegemonic multilingualism (cf. below) fuelled by politically and historically driven linguistic inequality, on the one hand, and (b) *de facto* multilingualism favouring linguistic diversity and equality between different (EU working) languages, on the other. However, a particular interest of this study is in deconstructing the status quo of the current *hegemonic multilingualism of/in the EU*.[3] The latter is conceived of as a process in which selected 'working languages' of the EU are ideologically preferred (or *de facto* more frequently used than other languages) in EU institutional practices. It is argued that such preferences arise from the history of the EU integration process and are driven mainly by political premises: they reflect the leading role of powerful states in the EU – principally, Germany, France and the UK – thus influencing the correspondingly increased use of German, French and English.[4] It is also argued that, despite some ideological appearances, hegemonic multilingualism is an ideological tool which effectively prevents actual or *de facto* multilingualism (based on the principle of equality and representation) from being developed and institutionally grounded within EU institutions.

Context

Since this chapter focuses on the debates on supranational issues in national public spheres, the context of this study must also be considered from both 'national' and 'European' perspectives.

Looking at the national (that is, German and Polish) contexts, we must take into consideration the fact that these countries have experienced very different types and paces of transformation in recent years (see Galasińska and Krzyżanowski 2008; Dailey-O'Cain and Liebscher, Jaworska and Wilkinson, this volume). While, in the aftermath of its unification in late 1990, Germany's transformation came in a more abrupt, top-down way – with the new federal states in the east (the former GDR) being incorporated into the western German state and economic structures – the Polish post-1989 transformation proceeded in a much more evolutionary, incremental, bottom-up (and frequently uneasy) manner (cf. Krzyżanowski and Galasińska 2008 for details). The post-1989 media landscapes of the two countries were (re)constructed accordingly: while in Germany the western German press and broadcasters took over their eastern counterparts (with the most notable arrival of commercial or private media), in Poland the entire media landscape had to be constructed anew with many similar tensions appearing between state-owned and private press and broadcasting organizations (see also Thomaß and Tzankoff 2001; Krzyżanowski 2006). However, the most important difference between the German and Polish transformation processes has above all been in the different pace of integration with the supranational structures of the EU. While eastern German regions automatically became part of the EU after merging with the Federal Republic in 1990, Polish EU membership took almost a decade (1994–2004) of difficult negotiations, which finally came to fruition when Poland joined the EU, together with several other Central and Eastern European countries, in May 2004 (see Krzyżanowski forthcoming).

Allowing for those differences, Germany and Poland are treated here as representative of 'old' (pre-2004) and 'new' (post-2004) EU member states respectively and are selected for analysis for several reasons. First, there are important demographic and linguistic grounds: the two countries are demographically the largest among 'old' and 'new' EU members respectively; they also have the largest number of speakers of German and Polish, the 'old' and 'new' members' most widely spoken languages. Second, there are significant political and historical reasons: while the frontiers of the two countries also demarcate the 'traditional' mental boundaries of Western and Central/Eastern Europe, there are many historical experiences and differences between Germany and Poland, which were to some extent reconciled by their involvement in the EU project and in particular by the 2004 enlargement (although many tensions remained or resurfaced, as Jaworska shows in this volume). Thus, by investigating public spheres in the countries whose 'national languages' were, or were about to become, very strongly represented in the institutions of the EU as of May 2004, this study aims to assess whether particular language ideologies which are tied to those languages and their role in the ongoing processes of nation-building (see Wright 2000) have also been 'enlarged' and projected on the future 'grand' construction (as well as, indeed, everyday functioning) of the institutions of the EU.

In terms of the 'European' (supranational) strand of our present context, the EU has been characterized by many political and institutional reforms ever since the EU began to develop into a political rather than a purely economic organization in the late 1980s (see Krzyżanowski and Oberhuber 2007). However, the most important occurrence of recent years has been the 2004 enlargement, which must be seen as one of the most pivotal points in the history of the European integration process. On the one hand, enlargement was a moment of crucial *political change* in the EU: it transformed the EU from a club of 'rich' Western European states into a supranational political organism which, as of 2004, incorporates several Central and Eastern European Countries (CEEC). Furthermore, perceived demographically, the EU following enlargement counted 74 million 'new' inhabitants from the CEEC. On the other hand, enlargement must also be seen as a point of pivotal *institutional change*: from 1 May 2004, the EU institutions started to incorporate representatives of the new CEEC member states (within, for example, all three core EU institutions),[5] which thus necessitated the introduction of new rules for the everyday practices of the EU institutions. That, in turn, was of paramount importance for the intra-institutional linguistic repertoire of the EU institutions and for the emergence of new forms of language planning regulating those practices.[6]

Throughout the last decade – that is, the time of preparation and eventual culmination of the eastward enlargement process – multilingualism has become one of the key focal points of EU policy. Once associated with non-EU areas of activity, multilingualism entered the EU agenda in the aftermath of the so-called Lisbon Strategy of 2000 (see European Council 2000). As the Strategy clearly listed (foreign) languages among the basic skills which, sustained through life-long learning, are to foster the EU's new goals, it was not long before related issues such as language learning, multilingualism and linguistic diversity in Europe/EU became central to the EU's agenda. In what followed, we have seen countless EU-initiated activities, action plans, declarations, resolutions, reports and surveys dealing with European multilingualism. Starting with the grand-scale set of actions of the 2001 European Year of Languages, through the European Commission's Action Plan 2004–6 on Promoting Language Learning and Linguistic Diversity (2003) or the recent document on Multilingualism: An Asset for Europe and a Shared Commitment (2008) – to mention just a few activities and documents – we have seen that the EU has made multilingualism and linguistic diversity one of its central topics.

However, it is also hard to overlook the fact that multilingualism became one of the EU policy buzzwords in the first decade of the twenty-first century, that is, not only at the time of the enlargement but also during the period when the EU found itself in one of the most turbulent stages of its development. Beset by ever-clearer internal crises, the EU was also increasingly criticized for its, by then, long-standing and ever-deeper 'democratic deficit' (cf. Majone 1994; Moravcsik 1998; Weiler, Begg and Peterson 2003; Follesdal and Hix 2006). Additionally, the project of the 'Big Bang' of the EU's 2004 and 2007 eastward enlargement also complicated the already uneasy EU internal situation. And although the EU has clearly recognized many of its current problems and forthcoming challenges by initiating *inter alia* its Constitutional project (cf. Krzyżanowski and Oberhuber 2007), it is certain that the development of the EU, once seen as an unending process (see Abélès 2000) has come to an unprecedented halt.

Methodology

The analytical methodology applied in this study is based on the methodological apparatus of Critical Discourse Analysis (cf. inter alia Fairclough and Wodak 1997), particularly in the 'discourse-historical' tradition (cf. Reisigl and Wodak 2001; Wodak 2001, 2008). Within this methodology, different context levels are taken into consideration, starting from the broader socio-political context (see above) and progressing to the (inter)textual context of, in our case, analysed press reporting (see below).

The discourse-historical methodology divides the analysis of discourses into two steps. Within the first step of the analysis, a scrolling of all analysed texts (here, press articles) is performed in order to devise lists of key 'topics of discourse', which are understood as text-semantic units which represent 'the most "important" or "summarizing" idea that underlies the meanings of a sequence of sentences... a "gist" or an "upshot" of such an episode...' (van Dijk 1984: 56, original emphasis; cf. van Dijk 1988, 1991). The main aim of the second, 'in-depth' step of analysis is to discover the qualitative features of those strands of discourse about the 2004 EU enlargement which debated this process from the point of view of 'languages', 'multilingualism' and other language-related issues, particularly in the focal context of the EU institutions.

Given the argumentation-oriented focus of the second step of analysis, its core analytical category is that of *arguments* (or *topoi*), which are identified in order to examine the ways in which arguments were structured and endowed with a discourse-pragmatic meaning. Based on both classical (Aristotelian) and modern argumentation theory (see van Eemeren and Grootendorst 1984, 1992; also Kienpointner 1992; Reisigl and Wodak 2001), *topoi* are defined here as 'structures of arguments', in which textual contents are positioned in a way that allows for the argument to lead to a particular (more or less logical) conclusion intended by the authors of the texts. Other categories of in-depth analysis were applied to support the examination of the key arguments described above. Those categories, previously applied in the discourse-historical analysis of transnational press reporting on Europe- and EU-related issues (cf. Oberhuber et al. 2005; Krzyżanowski 2009), included *inter alia* (a) *metaphors* and *metaphorical expressions*, approached here as chiefly linguistic-rhetorical devices supporting different arguments summarised by the topoi; and (b) strategies of *'nomination'* and *'predication'* as well as other strategies of *'self- and other presentation'* (Reisigl and Wodak 2001), which made it possible to discover how the image of different real-world objects and groups[7] was constructed in discourse, and how their varied degree of agency was thus portrayed and conveyed through the analysed media texts.

Empirical material

The newspaper corpora analysed in this study were compiled by obtaining articles in microfilm (Germany) and printed form (Poland). The newspaper search (the period of investigation) encompassed the ten days between 26 April and 5 May 2004, that is, five days before and five days after the date of the EU enlargement. During the search, the so-called large corpus of all of the identified newspaper articles reporting on the enlargement process was established. That corpus made it possible to identify the scope of the general newspaper interest in the enlargement as such by pointing to the diverse ways in which the different newspapers (liberal vs. conservative) and countries approached the issue.

The large corpus included the leading German liberal daily newspaper, the *Süddeutsche Zeitung* (SZ, published in Munich), as well as the largest conservative daily, the *Frankfurter Allgemeine Zeitung* (FAZ, published in Frankfurt am Main). The editions of the FAZ examined included the Sunday edition, the *Frankfurter Allgemeine Sonntagszeitung*. The Polish sub-corpus was drawn from the Polish liberal newspaper the *Gazeta Wyborcza* (GW, currently Poland's largest newspaper), and the key radical-conservative daily, the *Nasz Dziennik* (ND, closely tied to and co-owned by the equally radical Radio Maryja). Tables 2.1–2.4 provide an outline of the Polish and German corpora as well as of the frequency of reporting in the period of investigation (for further details, see Krzyżanowski and Wodak 2007).

Table 2.1   Reporting on the EU enlargement 2004 in *Süddeutsche Zeitung* (SZ)[8]

	26/04 MO	27/04 TU	28/04 WE	29/04 TH	30/04 FR	01/05 SA	02/05 SU	03/05 MO	04/05 TU	05/05 WE	TOTAL
NR	2	3	3	5	7	–	–	9	1	3	33
COM	5	4	2	5	10	–	–	3	–	3	32
EDIT	–	–	–	–	–	–	–	–	–	–	0
OT1	1	1	–	1	1	–	–	1	–	1	6
OT2	–	–	–	1	–	–	–	1	–	–	2
TOTAL	8	8	5	12	18	–	–	14	1	7	73

Table 2.2   Reporting on the EU enlargement 2004 in the *Frankfurter Allgemeine Zeitung* (FAZ)

	26/04 MO	27/04 TU	28/04 WE	29/04 TH	30/04 FR	01/05 SA	02/05 SU	03/05 MO	04/05 TU	05/05 WE	TOTAL
NR	5	2	2	4	5	–	5	11	1	–	35
COM	2	8	36	3	7	–	1	4	1	–	62
EDIT	1	–	1	–	1	–	1	2	–	–	6
OT1	–	–	4	–	1	–	1	1	–	–	7
OT2	–	–	1	–	1	–	1	–	–	–	3
TOTAL	8	10	44	7	15	–	9	18	2	0	113

Table 2.3   Reporting on the EU enlargement 2004 in *Gazeta Wyborcza* (GW)

	26/04 MO	27/04 TU	28/04 WE	29/04 TH	30/04–03/05 FR–MO	01/05 SA	04/05 TU	05/05 WE	TOTAL
NR	10	5	10	8	8	4	9	7	61
COM	2	–	1	7	6	25	5	3	49
EDIT	–	–	–	–	2	1	–	–	3
OT1	1	1	1	–	2	4	–	–	9
OT2	–	–	1	–	–	5	–	–	6
TOTAL	13	6	13	15	18	39	14	10	128

Table 2.4   Reporting on the EU enlargement 2004 in *Nasz Dziennik* (ND)

	26/04 MO	27/04 TU	28/04 WE	29/04 TH	30/04–03/05 FR–MO	04/05 TU	05/05 WE	TOTAL
NR	2	2	4	1	3	2	5	**19**
COM	1	4	3	6	4	2	3	**23**
EDIT	–	–	–	–	–	1	–	**1**
OT1	–	–	1	–	–	–	–	**1**
OT2	–	–	–	–	–	–	–	**0**
TOTAL	**3**	**6**	**8**	**7**	**7**	**5**	**8**	**44**

The large corpus was subsequently scaled down by screening the contents of all the newspaper articles and identifying those which (thematically) related to the issues of languages, multilingualism, and so forth. This selection included articles which focused specifically on languages/multilingualism and articles which referred to these issues among others. In both cases, the articles were identified by searching for keywords such as 'language', 'languages', 'multilingual' and 'multilingualism'.

The quantitative analysis of the small corpus (see Table 2.5) reveals that languages/multilingualism and related issues were very rarely discussed and were clearly perceived as marginal. Languages and multilingualism were mostly discussed (or actually mentioned or touched on) by means of scattered references (69 in total) as well as, though to a significantly lesser degree, by means of entire articles devoted to language-specific issues (ten in total). Of the Polish newspapers GW was most likely to refer to languages/multilingualism (32 articles and references in total, the largest number of references with 31). However, the German newspapers devoted more attention to the topic than their Polish counterparts (44 references/articles for SZ and FAZ combined); and SZ had the

Table 2.5   Key data on the small corpus on languages/multilingualism and related issues in the German and Polish press

	GERMANY		POLAND		TOTAL
	SZ	**FAZ**	**GW**	**ND**	
References	19	18	31	1	**69**
Articles	5	2	1	2	**10**
Sub-totals	24	20	32	3	–
TOTAL	**44**		**35**		**79**

most articles devoted principally or solely to multilingualism/languages (five in total). In terms of the liberal/conservative orientations, no clear discrepancies in referring to or describing language issues could be found in the German case, but in the Polish case the number of references/articles in the liberal GW (32 in total) clearly outnumbered those in the conservative ND (three in total).

Analysis[9]

Thematic analysis

In the German case, the large corpora of SZ and FAZ covered similar topics to debate the historical dimensions of the EU enlargement as well as several enlargement-related issues (Turkey and its eventual EU accession, the EU Constitutional process, the division of Cyprus, changes in Eastern/Western Europe before and after EU enlargement). Languages/multilingualism (in the small corpus) were widely put into the context of 'profiling' new/old EU members and merely describing them, albeit from the newspaper-specific liberal and conservative angles. Thus, the SZ concentrated mostly on socio-economic aspects of enlargement (in Germany and elsewhere in Europe) as well as on the then persistent post-Iraq 'Old Europe' vs. 'New Europe' debate, always with a very strong focus on selected acceding countries and their relations to Germany (here Poland received most attention). The FAZ, which also made its discourse clearly bilateral (by describing relationships between Germany and the accession countries), also focused on strictly EU-related matters (the Constitution, enlargement vs. development of European integration, and so on), whilst not neglecting specific areas of socio-political reality which would be affected (for example, the economy, education).

Therefore, the small corpus of the German newspapers put languages/multilingualism into the context of the larger topics/issues debated in conjunction with enlargement. They also marginalized language issues on the level of 'features' of countries or issues described in the texts. Hence, as was the case above, different countries were profiled in part by means of their languages and linguistic diversity (Slovenia, Cyprus, Latvia) while, for example, the frequent descriptions of the education sector (in Germany and elsewhere in the current/new EU countries) included many references to (SZ and FAZ), and several articles on (SZ), language tests, classes undertaken in various languages, translations of diplomas, language learning for future professional opportunities, and so forth. Importantly, within those rather marginal references to languages/multilingualism, little attention was paid to combining those issues with the changing EU institutions. In references which linked the two, the FAZ referred (3 May) to the growth of the number of EU working languages to 20, while the imminent growth of the European Commission's translation service was also described (27 April). For its part, the SZ (5 May) provided one full article about the changing linguistic situation in the EU institutions (analysed below).

Reporting in the Polish newspapers proved to be very diverse in terms of the intensity and scope of issues/topics discussed in connection with enlargement. On the one hand, as expected, the strongly pro-EU GW discussed enlargement from a number of perspectives, including topics pertaining to politics, society, economics and culture (both national and transnational) and to a very detailed profiling of the EU accession states. In that context, enlargement was perceived by the GW as an historical opportunity for both current and future EU members, while many historical and symbolic aspects of enlargement, such as the 'de facto breaking of the Cold War division of Europe' were thematized. On the other hand, the very anti-EU approach of the conservative ND (evident in, for example, its silence on enlargement as such) resulted in the fact that the enlargement process was perceived negatively, if at all, that is as a danger and a threat to Polish national independence (in political and economic terms and, very explicitly, to Polish national culture). In this context, many parallels were provided between, for example, the postwar Soviet domination of Poland and the current 'new domination' of the EU and its negative impact on Polish socio-political reality (see Jaworska, this volume).

The issues pertaining to languages and multilingualism occur in the Polish small corpus in a way that clearly reflects the general features of press reporting (both liberal and conservative) in Poland. Hence, the GW uses languages to describe the immensely positive and broad diversity of Europe. First, for example, in the country profiles provided, the reporting encompasses enlargement countries (such as Latvia and Slovenia) and the current EU member states with very 'characteristic' languages or linguistic landscapes (Finland with two official languages, the Netherlands with its language which is 'difficult' for Poles, the UK with its many dialects and sociolects of English, and so on). Second, the language skills of Polish citizens (mainly in English and German) were also described in the context of the new job opportunities for Poles in some of the 'old' EU countries. By contrast, in the ND, the specifically 'endangered' Polish language was mentioned in two articles (both 28 April) when Poland's ratification of the European Charter for Regional or Minority Languages was debated and (despite not having a clear link to EU politics as such) put into the context of the EU enlargement process and the ongoing 'Europeanization' of Poland. Again as expected, the EU institutions were linked with language issues only in the GW, specifically in a one-page article (5 May), which described the linguistic struggles in the EU institutions (see below for analysis).

Illustrative in-depth analysis

The key German article linking multilingualism/languages and the EU institutions was published in the SZ on the last day of the examined reporting, 5 May 2004.[10] This article, describing the EU translation service following enlargement, was entitled 'Heilbutt Maltesisch? Seit der EU-Erweiterung rotieren die Übersetzer in Brüssel' ('Halibut in Maltese? Since the enlargement of the EU the interpreters in Brussels are in a flap) and occupied about 20 per cent of the page.

The article, which describes the post-enlargement expansion of the EU translation service from the perspective of a Danish translator/interpreter (Mr Andersen), argues that, with enlargement, linguistic 'complexity has risen again' (*'nun ist die Komplexität nochmals gewachsen'*) due to the increase in the number of official languages:

Example 1

Mussten die Dolmetscher bisher nur mit elf Amtssprachen jonglieren, so sind es seit Anfang der Woche knapp doppelt so viele. Neun Sprachen sind mit der EU-Erweiterung am 1. Mai dazugekommen.

(Up to now the interpreters only had to juggle with eleven official languages, but since the beginning of this week there are twice as many. Nine further languages came with the enlargement of the EU on 1 May.)

Although this new linguistic situation is not described as a danger or a problem, it is clearly seen in uneasy terms as 'a challenge' (*'eine Herausforderung'*) which mainly boils down to the fact that not enough highly skilled translators could be found in time. As the article suggests, despite a very active search for new members of the translation service since 2003, the general 'marathon-like selection process' (*'[das] marathonartige[n] Bewerbungsverfahren'*) of the EU-specific 'Concours' resulted in the fact that, of all the enlargement countries, only Poland was able to engage enough translators and interpreters. In the case of other countries, particularly the small ones, among which Malta is mentioned as a key example, the question was asked whether it actually made sense to make their languages official languages of the EU.

Example 2

> Und angesichts der nur 400 000 Einwohner auf Malta denkt sich mancher in der EU wie absurd es war, der Hartnäckigkeit der Insel-politiker nachzugeben und Maltesich zur Amtssprache zu erklären, obwohl die meisten Bewohner der Mittelmeerinsel ohnehin Englisch sprechen.

> (And given that there are only 400,000 inhabitants in Malta, some people in the EU think it was absurd to give in to the intransigence of the island's politicians and declare Maltese an official language, despite the fact that most of those living on the Mediterranean island speak English anyway.)

Here the representative character of multilingualism in the EU is challenged in favour of one of the 'core' EU-15 working languages (English), and this challenge is crucially achieved by casting Maltese not as an element of Europe's culture but rather as a political tool used by Maltese politicians (whose 'intransigence' is overtly thematized) in the accession process. An unspecified quantifier is strategically used as the subject of the sentence, so that it is alleged that unidentified (though seemingly numerous) 'people in the EU' think that it was 'absurd' to allow Maltese to be made an official language.

Such arguments, which succinctly oppose the new linguistic diversity in EU institutions, are provided later in the article when a statement by the interviewed member of the translation service is quoted and interpreted:

Example 3

> Das Schöne an Europa ist die Vielfalt – auch die der Sprachen – erklärt Andersen die offizielle Linie. Es klingt wenig enthusiastisch.

> (The beauty of Europe is its diversity – including that of its languages – as Andersen explains the official line. It hardly sounds enthusiastic.)

Here, the interpretation of the statement as the 'official line' is crucial in identifying the newspaper's stance vis-à-vis the new, nominalized 'diversity' (*'Vielfalt'*) of languages in the EU. By claiming that the translator's statement 'hardly sounds enthusiastic' (*'klingt wenig enthusiastisch'*), the author presents it (which apparently remains objective) as a negative statement in support of the anti-diversity stance, which then becomes clearer in the article.

That stance is later developed when (for no apparent reason) the declining role of the French language in EU institutions is discussed. It is suggested, seemingly in line with the unspecified French media, that:

Example 4

Durch den Beitritt der osteuropäischen Länder schwindet der Einfluss des Französischen . . . Andersen bestätigt die Sorge der Franzosen: 'Von den Bewerbern aus dem Osten haben die meisten als erste Sprache Englisch gelernt, nicht Französisch.'

(Through the accession of the Eastern European countries French is losing its influence . . . Andersen confirms the concerns of the French: 'Of the Eastern candidates, most have English, not French, as their first [foreign] language.')

Here, the factual evidence of English being widely used among the representatives of the enlargement countries is, quite surprisingly, used as sufficient proof for the fact that French is 'losing its influence' (*'schwindet der Einfluss des Französischen'*). Importantly, French is hence portrayed as being engaged in a specific struggle with English, whereas, despite the fact that we are dealing with a German newspaper, the role of German in the EU institutions is never brought to the fore or even discussed (thus German appears to be outside the linguistic struggles taking place within the institutions of the EU). On the contrary, the importance of the role of English tends to be frequently referred to, as in the final part of the article which is devoted mainly to different translation-related anecdotes from EU institutions. It is suggested, for example, that English is frequently used in translation and interpreting as a bridging language, with debates being interpreted first into English and then into the other languages.

A somewhat different picture of the language-ideological debates in the EU emerges from a long commentary published in the Polish liberal daily *Gazeta Wyborcza* four days after enlargement, on 5 May 2004 (p. 11). In the article entitled 'Unijna Wierza Babel' ('The Union's Tower of Babel') and dealing with the linguistic situation within EU institutions, a set of language-based struggles is described as currently ongoing in the EU. Interestingly, unlike in the German case discussed above, the language-related issues are dealt with throughout the entire article (occupying a whole page) and are not relegated to selected (closing) paragraphs or parts of the text.

The article opens with a clear macro-proposition which summarizes its 'message'.

Example 5

Do mowiącej 11 językami unijnej wierzy Babel doszło teraz kolejne dziewięć języków ale rozszerzenie UE wzmocniło pozycję angiel-skiego. Wojna o językowy prymat wydaje się mało prawdopodobna, ale francusko-niemiecki opór przed dominacją angielskiego w UE przybiera coraz bardziej zorganizowane formy.

(The Union's Tower of Babel speaking in eleven languages has now been enlarged by nine further tongues, though the enlargement strengthened the position of English. A war over linguistic primacy is not very likely, although the French-German resistance to the domination of English in the EU is taking ever better organised forms.)

In this example, the opening statement alone is symptomatic: using several conceptual metaphors of war – mostly pertaining to different forms of combating ('war', 'resistance', 'positions'), but also to the description of the EU as a conflict-ridden 'Tower of Babel' – it portrays the EU and its institutions as an arena of ongoing (rather than past) struggle in which languages should eventually take priority. And while it is acknowledged that the position of English (which, as is argued later in the article, is said to be widely spoken among the representatives of the enlargement countries) as the key means of communication within the EU will be hard to overestimate, it is shown that there are other (though very few and selected) languages which are at least trying to recover their ground in the EU institutions.

Among the languages which are 'combating' the dominance of English, French emerges as the main opponent.

Example 6

Kilka miesięcy temu francuscy deputowani przegłosowali w Zgro-madzeniu Narodowym jednogłośnie rezolucję mierzącą w 'hege-monię języka angielskiego' w Unii.

(A few months ago French parliamentarians in the National Assembly unanimously passed a resolution against 'the hegemony of the English language' in the Union.)

However, this French resolution (described later as 'only wagging a finger') amounted to no more than the requirement that all French EU officials should be obliged to use 'French only' in their work in the EU's institutions. Such a plea is argued against later in the article since communication within the EU institutions would be significantly hindered if all EU officials used their native languages ('Germans and Austrians would start to speak in the Union's fora only in German, Spaniards only in Spanish', and so on).

Later, various ways of resolving the language-related struggles and 'wars' in EU institutions are described. Hence, the idea of being obliged to speak in a foreign language is first referred to as using a selected language (for example, English) as the medium of communication. Here, it is argued that choosing English as the EU lingua franca was indeed approached as an 'undemocratic heresy', while it is at the same time acknowledged that what counts is not that only 16 per cent of EU citizens are native speakers of English but that almost a third of the EU's citizens can freely communicate in that language. However, it is also argued that, in the EU context, the English-only option does give immense power to its native speakers, since they are then able to use their thorough native knowledge of the language to shape EU laws in their favour.

In the following part of the article, the history of the linguistic struggles in the EU is presented: here it is argued that with successive enlargements of the EU since 1973, when the UK joined the then European Community, and through the enlargement of 1995 when 'English-skilful Swedes and Finns joined', the position of French has been gradually decreasing within EU institutions (whilst '1 May 2004 has pushed French even closer to the margin').

Example 7

> Liczby mowią same za siebie – na początku lat 80. ponad połowa unijnych dokumentów urzędowych powstawała w języku francuskim, w latach 90. odsetek ten spadł tylko do 30 proc....Język Moliera dominował też wówczas na najsłynniejszej w Europie Sali prasowej – w Breydel, gdzie codziennie o 12 w południe zbiera się ponad 100 dziennikarzy akredytowanych przy Komisji Europejskiej. Wielkim szokiem było wprowadzenie angielskiego na salę prasową w drugiej połowie lat 90.
>
> (The numbers speak for themselves: at the beginning of the 1980s more than half of the EU documents were drafted in French, while

that number dropped to only thirty per cent in the 1990s....The language of Molière [French] dominated in Europe's most famous pressroom – in Breydel where more than a hundred journalists accredited by the European Commission gather every day at noon. It came as a great shock when English was introduced in the pressroom in the second half of the 1990s.)

However, it is not only French (referred to as 'the language of Molière') which remains in a state of struggle over its role within EU institutions. As the article also suggests 'the language of Goethe' (German) is also fighting to restore its importance, particularly vis-à-vis the ever-more powerful 'language of Shakespeare' (English). Despite being the EU's third official language, as well as the language with the most native speakers throughout Europe and in the EU, German is clearly losing ground.

Example 8

Zaledwie 3 proc. korespondencji unijnych urzędnikow z państwami członkowskimi oraz 1 proc. Korespondencji pomiędzy Komisją a pozostałymi instytucjami UE prowadzona jest po niemiecku.

(Only 3 per cent of correspondence between the Union's officials and the member states and only 1 per cent of correspondence between the European Commission and other EU institutions is conducted in German.)

But it is later argued that the Germans' motivation for recovering their language's role in EU institutions is not dictated by ideological or national identity reasons (as was suggested with reference to the French actions described above), but has some strictly practical implications.

Example 9

Niemcom chodzi nie tylko o prestiż, ale też o miejsca pracy w Unijnych organach, o dostęp do informacji i szanse w przetargach na realizacje europejskich zamówień publicznych.

(Germans are not so much concerned with the issues of prestige as they are with job opportunities in the Union's institutions, access to information and the good opportunities in European Union-funded public tenders.)

Finally, in its closing section, the article suggests that the language-related struggles in the EU remain (for the time being) unresolved, yet, as it is acknowledged:

Example 10

Na razie Unia działa na starych zasadach, ale niewykluczone, że rozszerzona Unia będzie musiała coś zrobić ze swą wieżą Babel.

(The Union is still working within its old rule, yet one cannot exclude the possibility that the enlarged Union will have to do something with its Tower of Babel.)

Thus, by referring elliptically once again to the EU as a metaphorical 'Tower of Babel' (as is the case in the title of the piece and in its opening sentence), the ongoing language struggle in the EU institutions is recognized, as is the fact that, in the future (with this and the forthcoming enlargement(s)), the unsatisfactory language policies of the EU institutions will need to be revised.

Illustrating our earlier claim about 'selective/hegemonic multilingualism' in EU institutions, the article clearly portrays the language-ideological debates taking place in the EU as limited to a set of core languages (English, French and German) which are represented and defended within the EU by their powerful 'representative' countries (the UK, France and Germany). Other languages are rarely, if ever, portrayed as contributing to the struggle since, implicitly, those who are set to represent them (namely, the respective countries) are not considered to be powerful enough to defend their languages. And while languages (other than those from the 'core group') such as Spanish and Italian are mentioned occasionally, the languages of the '2004 enlargement countries' are never thematized or referred to and, accordingly, their role (as well as that of the other non-core languages) is limited to that of quasi-bystanders in the ongoing EU language-ideological debates.

Conclusions

As has been demonstrated, despite their clear political salience as emphasized by the EU in recent years, the issues of languages and multilingualism were not prominent in the press reporting on the 2004 EU enlargement in Germany and Poland. In particular, the 'new' linguistic diversity and multilingualism of EU institutions were seldom discussed and only in a very limited number of articles and references. That in turn suggests a somewhat limited politicization of the issues of languages and multilingualism in the context of the EU institutions: this results in the fact that languages, particularly in the context of the EU institutional arrangements, are still approached in a highly marginal and mechanistic way (for example, as a way of translating and interpreting debates on other, more crucial issues). Languages, accordingly, are still set to make way for debates pertaining to politics, economics, education and other issues which are central to the processes of social and political transformation (particularly in the CEEC). That is, in turn, influential on the general perception of languages and multilingualism in the national public spheres of the two post-transformation countries analysed here: the latter are rarely interested in language(s) and related issues, which contributes to the generally low public perception of the salience of languages in the context of the EU and its recent enlargement(s).

However, the press reports on the 2004 EU enlargement analysed here generally acknowledge that the process is of prime importance to the growth of the broadly perceived diversity of the 'cultural space' of the EU. That diversity, as has been frequently described (mainly though by means of the few and incidental references described above), is reinforced by the growth of the linguistic capital of the EU after enlargement. That is to say, many of the analysed newspapers saw the EU enlargement as a process in which many new languages joined the EU while the cultural diversity of the EU was seen as increasing. However, while the increase in the number of official languages in the EU was perceived as a crucial and positive development in a broader European perspective, that diversity clearly was not transferred to the level of the focal EU institutions, in the context of which any further diversification of official/working languages was seen as an obstacle, perhaps as a 'challenge', but never as a positive development or an asset.

Hence, the following image of a multilingual Europe (or at least of a multilingual EU) was constructed by the German and Polish media. Despite placing multilingualism on its agenda in recent years, the EU is only eager to make 'broader' Europe linguistically diverse while, apparently for the purpose of political control, it would rather limit the multilingualism in its own institutions. Accordingly, the press analysis above shows an immense discrepancy between, on the one hand, descriptions of languages/multilingualism as positive (though clearly cultural, folklore-like) elements of the European cultural space and, on the other hand, the rather negative perception of the increased multilingualism of EU institutions. That discrepancy is neither arbitrary nor accidental: while 'allowing' for linguistic diversity (and the resulting multiplicity of visions and ideas of Europe) is permitted in the loosely defined, broad area of the European space, it is not allowed in the area of EU institutions (and politics), where the actual political interests and visions are realized and negotiated.

The analysis also shows that media-based German and Polish public spheres do not allow for the 'mirroring' of Europe's (also linguistic) diversity in the communicative and political space of EU institutions. That is, in turn, influential on the fact that the respective national publics are not able to see the EU institutions as inherently multilingual (that is, not as mirroring the linguistically ever more diverse EU-rope outside Brussels), since the media did not forge any public expectations about linguistic and other (e.g. political) diversity within EU institutions. Here, importantly, a strategic role for the media in post-transformation contexts must be recognized: they clearly highlight the role of enlargement as a crucial socio-political change (in 'Europe') and foster public expectations about the growing diversity of the European space. At the same time, however, the media clearly play down the role of the 2004 enlargement as a crucial moment of political-institutional change in the EU institutions, where the status quo is still keenly and actively defended and any fundamental change is prevented.

The 'Europe vs. EU discrepancy' (see Krzyżanowski and Oberhuber 2007) is crucially reflected in the general picture of diverse language ideologies which, as shown in the analyses, were, as hypothesized, inscribed in several language-ideological debates. On the one hand, within the broader level of Europe/European space, where languages were perceived positively, language ideologies were scarce and, if considered at all, were clearly supporting *de facto* multilingualism. Within the latter, 'positive' language ideology, the plurality of languages within EU-ropean space (*not* EU institutions) was considered as an asset since it emphasized the unique richness of the cultural space of the EU member states. Importantly, however, that ideology was actually not so much constructed as merely represented in the analysed instances of discourse: as we have seen, languages were only among the 'primordial features' of the enlarging and ever more diverse EU-rope, and were simply 'described' rather than championed. Further, and still within the broad area of Europe, we have seen that, if thematized, some language ideologies pertained to selected national landscapes and the role of particular languages within them. Here, a peculiar (though fairly traditional) ideology of nationalistic monolingualism came to the fore in the Polish conservative press, which opposed the EU in general and its enlargement in particular as a threat to Polish culture and to its core element, that is, the Polish language. However, since it was rooted in the overt opposition to the idea of any transnational European integration as such, that 'nationalistic' ideology also could not be considered as viable for different conceptions of multilingualism in EU institutions.

On the other hand, as expected, the most salient ideological stance which was elaborated and championed in the context of the EU institutions was the previously hypothesized hegemonic multilingualism. Discursively, that ideology was constructed by means of debating the contested state of competition between English, German and French for primacy among the EU's most commonly used and most important (working) languages (cf. also van Els 2001, 2005; Phillipson 2003; Ammon 2006). Hegemonic multilingualism was mainly encountered in different examples of the liberal press (in the then 'old' EU country of Germany as well as in the accession state of Poland) clearly reflecting the pre-enlargement linguistic status quo of the EU – with the key 'working languages' of English, German and French – which, as was frequently suggested, should continue in the aftermath of the big socio-political change marked by 1 May 2004. Despite promoting more than one language, that ideology was far from the actual multilingual stance that would allow all languages of the EU member states to be fully represented in the EU institutions and their everyday functioning. On the contrary, while it was acknowledged within various displays of hegemonic multilingualism that several languages of the enlarged EU should be given some symbolic status as the EU's 'official languages', it was even more strongly argued that only selected 'core' languages – which apparently do not include any of languages of the 2004 EU enlargement countries – will (and should) remain the *de facto* 'working languages' used in the everyday functioning of the political organism of EU institutions.

Notes

1. This chapter is based on research conducted within the EU Sixth Framework Integrated Project 'DYLAN: Language Dynamics and Management of Diversity' (www.dylan-project.org).
2. For other extensive analyses of media coverage of the 2004 EU enlargement, see de Vreese and Boomgarden (2006); Krzyżanowski and Wodak (2007); Schuck and de Vreese (2006).
3. Ruth Wodak and I coined the notion of 'hegemonic multilingualism' (see Krzyżanowski and Wodak 2007).
4. Those premises would, however, be rarely highlighted as *de facto* reasons for linguistic inequality, and instead other legitimating strategies, such as 'efficiency', 'simplification of procedures', and so on, would be used to

justify them. See also Phillipson (2003) for further arguments on the debate surrounding the increased use of English in EU politics and institutions.

5. The *de facto* enlargement of the European Parliament took place in the aftermath of the first post-EU enlargement elections which were held in mid-June 2004. However, it must be noted that representatives of the acceding CEEC states were also present as EP observers as of mid-2003 or as members of the 2002–3 Convention on the Future of Europe (see Krzyżanowski and Oberhuber 2007 for further details).

6. The 2004 EU enlargement is also seen as a process exemplary of the enactment of new language-based institutional patterns and procedures. The later enlargements (e.g. 2007 involving Bulgaria and Romania) clearly followed the procedures of enlarging the linguistic repertoire of the EU worked out and implemented in the aftermath of 2004.

7. For a specifically actor-oriented analysis of a construction of different social groups in discourse, see van Leeuwen (1996).

8. Abbreviations in Tables 2.1–2.4: NR = News Report; COM = Commentary; EDIT = Editorial; OT 1 = Other 1; OT 2 = Other 2. Other 1 and Other 2 denote different genres used variably in the newspapers analysed here.

9. Due to limitations of space, I only analyse language-related debates pertaining to the EU institutions and disregard other language-related debates.

10. Importantly, despite discussing languages/multilingualism in the broader context of the enlargement, none of the articles published in the FAZ related those issues to EU institutions, while only several minor 'statistical references' on the growing number of EU official languages were provided.

References

Abélès, M. (2000) 'Virtual Europe', in Bellier and Wilson (2000), 31–50.

Ammon, U. (2006) 'Language conflicts in the European Union', *International Journal of Applied Linguistics* 16(3), 319–38.

Bellier, I. and Wilson, T. M. (eds) (2000) *An Anthropology of the European Union: Building, Imagining and Experiencing the New Europe* (Oxford: Berg).

Blackledge, A. (2005) *Discourse and Power in a Multilingual World* (Amsterdam: John Benjamins).

Blommaert, J. (ed.) (1999a) *Language Ideological Debates* (Berlin: Mouton de Gruyter).

Blommaert, J. (1999b) 'The debate is open', in Blommaert (1999a), 1–39.

Bruhn-Jensen, K. and Jankowski, N. (eds) (1991) *Handbook of Qualitative Methods in Mass Communication Research* (London: Routledge).

Caldas-Coulthard C-R. and Coulthard, M. (eds) *Texts and Practices. Readings in Critical Discourse Analysis* (London: Routledge).

de Cillia, R., Krumm, H-J. and Wodak, R. (eds) (2003) *The Costs of Multilingualism: Globalisation and Linguistic Diversity* (Vienna: Austrian Academy of Sciences).

de Vreese, C. H. and Boomgarden, H. (2006) 'Media effects on public opinion about the enlargement of the European Union', *Journal of Common Market Studies* 44(2), 419–36.

European Council (2000) *Presidency Conclusions – Lisbon European Council of 23 and 24 March 2000* (Brussels: Council of the European Union).

Fairclough, N. and Wodak, R. (1997) 'Critical Discourse Analysis', in van Dijk (1997), 258–84.

Follesdal, A. and Hix, S. (2006) 'Why there is a democratic deficit in the EU: a response to Majone and Moravcsik', *Journal of Common Market Studies* 44(3), 533–62.

Fossum, J. E. and Schlesinger, P. (eds) (2007) *The European Union and the Public Sphere. A Communicative Space in the Making?* (London: Routledge).

Gal, S. (1998) 'Multiplicity and contestation among linguistic ideologies', in Schieffelin et al. (1998), 317–31.

Gal, S. (2005) 'Language ideologies compared: metaphors and circulations of public and private', *Journal of Linguistic Anthropology* 15 (1), 23–37.

Gal, S. (2006) 'Migration, minorities and multilingualism', in Mar-Molinero and Stevenson (2006), 13–28.

Galasińska, A. and Krzyżanowski, M. (eds) (2008) *Discourse and Transformation in Central and Eastern Europe* (Basingstoke: Palgrave Macmillan).

Kienpointner, M. (1992) *Alltagslogik: Struktur und Funktion von Argumentationsmustern* (Stuttgart: Frommann-Holzboog).

Krzyżanowski, M. (2006) *Media Research: Poland and Austria. Report Prepared for The European Commission within EU-FP6 'EMEDIATE: Media and Ethics of the European Public Sphere'* (Lancaster: Lancaster University), (http://www.iue.it/RSCAS/Research/EMEDIATE).

Krzyżanowski, M. (2009) 'Europe in crisis: discourses on crisis-events in the European press 1956-2006', *Journalism Studies* 10(1) (special issue on 'Questioning European Journalism' ed. H. Örnebring).

Krzyżanowski, M. (forthcoming) *Becoming European: Discourses of Identity and Social Change in Polish Politics after 1989* (Amsterdam: John Benjamins).

Krzyżanowski, M. and Galasińska, A. (2008) 'Introduction: discourses of social and political transformation in the "New Europe"', in Galasińska and Krzyżanowski (2008).

Krzyżanowski, M. and Oberhuber, F. (2007) *(Un)Doing Europe. Discourses and Practices of Negotiating the EU Constitution* (Brussels: P.I.E.-Peter Lang).

Krzyżanowski, M. and Wodak, R. (2007) *Multilingual European Institutions and the Discourse on the EU Enlargement in the National Public Spheres: A Pilot Study. Report Prepared for the European Commission within EU-FP6 'DYLAN: Language Dynamics and Management of Diversity* (Lancaster: Lancaster University).

Langenbucher, W. R. and Latzer, M. (eds) (2006) *Europäische Öffentlichkeit und Medialer Wandel* (Wiesbaden: VS Verlag für Sozialwissenschaften).

Majone, G. (1994) 'The European Community as a regulatory state', *European Community Law* 1, 321–419.

Mar-Molinero, C. and Stevenson, P. (eds) (2006) *Language Ideologies, Policies and Practices: Language and the Future of Europe* (Basingstoke: Palgrave Macmillan).

Moravcsik, A. (1998) *The Choice for Europe: Social Purpose and State-Power from Messina to Maastricht* (New York: Cornell University Press).

Oberhuber, F., Bärenreuter, Ch., Krzyżanowski, M., Schönbauer, H. and Wodak, R. (2005) 'Debating the European Constitution. On representations of Europe/the EU in the press', *Journal of Language and Politics* 4(2), 227–71.

Phillipson, R. (2003) *English-Only Europe? Challenging Language Policy* (London: Routledge).

Reisigl, M., and Wodak, R. (2001) *Discourse and Discrimination* (London: Routledge).

Ricento, T. (ed.) (2005) *An Introduction to Language Policy: Theory and Method* (Oxford: Blackwell).

Schieffelin, B., Woolard, K. and Kroskrity, P. (eds) (1998) *Language Ideologies: Practice and Theory* (Oxford: Oxford University Press).

Schuck, A. and de Vreese, C. H. (2006) 'Framing the EU enlargement. News media content and effects', in *European Journal of Communication* 21(1), 5–32.

Shohamy, E. (2006) *Language Policy: Hidden Agendas and New Approaches* (London: Routledge).

Silverstein, M. (1998) 'The uses and utility of ideology. A commentary', in Schieffelin et al. (1998), 123–45.

Spolsky, B. (ed.) (2004) *Language Policy* (Cambridge: Cambridge University Press).

Thomaß, B. and Tzankoff, M. (eds) (2001) *Medien und Transformation in Osteuropa* (Wiesbaden: Westdeutscher Verlag).

Trenz, H-J. and Eder, K. (2004) 'The democratising dynamics of the European public sphere: towards a theory of democratic functionalism', *European Journal of Social Theory* 7(1), 5–25.

Triandafyllidou, A., Wodak, R. and Krzyżanowski, M. (eds) (2009) *The European Public Sphere and the Media: Europe in Crisis* (Basingstoke: Palgrave Macmillan).

van Dijk, T. A. (1984) *Prejudice in Discourse* (Amsterdam: John Benjamins).

van Dijk, T. A. (1988) *News as Discourse* (Hillsdale, NJ: Lawrence Erlbaum Associates).

van Dijk, T. A. (1991) 'The interdisciplinary study of news as discourse', in Bruhn-Jensen and Jankowski (1991), 108–20.

van Dijk, T. A. (ed.) (1997) *Discourse as Social Interaction* (London: Sage).

van Eemeren, F.H and Grootendorst, R. (1984) *Speech Acts in Argumentative Discussions* (Dordrecht: Foris Publications).

van Eemeren, F.H. and Grootendorst, R. (1992) *Argumentation, Communication and Fallacies* (Hillsdale, NJ: Lawrence Erlbaum Associates).

van Els, T. (2001) 'The European Union, its institutions and its languages: some language political observations', *Current Issues in Language Planning* 2(4), 311–60.

van Els, T. (2005) 'Multilingualism in the European Union', *International Journal of Applied Linguistics* 15(3), 263–81.

van Leeuwen, T. (1996) 'The representation of social actors', in Caldas-Coulthard and Coulthard (1996), 32–70.

Weiler, J. H. H., Begg, I. and Peterson, J. (eds) (2003) *Integration in an Expanding European Union. Reassessing the Fundamentals* (Oxford: Blackwell).

Wodak, R. (2001) 'The discourse-historical approach', in Wodak and Meyer (2001), 63–94.

Wodak, R. (2008) 'Introduction: discourse studies – important concepts and terms', in Wodak and Krzyżanowski (2008), 1–29.

Wodak, R. and Koller, V. (eds) (2008) *Handbook of Communication in the Public Sphere, Handbook of Applied Linguistics* Vol. IV (Berlin: Walter de Gruyter).

Wodak, R. and Krzyżanowski, M. (eds) (2008) *Qualitative Discourse Analysis in the Social Sciences* (Basingstoke: Palgrave Macmillan).

Wodak, R. and Meyer, M. (eds) (2001) *Methods of Critical Discourse Analysis* (London: Sage).

Wodak, R., and Wright, S. (2006) 'The European Union in cyberspace: multilingual democratic participation in a virtual public sphere', *Journal of Language and Politics* 5 (2), 251–75.

Wright, S. (2000) *Community and Communication: The Role of Language in Nation-State Building and European Integration* (Clevedon: Multilingual Matters).

Wright, S. (2004) *Language Policy and Language Planning: From Nationalism to Globalisation* (Basingstoke: Palgrave Macmillan).

Part II
Border Crossings

3
The German Language in Poland: the Eternal Foe and the Wars on Words[1]

Sylvia Jaworska

Introduction: language as symbolic capital

'A language is worth what those who speak it are worth.'

Bourdieu (1977: 652)

The aim of this chapter is to examine the current status of the German language in Poland and to envisage its future standing in the linguistic marketplace in this part of Europe. Some may wonder why such an undertaking is necessary. After all, German is a prestigious language in this part of Europe – a new lingua franca. Indeed, for some time there has been a widespread belief that German is a language of intercultural communication in Poland, as it is elsewhere in Central and Eastern Europe (cf. Pfeiffer 1992; Darquennes and Nelde 2006). For many, this was evidenced by the proximity of the German-speaking communities, the presence of German minorities and the high number of learners of German as a foreign language. In particular, the latter is flagged as proof of the high status that German has: Poland is, according to data provided by StaDaF (Goethe Institut 2005), a country where German is widely taught and learnt. However, the quantitative data is highly decontextualized and based on figures from one sector only: state education. It presents a homogeneous picture and does not reveal many of the dynamic mechanisms and nuances which are emerging in this context, and appear to indicate significant changes in linguistic practices. While I would agree that some quantification is necessary to capture tendencies and developments in 'linguistic marketplaces', such data often only scratches the surface (Holliday 1994: 5).

Linguistic practices are not stable 'units' that occur in laboratories. They are always embedded in multifaceted and dynamic contexts and are shaped by historical, social and political factors. Recent work, particularly within a poststructuralist framework, has demonstrated the relevance of social and political dynamics, as well as of social boundaries in the process of language choice, learning and use (Norton-Peirce 1995; Lantolf 2000; Norton 2000; Norton and Toohey 2002). By drawing on Bourdieu (1977, 1991), the poststructuralist framework recasts linguistic practices as forms of symbolic capital inevitably bound to the issues of power, domination and struggle in the relationship between individuals and communities. Against this background, language is conceptualized as an investment which provides access to various symbolic and material resources, such as education or employment (Norton-Peirce 1995). Thus, individuals are likely to 'invest' in (i.e. learn and practise) another language or linguistic variety if they expect it to yield good returns, namely access to wide range of opportunities and consequently an increase in their cultural capital (ibid.: 17).

The notion of language as investment should not be confused with the now classic concept of instrumental motivation developed within the socio-psychological paradigm, which assumes motivation to be a stable variable (Gardner and Lambert 1959; Schumann 1978). Rather, it endeavours to capture the dynamic relationship between individual choices and the ever-changing society, which can set positive or negative conditions for language choice and use (Norton-Peirce 1995; Pavlenko 2002).

In the poststructuralist view, a language is always imbued with values attached to the community of those who speak it within a multilingual environment, particularly to the perception of what the *other* linguistic community is, what it has, what it does and what it offers (Carli et al. 2003). If a particular community offers access to its symbolic and material resources, which in turn could bring desired returns, then the value of its language is perceived as high. It becomes a prestigious variety, likely to be learnt and to become a tool of intercultural communication (see Pavlenko 2002; Carli et al. 2003). Conversely, if a community does not provide desired resources or simply restricts access to them through, for example, various gatekeeping mechanisms and hence limits opportunities for participation and interactions, its language could soon be viewed as being of little symbolic and material value, and hence not worth acquiring.

Perceptions on values and prestige are collective judgements which result from asymmetries between the linguistic communities involved, and are elements of a complex and ongoing power-game (Carli et al. 2003). Power relations and asymmetries can be indicated on the basis of quantitative data, normally the number of speakers or learners (ibid.). However, such data says little about the collective value judgements and attitudes towards languages that are detrimental to the *actual symbolic* value of a language. Thus, if one wants to understand the challenges faced by linguistic practices, one needs to move beyond the quantitative data and explore how a community indexes other communities and what values and attributes it ascribes to them and their languages.

By considering language as a form of investment, and the role of the socio-political context as pivotal in setting conditions for language choice, learning and use, this chapter examines the mechanisms that determine the status of German in Poland. The material presented for this analysis is interesting in many ways. Germany and Poland are neighbouring states and their border is recognized as one of the 'fault lines' of Europe – the German-Slavic linguistic zone of conflicts and asymmetries (Chilton 1998: 5). This geographical positioning, and the historical baggage that goes with it, already hint at a fractious interactional space (see Wilkinson, this volume). Indeed, the vicissitudes of history have largely influenced the status of German and the attitudes to it in Poland.

From being simply a contact language with a direct neighbour – a medieval trader – German became, over the centuries, the language of an enemy and oppressor associated with aggression and violence (Grucza 2002). From the early 1990s onwards, a rather dramatic change in attitudes towards the Germans and their language took place in Poland. This was accompanied by the development of a new discourse, in which the key words were reconciliation, partnership and dialogue. At the same time, the number of people learning German in Poland doubled, and some even celebrated it as a new lingua franca (cf. Pfeiffer 1992). And yet, at the beginning of the new millennium, we are confronted with a different picture. Instead of advancing the dialogue of the 1990s, a monologue of resentments is being increasingly heard in Poland. The number of people learning German in state education is still high and various institutions, German and non-German, are keen to promote the language as an important communication tool in this part of Europe.[2] However, one has to be cautious when treating German as a lingua franca in Central and Eastern Europe solely on the basis of the number of learners. As discussed above, the statistical data masks some of the salient features and needs to be offset and complemented by an analysis of attitudes and collective value judgements associated with the Other, that is to say, with the Germans, Germany and the German language. The print media play a critical role in this respect, as they reproduce and disseminate the discourse of the Other, and in so doing make salient certain values and iconic representations. Thus, this chapter starts with an examination of the representation of Germanness (that is the German language, culture and society) in public discourse in Poland by analysing a corpus of articles published in the period 2003–7 in the three Polish newspapers with the largest readership: the liberal and pro-European daily *Gazeta Wyborcza* (GW), the conservative daily *Nasz Dziennik* (ND) and the weekly magazine *Wprost* which has a conservative but liberal orientation. Drawing on a discourse-analytical methodology (Chilton and Schäffner 1997; Schäffner 2002), the analysis focuses on the key topics which are discussed in relation to Germany and the Germans, and the ways in which the Other is linguistically constructed. Of particular interest is the question of how the German language is positioned in the public discourse and what value judgments, if any, are made about it. In the second section, I look at the popularity of German in Polish educational institutions and the position of German as a minority language. In doing so, this chapter ultimately endeavours to assess the role of the German language in the linguistic marketplace in this part of the EU and to consider how the situation may change in the future. Will German become a tool of intercultural communication, and what are the conditions which could block or facilitate this process?

From the discourse of reconciliation to the rhetoric of war and Germanization

Following the collapse of the Eastern Bloc, Poland underwent radical political, social and economic changes. It emerged as a democratic country with a free market economy and political pluralism. All of this was accompanied by rapid cultural and linguistic changes. The regime of the Russian language was overthrown and Western languages were enthusiastically welcomed. In line with the ideals of egalitarianism and transparency, and as an antidote to the old political jargon, new forms of discourse have developed in the public sphere (Duszak 2006). These were characterized by more dialogic and open communication patterns (ibid.).

However, these positive and open attitudes slowly gave way to disillusionment. For many Polish citizens, the pro-Western transformations proved to be the equivalent of shock treatment. It soon became clear that not everyone was benefiting from the market economy. In fact, unemployment was rising dramatically, while at the same time, social security networks were dramatically scaled down. Fears, insecurities and social disparities started to shape Poland. Thus, at the eve of accession to the EU and immediately afterwards, the pro-Western stance underwent a process of re-evaluation. The positive discourse of gains, winners and opportunities was supplemented by a discourse of losses, losers and barriers. Increasingly, Europeanization and globalization were seen as threats to the Polish national identity, cultural values and language (Skotnicka-Illasiewicz 2000). As Duszak (2006) observes, Polish society finds itself in a state of axiological dualism, divided between a pro-European, liberal orientation and a protective, nationalist stance. The general election in 2005 clearly demonstrated this.[3]

In all of these processes, Germany played a significant role. This western neighbour strongly supported Poland's attempts to join the EU and NATO. This was accompanied by a host of political landmarks in bilateral relations, such as the Treaty of Good Neighbourliness in 1991 and an agreement finalizing the controversial issue of the Oder–Neisse border, which was ratified in 1992. These treaties and ongoing support accelerated cultural and economic cooperation, which in turn increased the level of positive attitudes towards the western neighbour (Bingen and Malinowski 2000; Holzer and Fiszer 2001). The transformation was perceived as an enormous political success and was directly reflected in the changing way in which Germans and Germany were portrayed in public discourse.

During the period immediately after 1945, Germany was (for obvious reasons) demonized; and this was mirrored and reinforced in the terminology used to describe Germans. As Wolff-Powęska (2005: 70) observes, the function of the language was to punish. Germans were never presented as individuals but as a collective and abhorrent mass of Nazis and aggressors, while the Polish word for Germans was spelt with a lower case initial to emphasize the contempt with which they were viewed. In addition, there was a strong belief that aggression was an inherent and age-old characteristic of the German nation from the Middle Ages onwards. Hence, other images frequently used were those of the Teutonic Knights and the Prussians, both of which are connected in the Polish collective memory with negative experiences, particularly with the *Drang nach Osten* (Drive to the East), oppression and Germanization.[4] Phrases such as *alle raus, Hände hoch* and *halt* (everyone out, hands up, stop) in their original German forms were frequently employed to keep alive the memory of the shouting, belligerent Nazis and indexed German as a language of commands and orders. This anti-German stance was also reflected in the language policy of the period: the teaching of German was reduced to an absolute minimum and actually forbidden in the regions that were part of Germany before 1945.

A substantial change of attitude and a new discourse emerged following the collapse of the Eastern Bloc. A completely new phraseology, unthinkable before 1989, entered the discourse on Polish–German relations. Reconciliation, partnership, dialogue and the Polish–German community of interests were the new key words, while *raus* and *halt* disappeared. At the same time, there was a growing interest in the German language which, instead of being seen as the language of the eternal enemy, was increasingly perceived as a passport to the West and the instrument of westernization.

During the 1990s, the number of learners of German in state schools doubled. As a study by Walenczak and Wróblewska-Pawlak (1997) on language preferences of Polish pupils reveals, the main reason for learning German was the perceived work opportunities that the language could offer in both countries and beyond. Thus, Germany was seen as a country of opportunities, while the language, despite the common perception of it as being harsh and difficult to learn, was now regarded as a tool granting access to new symbolic and material resources. The vision of Germany as an open, welcoming country disseminated by the print media played a significant role in reinforcing such attitudes.

The situation changed on the eve of Poland's accession to the EU. Just at the point when Germany and Poland seemed to be reaching reconciliation, numerous incidents caused tensions and overshadowed the good relationship established in the 1990s. The trigger points were the activities of the German organization *Preußische Treuhand* (Prussian Trust). This organization began numerous legal actions demanding compensation for, or the return of, property which belonged to the Germans before 1939. At the same time (in 1998 to be exact), Erika Steinbach, a relatively unknown CDU politician in Germany, was elected head of *Der Bund der Vertriebenen* (League of Expelled People). She demanded recognition for Germans expelled from the (now) Polish western territories. This generated a great deal of controversy in Poland and was widely reported in the Polish print media.

In 2003, the liberal weekly magazine *Wprost* addressed the topic by putting a picture presenting Steinbach in a Nazi uniform on the front page. The Germans were portrayed as a malicious and aggressive enemy, who only masqueraded as a friend in order to gain material assets at the expense of Poles. This was symbolized by a portrait of Germany as a Trojan horse (*Wprost* 38, 2003), by making explicit references to the

Nazi Reich and the Prussian state, and the use of phraseology associated with war and battles, for example, 'Bomba Steinbach' (Bomb of Steinbach, *Wprost* 39, 2003), 'Kły IV Rzeszy' (Tusks of the Fourth Reich, *Wprost* 31, 2004), and 'Zimna Wojna Polsko-Niemiecka' (Polish-German Cold War, *Wprost* 35, 2006).

The *Gazeta Wyborcza* (GW), a liberal and pro-European daily newspaper, approached the issue with disbelief at first, as the headlines 'Sąsiedzi, zróbcie coś!' (Neighbours, do something! GW, 3 July 2003) and 'Co się stało, sąsiedzi?' (What has happened, neighbours? GW, 21 January 2004) illustrate. The Germans were still seen as neighbours, and not as the enemy. However, over the course of time, even GW's tone became more heated, and references were made to Prussia, war, devils and other negative attributes, for example 'Pruski Atak' (Prussian attack, GW, 4 August 2004), 'Debata upiorów' (Debate of the devils, GW, 22 September 2004) and 'Ci podstępni Niemcy' (These perfidious Germans, GW, 4 October 2004).

The concept of the Polish–German community of common interests, widely used in the 1990s, was overtaken by the concept of 'polsko-niemiecka wspólnota kłopotów' (Polish–German community of problems, GW, 10 December 2005), of which the most crucial were a lack of communication and dialogue. Indeed, Germany and Poland were frequently portrayed in GW as nations unable to talk and listen to each other. In fact, the dialogue initiated in the 1990s had become a 'dialogue of the deaf' ('Jak rozmawiać z Niemcami?', How to talk with the Germans? GW, 30 October 2006). Even when attempts are made, for example on the local level through school exchanges, there seems to be a solid wall between the two communities, as GW reported in an article with a headline in German 'Keine Grenzen?' (No borders?, GW, 28 June 2003).[5] The River Odra, which functions as a border between Germany and Poland, is seen as the mythological River Styx. For both sides crossing the river means a journey into the underworld.

The conservative Catholic daily *Nasz Dziennik* (ND) dedicated a large number of articles to Erika Steinbach and the demands of the Prussian Trust. However, in contrast to GW, which tried to analyse and understand the problem, ND always presented the issues as an attack on Poland, as the headlines 'Prusacy szykują nowe skargi na Polskę' (Prussians are preparing new claims against Poland, ND, 15 March 2007) and 'Erika Steinbach atakuje polski rząd' (Erika Steinbach is attacking the Polish government, ND, 27 June 2007) exemplify. References were also made to the Bismarckian *Kulturkampf*, which in the Polish collective memory is closely associated with the imposition of German as a first language ('Od Wrześni[6] do Kolonii', From Września to Cologne, ND, 21 August 2007). Some references suggest that the activities of the Prussian Trust and Erika Steinbach are seen as a continuation of the aggressive Germanization policy that affected the Polish population in the territories annexed by the Prussian state in the nineteenth century. For example, Germany was described as *Hakata*, the popular name given by Poles to denote the Prussian nationalist organization *Deutscher Ostmarkenverein*, established in 1894 in Poznań to expand the German national spirit and language in this region ('Od Wrześni do Kolonii', From Września to Cologne, ND, 21 August 2007).[7]

For ND, there has never been any genuine reconciliation between the two nations, and the Poles had been brainwashed into believing that Germany was supporting Polish interests:

> W to, że stosunki polsko-niemieckie są idealne, nie wierzy już chyba nikt - choć tak niedawno niewiara w ten dogmat była oznaką 'oszołomstwa' i 'szowinizmu'. Przez kilkanaście lat twierdzono, że mamy 'historyczne pojednanie' i 'adwokata' w Unii.

> (People no longer believe that Polish-German relations are all that wonderful. Not so long ago, such a statement would have been taken as a sign of 'stupidity' and 'chauvinism'. For many years, it has been claimed that we have a 'historical reconciliation' and a 'supporter' in the EU.)

> (Jasiński, *Nasz Dziennik*, 22 January 2007)

Another sign of creeping Germanization for the Polish media was the exclusion of Polish as a language of communication for/among children born to Polish-German families living in Germany. According to Polish newspapers, some local branches of the German *Jugendamt* (Youth Welfare Office) issued a ban on the use of Polish in cases where Polish-speaking parents separated from their German spouses. Polish-speaking parents were not allowed to use their mother tongue when visiting their children; conversations had to be in German. The Polish media described this as a new Germanization process or made references to the Nazis' notorious *Lebensborn* policy, as some of the headlines in all three newspapers illustrate: 'Twój syn będzie Niemcem, czyli nowy Lebensborn' (Your son will be a German: a new *Lebensborn*, GW, 3 November 2003), 'Nowa Germanizacja' (New Germanization, *Wprost* 31, 2006), 'Polnisch verboten!' (Polish forbidden! *Wprost* 33, 2004). There is no doubt that the decision of the *Jugendamt* offices in question was discriminatory. However, it is difficult to estimate to what extent such practices were a widespread phenomenon and whether any other family problems were involved. In fact, the issue was brought to the European Parliament in 2006, when some Polish-speaking parents submitted petitions alleging discrimination on the grounds of language (European Parliament 2007). The European Parliament ruled out that such language arrangements may have been justified by 'objective considerations independent of the nationality of those concerned and proportional to the legitimate objective of protecting the overriding interests of the child' (ibid.: 4), for example, the fact that the visits had to be supervised. In the Polish media the issue was presented from the point of view of the Polish parents, while the German partners were often linked with Nazi Germany. The problem was seen as a political confrontation between two nations, Poland and Germany, and as a continuation of the racist doctrine of Nazi Germany practised by the *Jugendamt*, as an example from ND illustrates:

Urzędy te zostały utworzone jeszcze przez hitlerowców do wychowywania 'czystych rasowo' dzieci.

(These offices [*Jugendamt*] were established by the Nazis for the purpose of rearing 'racially pure' children.)

(Maszewki, Nasz Dziennik 1 April 2007)

This topic also triggered a strong perception of the asymmetry of treatment and linguistic discrimination. In many articles it was emphasized that in Poland, the German minority is privileged in German-speaking schools, radio stations, various print media publishing houses and representatives in the Polish parliament. In contrast, citizens of Polish descent living in Germany do not enjoy such privileges, and are discriminated against if they use their mother tongue ('Pomniejszanie mniejszości', Making the minority smaller, *Wprost* 42, 2003, 'Zewsząd bariery', Barriers everywhere, ND, 18 August 2007). Language here is clearly a tool of division or even repression.

Apart from these historical, cultural and linguistic asymmetries, there are also economic barriers which have given rise in Poland to negative attitudes towards Germany. Whereas after EU enlargement the vast majority of European countries were gradually opening their labour markets to the newcomers, Germany and Austria restricted access, and continue to do so. This issue is portrayed as a bitter pill for Poles to swallow and as political cowardice on the part of Germany and Austria.

ND portrays the barrier, ironically, as an example of 'true German hospitality' (ND, 1 May 2008), while *Wprost* (12, 2004) describes it as *Rauspolitik* (actually using this German term). Even those who succeed in obtaining work in Germany or work for German companies in Poland are not equally treated. For example, *Wprost* (12, 2004) cites various cases of Polish workers being sacked unfairly by their German bosses, while GW refers to numerous and extra controls exercised on Polish workers working legally in Germany. As reported in the newspaper ('Nie kontrolujcie Polaków aż tak!' Don't control Poles so much, GW, 5 June 2007), the Germans always mistrust Polish workers and automatically assume that they must be breaking the law. One story which hit the front pages was the case of an employee at a German company based in Poland. He was sacked because he refused to speak German with his Polish co-workers. As highlighted in an article in GW entitled 'Hier wird nur Deutsch gesprochen!!! – Tutaj rozmawia się tylko po niemiecku!!!' (Only German is spoken here!!!, GW, 22 January 2007), the German company requested all workers to use German only, because customers, mainly Germans, might not react positively if they heard an East European language being spoken in the background. The management of the company denied this and argued that they simply wanted to give the workers the opportunity to use German all the time so that they could increase their command of the language. The Polish court ruled that there was a case of discrimination and the German company had to pay compensation.

The scope of this chapter does not allow for the discussion of more newspaper data. However, the examples chosen are symptomatic and demonstrate the linguistic, cultural and economic boundaries and asymmetries the current discourse on Polish-German relations is woven around. In fact, the discourse portrays both countries as homogenized, national unities: *they* – the Germans – have been always a threat to *us* – the Poles – and whatever they do is a continuation of their aggressive and long-established *Drang nach Osten*. There is an almost fatalistic belief that history always repeats itself, as reflected in the frequent use of the word 'again' in headlines, or references to symbolic historical events such as the Bismarckian *Kulturkampf* or *Hakata*. Indeed, history always seems to be the key to the interpretation of controversial events; the discourse always takes the reader back to the past, while the future of the relationship is presented as uncertain.

The more right-wing the newspaper, the stronger the focus on the past and on the Germans as oppressors. All in all, the discourse has visibly shifted from the concept of the German as a good neighbour (widely used in 1990s) to the German as an enemy. Moreover, Germany is perceived as a country which, through various barriers and restrictions, is trying to erect a wall along its eastern border, which seriously limits the opportunity for direct contacts and interaction.

Against this background, it is not surprising to see that the Polish media foreground the concept of the 'dialogue of the deaf' (GW, 30 October 2006), which symbolizes a lack of communication and understanding. The German language as such is not a matter for much debate. However, when it is discussed, it is seen as a tool of Germanization and oppression, as a language which is enforced. The negative connotations are highlighted by using words such *raus* or *verboten* in their original German forms, which are associated with a domineering Nazi and strengthen the perception of German as a language of orders and oppression.

The ways in which Germany and the Germans are portrayed in the public discourse may not directly and immediately influence the status of the German language in Poland. However, as a study by Wróblewska-Pawlak and Strachanowska (2000: 109) demonstrates, the major obstacles to learning German among school pupils are psychological aversion towards the language, connotations with Nazi Germany, harsh sounds and strident speech associated with it. These are precisely the images disseminated by Polish print media and thus they might further entrench such negative attitudes. Above all, the images leave a strong feeling of asymmetries and distrust.

Building walls and emphasizing divisions deepens the gulf between the two communities. The language of a neighbouring country could function as a bridge. However, given the few interactional opportunities, one may ask whether German is a good investment. Maybe it is worth looking East instead of West? As the next section demonstrates, the socio-economic dynamics may alter the status of the German language in Poland in the near future.

The current status of German as a foreign and minority language

German as a foreign language

Over the past 15 years, the foreign language sector in Poland has undergone substantial changes. The result of the democratic reforms of 1989 was that Russian (which until 1990 was the compulsory first foreign language in all educational institutions) lost its importance almost overnight, while interest in Western languages, particularly English and German, increased (Wróblewska-Pawlak and Strachanowska 2000). Such a scenario was common to many post-communist countries in Central and Eastern Europe (Nekvapil and Sherman and Maitz and Sándor, this volume).

By 1993–4, the number of pupils learning English and German was six times and four times greater respectively, compared with 1986–7 (ibid.). The situation has stabilized substantially since then. In 2004–5, there was a slight decrease in the number of German learners. At the same time, the number of learners of Spanish and Italian rose (Polish Ministry of Education 2005). Nevertheless, in the rank order of languages, English remains the most widely taught language, and further measures are being undertaken to strengthen its position in primary schools (i.e. starting at the age of seven). Currently, the first foreign language is introduced in grade four (pupils aged ten).

According to educational data, German has secured its position as the second foreign language in Poland (see Table 3.1). If we consider the aspect of language choice however, then the situation is less rosy. In fact, when two languages are compulsory (as in upper secondary education institutions) the difference in the number of German and English learners is appreciable, with 97.1 per cent learning English and 71 per cent learning German. Yet, in situations where only one language can be studied, English is well ahead. For example, in lower secondary schools where only one language is mandatory, 72.2 per cent of pupils opt for English, while only 30 per cent choose German (Polish Ministry of Education 2005). The high prestige of English is also reflected in the booming private language sector, which alongside regular language classes offers preparatory courses for candidates who wish to obtain widely recognised certificates (ibid.). Certificates in English are clearly in the lead: in 2004/5 there were 16,405 candidates taking an exam in

Table 3.1 The total number of school pupils (in %) learning foreign languages in Polish state education, 1992–2005

Year	English	German	French	Russian
1992/1993	18.2	16.0	3.2	34.0
1997/1998	32.5	23.9	4.0	19.7
2002/2003	62.4	34.8	3.8	9.7
2004/2005	65.3	34.2	3.4	6.7

Source: Polish Ministry of Education (2005) *Edukacja językowa w Polsce*, p. 11.

Table 3.2 The number of candidates registered for certificates in English and German, 2004/2005

English		German	
Certificates	**Candidates**	**Certificates**	**Candidates**
Cambridge First Certificate in English (FCE)	6,213	Zentrale Mittelstufenprüfung (ZMP)	56
Cambridge Certificate of Proficiency in English (CPE)	654	Zertifikat Deutsch	1,596
London Chamber of Commerce and Industry (LCCI)	4,258	Zentrale Oberstufenprüfung	162
Cambridge Certificate in Advanced English (CAE)	3,987		
Test of English as a Foreign Language (TOEFL)	1,293		
Total	**16,405**	**Total**	**1,814**

Source: Polish Ministry of Education (2005) *Edukacjajęzykowa w Polsce*, p. 26.

(British) English and only 1,814 in German (see Table 3.2). The most popular certificates are: the Cambridge First Certificate in English (FCE) and the London Chamber of Commerce and Industry Certificate (LCCI). The latter is professionally oriented and widely recognized as a passport to employment. These figures suggest that people in Poland are certainly more likely to invest their time and a substantial amount of money in English than in German.

If we look at the numbers of learners of German in each region of Poland, substantial disparities emerge. In western Poland, in the regions closest to the German border, German is learnt and taught on roughly equal terms with English: between 50 per cent and 60 per cent of pupils learn German. The further east we move, the fewer the number of learners of German. This reaches a low of 30 per cent in the regions near the Russian border. In these eastern regions, English is learnt by over 80 per cent of pupils (ibid.). The strong position of German in the regions near the German border can be explained by the presence of the German-speaking minority and the intensification of contacts between Germans and Poles in these regions after 1989 (see Wilkinson, this volume). The indifference to German in the east can be attributed to fewer direct contacts. The political views of the population in each region may also have an impact on language choice. It is striking that the regional distribution of the preference for German is almost identical to electoral preferences. In the regions where German is on a par with English, liberal and pro-European parties win. Conversely, in regions where German is less popular, national-conservative parties with their anti-European and anti-German allies are strongly supported. These regional differences undermine the frequent portrayal of German as a language widely learnt in Poland. Moreover, the quantitative data does not reveal the quality of teaching and the actual communicative potential of German, that is to say, the extent to which it is understood and used for communicative purposes.

A report entitled 'Eurobarometer: Europeans and their languages' (2006) presents some interesting findings in this respect. In Poland, 57 per cent of the respondents stated that they can hold a conversation in one foreign language, and 32 per cent in two languages. This positions Poland roughly in the middle of the other EU countries. As far as the range of languages spoken is concerned, English comes first with 29 per cent, followed by Russian with 26 per cent. German comes third with 19 per cent, the lowest percentage for German among the new EU member states. As evidenced by Wilkinson (this volume), even in the border regions where German enjoys very high status, it is not necessarily a successful tool of intercultural communication.

The relatively high percentage for Russian can be partly explained by its compulsory status between 1945 and 1989. However, there are also some signs that Russian is slowly making a comeback. The number of people learning it, particularly in non-state institutions, has recently increased because of the occupational prospects the language offers (BBC, Poles return to Russian language, 2007). While one should not overestimate this rise, the data demonstrates that Russian is once again being perceived as useful. The interest in the language may also be rising with the currently increasing economic, cultural and political ties with the former Soviet republics, particularly Ukraine. In this respect, it is important to note that Poland opened its labour market not only to workers from the new member states, but also to workers from non-EU countries such as Russia, Ukraine and Belarus.

Undoubtedly, the position of German in Poland is still strong, but its use as a means of communication is not as widespread as one might assume on the basis of the data on the number of learners. This can be partly explained by the fewer interactional opportunities that exist between the two countries. As discussed in the introduction, languages are increasingly perceived as investments, which should give 'access to hitherto unattainable resources' (Norton-Peirce 1995: 17). In this respect, English is seen from the Polish perspective as a better investment than German, as it permits access to the material and symbolic resources of the English-speaking countries in Europe, and therefore offers an opportunity to increase one's cultural capital.[8]

In contrast, the German-speaking countries restrict access to their resources for people from the new member states. German does not therefore guarantee as good a return on investment as English, and may even decline in the future. German is no longer perceived as a passport to the West. The restrictions imposed by Austria and Germany, combined with negative images associated with Germany, particularly the perceived discrimination and asymmetries, could further reduce its value in the linguistic marketplace in this part of Europe.

The problem of asymmetries and attitudes towards language can also be observed when considering German as a minority language within Poland – a topic discussed in the next section.

German as a minority language

The German-speaking minority constitutes the largest ethnic minority group in Poland, although their precise numbers are difficult to estimate and vary according to the sources. The Polish Ministry of Education (2005) estimates the German minority at about 150,000, while German sources quote figures closer to 600,000 (Rogall 2008). Whichever figure is more accurate, this still represents a very small proportion (ranging from 0.4 to 0.8 per cent) of the total population of Poland.

The fate of ethnic Germans in Poland immediately after 1945 was extremely difficult. The shift of the Polish border towards the West – a decision imposed by the Allies – was accompanied by the expulsion and transfer of millions of people. Germans were forced to evacuate the western Polish territories, which began to be occupied by Poles resettled from Poland's former eastern territories (which had been annexed by the USSR). Some of the German-speaking people who remained (mainly in Upper and Lower Silesia) were classified as Germanized Poles, whose true Polish identity (in the view of the communist regime) had been diluted by a long period of Germanization (Cordell and Wolff 2005). Thus, an intensive process of re-Polonization was launched. However, the Polish arrivals in the new western territories saw those Germanized Poles as Germans, and many acts of discrimination were recorded (Fleming 2003). As a result of the tensions between Bonn and Warsaw in the following decades, the Polish communist government increasingly sought to eject Germans. In fact, many emigrated to Germany, and by 1963 the Polish government officially declared that the German minority in Poland had ceased to exist. Thus, it came as a big surprise after 1989 when some groups in Upper and Lower Silesia unexpectedly and publicly disclosed their German origins. This was not welcomed and gave rise to anti-German feelings and tensions within the region (often expressed by slogans written on walls). Fleming (2003: 395) provides some examples: 'Nie chcemy Niemca: Śląsk – Polski' (We don't want Germans: Silesia – Polish), 'Szwaby do domu' (Krauts go home) or 'Nie głosuj na Szkopa' (Don't vote for the Hun). Due to some significant political landmarks in bilateral relations, particularly the Treaty of Good Neighbourliness (ratified in 1991), these tensions subsided to some extent. Soon afterwards, the German-speaking groups were recognized as a minority and were given the right to foster their culture, language and traditions. In fact, the German minority became very active in cultural and political terms, gaining two seats in the Polish parliament. The number of schools offering German as a minority language rose in Poland from zero to 385 by 2005 (Ministry of Interior and Administration 2007). All this led many to believe that there was a genuine revival of the German minority, its language and traditions (Fleming 2003). Certainly, there were some improvements, at least in economic terms. Ethnic Germans could claim dual nationality and hence obtain a German/EU passport, which in turn allowed them to take up temporary employment opportunities in Germany. The fact that they are dual passport holders and can speak German has been flagged as a significant advantage, which tangibly improves their material status. It is not surprising that such asymmetries have resulted in envy among the Poles, and antipathy towards their German neighbours. These tensions have very recently come to the fore, when the Polish Ministry of Interior and Administration allowed the use in some villages of place-name signs in both languages, Polish and German. This has not been welcomed by the Polish population, who openly resist the restoration of the former German names. For some, this is another sign of Germanization and a return of the German devils (Dżon 2008). The German minority, particularly the older generation, see the introduction of bilingual signs as something that could strengthen the roots of their identity in this region. There are indeed some indications that the links with Germany and the German language and culture have considerably weakened, particularly among the younger generation, whose competence in German is often very rudimentary. As emphasized in the Strategy for the Development of Education of the German Minority (Ministry of the Interior and Administration 2007), German is taught as a foreign language in the vast majority of schools attended by the members of the German minority, and the same classes are offered to pupils from the majority group. Only a few schools offer bilingual programmes or use German as the sole medium of instruction. This is justified by the lack of competence in German among the minority group pupils (ibid.). Thus, the enthusiasm about the growing number of schools offering German as a minority language has to be taken with a pinch of salt.

Fleming (2003) currently observes a process of alienation from Germanness, and the discontent which is, in his opinion, a result of temporary migration to Germany (many ethnic Germans, particularly the younger ones, cross the border into Germany to take up work opportunities). There is evidence to suggest that these Germans are othered or even discriminated against on the other side of the border (that is in Germany) on the basis of their foreignness, particularly their 'awkward' German or limited fluency in the language (Fleming 2003). They are seen as Poles speaking bad German. This is often the reason why they are marginalized and excluded from social mobility. For Fleming (2003), this is a considerable disincentive to adopt a German identity and the German language.

Conclusions

Central and Eastern Europe has always been an arena of tension and violent confrontation between linguistic communities, resulting in linguistic shifts in every case. Nowadays, European integration and globalization are both challenging linguistic practices, particularly the continuum between stigma and prestige. In some contexts, the long-stigmatized communities and their languages are acquiring a new, higher value, while the prestige of some dominant languages seems to have weakened. Such changes are inevitably linked with economic and socio-political shifts that have created asymmetries and ultimately influenced perceptions of the communities and their languages. These are, in turn, directly involved in creating negative or positive conditions for language choice, learning and use.

The case of German in Poland is a good example to illustrate the significance of socio-political dynamisms and perceptions of the Other on linguistic practices. In the 1990s, Germany – the admired neighbour – was seen as Poland's strongest supporter in the EU, and hence German was perceived as the key to open European doors and the wider world.

Learning German was, in the public perception, a good investment likely to yield substantial returns and increase one's cultural capital (cf. Walenczak and Wróblewska-Pawlak 1997). It became the second foreign language in Polish state education and in some parts of Poland a serious competitor to English.

At the beginning of the new millennium, enthusiasm for Germany and the German language seems to have cooled down. The barriers posed by Austria and Germany restrict interactions and mobility between the two linguistic communities creating a feeling of strong asymmetries. Instead of the rapprochement and good neighbourliness emphasized in the discourse of the 1990s, distance has grown and there is little communication, as symbolized by the phrase 'dialogue of the deaf'. In the current discourse Polish-German encounters are frequently indexed as sites of struggle and are interwoven with stereotypical, predominantly negative images of Germany and Germans, while the German language is foregrounded as a tool of discriminatory practices.

In their extensive overview of the position of German as a lingua franca, Darquennes and Nelde (2006: 74) conclude that the international standing of German would improve if language policy-makers from the German-speaking countries put more effort into developing 'innovative language spread strategies'. While the efforts of language policy-makers could certainly contribute to the promotion of German abroad, I believe that changes in the political domain (for example, lifting some of the restrictions and barriers) could potentially have a more profound effect. However, it remains to be seen what directions the German-speaking countries will assume in future and to what extent the balance between the protection on national interests and the free movement of people (and languages) in the EU will be redressed.

Notes

1. I would like to thank Ramesh Krishnamurthy and Jane Wilkinson for proofreading an earlier version of this chapter and providing many useful comments.
2. Promotional materials distributed by universities and colleges in English-speaking countries frequently highlight the importance of German as a language of communication and business in Central and Eastern Europe. Here are a few examples from a rather long list: http://www.ed.ac.uk/studying/undergraduate/finder/subject.php?id=3,45, http://www.mml.cam.ac.uk/german/courses/ugrad/initio.html, http://www.odu.edu/al/lang/german.htm, http://www.bu.edu/mlcl/about/why-study/german.html, http://www.languages.uconn.edu/programs/german/. Accessed 26 June 2008.

3. Just a year after accession to the EU, a general election was held in Poland, in which the nationalist-conservative Law and Justice Party won, with 54 per cent of all votes. Its opponent, the liberal and pro-European Civic Platform, gained 46 per cent.
4. The first book published in Poland after the war was the novel *Krzyżacy* (Teutonic Knights), written by the Nobel Prize winner Henryk Sienkiewicz (1846–1916). The book was written as a protest against Germanization. Its main motif was the defeat of the Teutonic Knights by the Polish-Lithuanian king Jagiełło in the battle of Grundwald in 1410 – an historical event which became a symbol of national glory.
5. The title of the article alludes to a trilingual Polish-German-Russian song with the same title written by Polish and German musicians. It was sung by the Polish group 'Ich Troje' at the Eurovision Contest in 2003.
6. Września is the name of a town in west Poland, which is a symbol of the Polish protests against Germanization at the beginning of the twentieth century.
7. The name *Hakata* is derived from the initials of the founders of Deutscher Ostmarkenverein: Ferdinand von Hansemann, Hermann Kennemann and Heinrich von Tiedemann-Seeheim. In the Polish collective memory, *Hakata* has negative associations; it is a symbol of the aggressive Germanization policy practised on the Polish territory annexed by Prussia in the nineteenth century (Wiktorowicz 2002).
8. The fact that for some English offers access to desirable resources and therefore could give life-changing opportunities is omitted from current discourse on English as a global language, which give rise to more negative reactions (Joseph 2004).

References

BBC (2007) 'Poles return to Russian language', http://news.bbc.co.uk/1/hi/world/europe/6233821.stm. Accessed 10 September 2008.

Bingen, D. and Malinowski, K. (eds.) (2000) *Polacy i Niemcy na drodze do partnerskiego sąsiedztwa* (Poznań: Instytut Zachodni).

Bourdieu, P. (1991) *Language and Symbolic Power* (Cambridge: Polity Press).

Bourdieu, P. (1977) 'The economics of linguistic exchanges', *Social Science Information* 16, 645–68.

Carli, A., Guardino, C., Kaučič-Baša, M., Sussi, E., Tessarolo, M. and Ussai, M. (2003) 'Asserting ethnic identity and power through language', *Journal of Ethnic and Migration Studies* 29(5), 865–83.

Chilton, P. (1998) 'The role of language in human conflict: prolegomena to the investigation of language as a factor in conflict, causation and resolution', in S. Wright (ed.), *Language and Conflict: A Neglected Relationship* (Clevedon: Multilingual Matters), 3–17.

Chilton, P. and Schäffner, Ch. (1997) 'Discourse and politics', in T. van Dijk (ed.), *Discourse as Social Interaction* (London: Sage), 206–30.

Cordell, K. and Wolff, S. (2005) 'Ethnic Germans in Poland and the Czech Republic: a comparative evaluation', *Nationalities Papers* 33(2), 255–76.

Darquennes, J. and Nelde, P. (2006) 'German as a lingua franca', *Annual Review of Applied Linguistics* 26, 61–77.

Duszak, A. (2006) 'Why new newspeak? Axiological insights into language ideologies and practices in Poland', in C. Mar-Molinero, and P. Stevenson (eds.) *Language Ideologies, Policies and Practices* (Basingstoke: Palgrave Macmillan), 91–103.

Dżon, B. (2008) 'Kogo bolą oczy od niemieckich nazw', *Przegląd* 21, http://www.przeglad-tygodnik.pl/index.php?site=reportaz&name=221.   Accessed 10 September 2008.

Eurobarometer (2006) *Europeans and their languages*,http://ec.europa.eu/public_opinion/archives/ebs/ebs_243_en.pdf. Accessed 10 September 2008.

European Parliament (2007) *Petition 0038/2006 by Wojciech Pomorski concerning discrimination regarding visiting rights on grounds of language.*

Fleming, M. (2003) 'The limits of the German minority project in post-communist Poland: scale, space and democratic deliberation', *Nationalities Papers* 31(4), 391–411.

Gardner, R. and Lambert, W. (1959) 'Motivational variables in second-language acquisition', *Canadian Journal of Psychology* 13, 266–72.

Goethe Institut (2005) *Deutsch als Fremdsprache weltweit. StaDaF Datenerhebung 2005* (München: Goethe Institut).

Grucza, F. (2002) 'Deutschunterricht und Germanistikstudium in Polen', in G. Helbig, L. Götze, G. Henrici and H. J. Krumm (eds.), *Deutsch als Fremdsprache. Ein internationales Handbuch. 2. Halbband* (Berlin and New York: Walter de Gruyter), 1528–43.

Holliday, A. (1994) *Appropriate Methodology and Social Context* (Cambridge: Cambridge University Press).

Holzer, J. and Fiszer, J. (eds.) (2001) *Rola Niemiec w procesie Integracji Polski z Europą* (Warszawa: Polska Akademia Nauk).

Joseph, J. E. (2004) 'Linguistic identity and the limit of global English', in A. Duszak and U. Okulska, *Speaking from the Margin. Global English from a European Perspective.* (Frankfurt am Main: Peter Lang), 17–33.

Lantolf, J. P. (2000) *Sociocultural Theory and Second Language Learning* (Oxford: Oxford University Press).

Ministry of Interior and Administration (2007) *Strategia Rozwoju Oświaty Mniejszości Niemieckiej w Polsce*, http://www.mswia.gov.pl/portal/pl/312/. Accessed 10 September 2008.

Norton, B. (2000) *Identity and Language Learning: Gender, Ethnicity, and Educational Change* (London: Longman).

Norton, B. and Toohey, K. (2002) 'Identity and language learning', in R. Kaplan (ed.), *Oxford Handbook of Applied Linguistics* (Oxford: Oxford University Press), 115–23.

Norton-Peirce, B. (1995) 'Social identity, investment, and language learning', *TESOL Quarterly*, 29(1), 9–31.

Pavlenko, A. (2002) 'Poststructuralist approaches to the study of social factors in second language learning and use', in V. Cook (ed.), *Portraits of the L2 User* (Clevedon: Multilingual Matters), 277–302.

Pfeiffer, W. (1992) 'Aktuelle Probleme der Sprachpolitik und des Sprachunterrichts: Beispiel Polen', in C. Gnutzmann, F. G. König and W. Pfeiffer (eds.), *Fremdsprachenunterricht im internationalen Vergleich: Perspektive 2000* (Frankfurt am Main: Diesterweg), 90–101.

Polish Ministry of Education (2005) *Edukacja językowa w Polsce*, http://www. men. gov.pl/wspolpraca/rada_europy/country_profile.php. Accessed 10 September 2008.

Rogall, J. (2008) 'Die Deutschen in Polen', in *Informationen zur politischen Bildung*, http://www.bpb.de/publikationen/0114278051821920091161108698 5322,6,0, Die_Deutschen_in_Polen.html. Accessed 10 September 2008.

Schäffner, Ch. (2002) 'Auf der Suche nach dem Feind – Anmerkungen zum NATO-Diskurs', in O. Pangal and H. Stürmer(eds.), *Politische Konzepte und verbale Strategien. Brisante Wörter – Begriffsbilder – Sprachbilder* (Frankfurt am Main: Peter Lang), 169–84.

Schumann, J. (1978) 'The acculturation model for second language acquisition', in R. Gingras (ed.), *Second Language Acquisition and Foreign Language Teaching* (Washington, DC: Centre for Applied Linguistics), 27–50.

Skotnicka-Illasiewicz, E. (2000) 'Może tu Wschód, a może Zachód...?', *Studia Europejskie* 14(2), 11–20.

Walenczak, I. and Wróblewska-Pawlak, K. (1997) 'Języki obce w Polsce – próba bilansu', *Studia Europejskie* 1, 135–54.

Wiktorowicz, J. (2002) 'Die deutsch-polnische Nachbarschaft und ihre Widerspiegelung in der polnischen Sprache', in D. Cherubin, K. Jakob and A. Linke (eds.), *Neue deutsche Sprachgeschichte. Mentalitäts-, kultur- und sozialgeschichtliche Zusammenhänge* (Berlin and New York: Walter de Gruyter), 337–48.

Wolff-Powęska, A. (2005) 'Wojny na słowa: Co Niemiec, to odmieniec', in *Polityka* 18, 70.

Wróblewska-Pawlak, K. and Strachanowska, I. (2000) 'Preferencje językowe młodzieży polskiej w okresie transformacji: 1990–1999', *Studia Europejskie* 1, 99–114.

Newspaper articles

'Bruksela: nie kontrolujcie Polaków aż tak!' (*Gazeta Wyborcza*, 5 June 2007).

'Twój syn będzie Niemcem, czyli nowy Lebensborn' (*Gazeta Wyborcza*, 13 November 2003).

'Zewsząd bariery' (*Nasz Dziennik*, 18 August 2007).

Buras, P. (2005) 'Polsko-niemiecka wspólnota kłopotów' (*Gazeta Wyborcza*, 10 December 2005).

Cywiński, P. (2004) 'Debata upiorów' (*Gazeta Wyborcza*, 22 September 2004).

Cywiński, P. (2004) 'Polnisch verboten!' (*Wprost*, 33, 2004) http://www.wprost.pl/ ar/64635/Polnisch-verboten/?I=1133. Accessed 10 September 2008.

Cywiński, P. (2006) 'Nowa Germanizacja' (*Wprost*, 31, 2006) http:// www.wprost.pl/ar/94195/Nowa-germanizacja/?I=1234. Accessed 10 September 2008.

Grzebałkowska, M. (2003) 'Keine Grenzen?' (*Gazeta Wyborcza*, 28 June 2003).

Jasiński, K. (2007) 'Matrix Pawelki' (*Nasz Dziennik*, 22 January 2007).

Jasiński, K. (2007) 'Od Wrześni do Kolonii' (*Nasz Dziennik*, 21 August 2007).

Kalicki, W. (2006) 'Jak rozmawiać z Niemcami?' (*Gazeta Wyborcza*, 30 October 2006).

Kowalewska, J. (2007) 'Hier wird nur Deutsch gesprochen!!!' (*Gazeta Wyborcza*, 22 January 2007).

Krysiak, P. (2004) 'Ci podstępni Niemcy' (*Gazeta Wyborcza*, 4 October 2004).

Kudzia, P. (2003) 'Bomba Steinbach' (*Wprost*, 39, 2003) http://www.wprost. pl/ar/49710/Bomba-Steinbach/?I=1087. Accessed 10 September 2008.

Maszewski, W. (2007) 'Erika Steinbach atakuje polski rząd' (*Nasz Dziennik*, 27 June 2007).

Maszewski, W. (2007) 'Niemcy chcą chipować dzieci' (*Nasz Dziennik*, 1 April 2007).

Maszewski, W. (2007) 'Prusacy szykują nowe skargi na Polskę' (*Nasz Dziennik*, 15 March 2007).

Rubinowicz-Gruendler, A. (2003) 'Sąsiedzi, zróbcie coś!' (*Gazeta Wyborcza*, 3 July 2003).

Semka, P. (2006) 'Zimna Wojna Polsko-Niemiecka' (*Wprost*, 35, 2006) http://www.wprost.pl/ar/94385/Zimna-wojna-polsko-niemiecka/?I=1237, date accessed 10 September 2008.

Sieradzki, S. (2003) 'Pomniejszanie mniejszości' (*Wprost* 42, 2003) http://www. wprost.pl/ar/50778/Pomniejszanie-mniejszosci. Accessed 10 September 2008.

Sieradzki, S. (2004) 'Rauspolitik' (*Wprost*, 12, 2004) http://www.wprost. pl/ar/57646/Rauspolitik. Accessed 10 September 2008.

Tobolski, T. (2008) 'Niemiecka gościnność' (*Nasz Dziennik*, 1 May 2008).

Wolff-Powęska, A. (2004) 'Co się stało, sąsiedzi?' (*Gazeta Wyborcza*, 21 January 2004).

Zagrodzka, D. Karski, K and Cieśliński, A. (2004) 'Pruski Atak' (*Gazeta Wyborcza*, 4 August 2004).

Zieleniewski, M. (2004) 'Kły IV Rzeszy' (*Wprost*, 31, 2004) http://www.wprost.pl /ar/63922/Na-stronie-Kly-IV-Rzeszy/&I=1131/. Accessed 10 September 2008.

4
'Die härteste Sprachgrenze Europas?' Negotiating the Linguistic Divide in Theatres on the German–Polish Border

Jane Wilkinson

Introduction: the German–Polish borderland

The German–Polish border is frequently referred to as 'die härteste Sprachgrenze Europas' (the hardest language boundary in Europe) (see Matthiesen 2002; Glante 2003: 3), not only because the two languages are so different, but also because very few Germans and Poles can speak both languages fluently. The resulting communication problems, particularly in the border region itself, only serve to exacerbate an already problematic relationship between two nations that have shared a shifting border and fought several wars over the centuries. Indeed, this problematic relationship is both the result and the cause of the widespread lack of language skills: reciprocal fears, prejudices and resentments mean that many Germans and Poles have little interest in learning the language of their neighbour – although German's 'prestige' as a western, international language means that considerably more Poles learn German than vice versa – and that they use their own language 'in the push and pull struggle to define some version of "self" over and against some "other"' (Artega 1994: 1; see also Jaworska, this volume). Put differently, language functions as an important 'identity marker' (Blommaert and Verschueren 1998: 192) or 'identity-constituting marker' (Meinhof 2003b: 792), which distinguishes Germans from Poles in the border region, where the national Other is in such close, and potentially threatening, proximity (cf. Bauman 2000: 176).

At a time when Europe, or at least the European Union, is moving towards greater political, economic and cultural integration, the

73

two functions of language as a means of communication and as an identity marker need to be balanced, particularly in border regions. For, as Paasi (2001: 17) explains, boundaries embody precisely this duality: 'Boundaries also mediate contacts between social groups, and not only separate them.' In the divided communities[1] of Frankfurt (Oder)/Słubice and Görlitz/Zgorzelec, situated right on the German–Polish border, one of the ways in which this balance is sought is through the staging of transborder cultural events, including theatre festivals and projects. As a live cultural form, theatre can bring people together in one place at one time for one purpose and thus holds considerable potential for breaking down boundaries and creating an at least temporary sense of equality and sharing; a state which the theatre anthropologist Victor Turner (1982) calls communitas. Theatre can construct a liminal or 'third' space (cf. Bhabha 1994) in which intercultural, cross-border communication and interaction ought to be possible (see also Schneider, this volume). However, at 'Europe's hardest language boundary', a cultural form which relies fairly heavily on language faces a number of problems, the most basic being which language(s) to use so that the audience can follow what is happening on stage.

The majority of the cultural institutions, including theatres, in the German–Polish border region are to be found in Germany; not least because the larger parts of the towns Frankfurt (Oder) and Görlitz were on the German side of the Oder and Neiße rivers respectively when the current border was drawn in 1945. This means that most transborder cultural projects are organized, or at least initiated, by Germans, be they individuals, groups or institutions, with the risk that some initiatives can be seen as being imposed on the neighbouring Polish communities. Consequently the choice of performance language is a sensitive issue embodying a complex web of language ideologies and policies. If theatres choose German as the language of production, they could be accused of closing themselves off from a Polish audience and of (re)asserting the dominance of their language, culture and identity in the borderland. This could reinforce the existing 'asymmetry' between Germany and Poland (see Holly et al. 2003) and deepen the 'socio-economic fault-line' (Meinhof 2003b: 789) that still runs the course of the former Iron Curtain. This is recognized by most directors and project managers in German theatres, who look for alternatives when organizing transborder events. These alternatives form the focus of this chapter, which examines the way in which the linguistic and cultural border between Germany and Poland is negotiated, and in some cases reconstructed, through decisions concerning language use in theatre. For, as Berg and van Houtum (2003: 2) so eloquently explain, since the end of the Cold War, 'borders have become predominantly interpreted as the communication of practices, as stories narrated by some for some and believed, identified with or contested by others'.

Since the lifting of the Iron Curtain in 1989 and, to an even greater extent, since EU expansion in 2004 and the extension of the Schengen area of 'borderless' travel[2] to include the first new member states in 2007, 'security borders' across Western and Central and Eastern Europe now exist only nominally (cf. Laitinen 2003). The boundary lines demarcating nation-state territories have not been erased; they are still to be found on any map of Europe and are, in most cases, still marked by 'welcome to' signs, flags and border posts on the ground. However, these boundary lines are no longer policed; after crossing the new outer border of the EU, now shifted significantly to the east, people, goods and money can travel freely between all member states signed up to the Schengen Agreement of 1985. But what does this relatively rapid dismantling of security borders across Europe mean for the inhabitants of borderlands? In their most basic function, nation-state boundaries may 'only...mark the limits of sovereignty' (Prescott 1987: 80), but in so doing they also mark and even create social, cultural and linguistic differences, which, as Laitinen (2003: 17) explains, cannot be erased with the same speed and ease as security controls:

> Practically, the transitional phase in the context of the security border means that there may be a rather rapid development in the field of economics or even in the political agenda, which again does not mean that the social or cultural sphere would follow at the same pace.

In their Border Identities project conducted in divided communities along the former Iron Curtain between 2000 and 2003 (immediately prior to EU expansion), Meinhof et al. found considerable discrepancies between the 'official' political rhetoric of European integration and the personal experiential narratives of borderland inhabitants (see Meinhof and Galasiński 2002; Meinhof 2002, 2003a, 2003b). Despite the establishment of cross-border 'Euroregions' and the funding of numerous transborder projects designed to bring people together, many interviewees still felt themselves to be separated and even distant from their neighbours across the border. Among the many reasons cited for this was the surviving linguistic divide (see Carli et al. 2003). Such findings reflect Ehlers, Buursnick and Boekema's (2001: 1) contention that 'the mental and emotional meanings of borders are becoming more important' and support Laitinen's (2003: 17) assertion that 'it takes time to "re-imagine" the political space we live in'. This chapter builds on the seminal research of Meinhof et al. and takes it forward by moving into the post-2004 period and by focusing on the role of cultural, specifically theatrical, production and language choice in the 're-imagining' of borderland spaces.

German versus Polish: a linguistic 'asymmetry'

It may seem obvious to suggest that good German–Polish relations in the border region are reliant on effective cross-border communication and that effective cross-border communication in turn demands adequate language skills on both sides. However, such assertions are frequently and necessarily repeated by politicians and academics concerned with language learning and language policy in Europe's border regions, including this one. Krumm (1999: 115), for example, states quite simply: 'Für die Pflege guter Nachbarschaft sind Sprachen das unentbehrliche Kommunikationsmittel' (Languages are the vital means of communication for the promotion of good neighbourly relations). Oppermann (2002b: 9) echoes these sentiments:

> Der gegenseitige Austausch von Fremdsprachenkenntnissen, zumal auf der Ebene der kulturberührenden Nachbarsprachen, ist dabei die conditio sine qua non europäischer Existenz.
>
> (The reciprocal exchange of foreign language skills, especially on the level of culturally contiguous neighbouring languages, is therefore the *conditio sine qua non* of European existence.)

In the German–Polish borderland itself, Krzysztof Wojciechowski (2002: 83–4) (director of the *Collegium Polonicum* in Słubice) argues that, 'die Fähigkeit zur Kommunikation bedeutet...die Fähigkeit, sprachliche Brücken zu bauen und über diese Brücken Inhalte zu transportieren' (the ability to communicate means...the ability to build linguistic bridges and to transport content across these bridges). He then laments that such linguistic competence, necessary for effective intercultural communication, is not possessed by the majority of people living in the German–Polish borderland, particularly on the German side.

Meinhof (2003b: 792) maintains that:

> Border communities constitute *per se* a reservoir of 'natural' multilingual and multicultural experiences. Yet as a result of a whole range of

socio-linguistic factors, these are very often restricted to an 'artificial' monolingualism.

Spending any time in the German–Polish borderland one very quickly notices such an 'artificial monolingualism', one that favours German. German dominates as the language of transborder communication on a number of levels: from the presence of German-language street signs and menus on the Polish side and the conspicuous absence of Polish-language equivalents on the German side, to the ability of many Polish administrators (for example, in the town halls of Słubice and Zgorzelec) to speak fluent German and the inability of their German counterparts to speak Polish.

There are several reasons for this linguistic 'asymmetry' (Holly et al. 2003) in the German–Polish borderland, many of which have already been substantially investigated and documented elsewhere (see e.g. Wojciechowski 2002; Carli et al. 2003, Meinhof 2003b; Jaworska and Krzyżanowski, this volume). One obvious and practical reason is the lack of Polish-language education in German schools, even in the *Länder* Brandenburg and Saxony in which our border towns of Frankfurt (Oder) and Görlitz are situated. As Hessky (1995: 65) points out, an important – and basic – motivation in language learning is 'erreichbare Lernangebote' (accessible learning opportunities). The *Brandenburgische Bildungsserver* (2008) may celebrate the fact that 'more than 1200' pupils in Brandenburg are now learning Polish, but, as of April 2008, Polish is still only offered at 37 Brandenburg schools (of which 19 are primary schools). A total of 1,772 non-specialist schools are listed in the official statistics of the *Land* Brandenburg, including 101 *Gymnasien*, in which at least one foreign language is compulsory for successful completion of the *Abitur* (school-leaving exam) (Statistik Berlin-Brandenburg 2007–8: 11). Similarly, Saxony's official statistics for the 2007–8 academic year list 1,498 schools, of which 140 are *Gymnasien*, but in which only 972 pupils are learning Polish, ranking it as the seventh foreign language behind English (239,809 learners), French (36,403 learners), Latin (15,097), Russian (11,414 learners), Spanish (4,678 learners) and Czech (2,114 learners) (Statistik Sachsen 2007–8).

However, it is not simply the limited Polish-language provision that is the problem: behind a lack of supply is often a lack of demand, and there is simply not the demand for Polish language classes in Germany. In contrast, German is offered and taken as the first or second (behind English) foreign language in most Polish schools near the border. According to the Polish Ministry of Education, in the region of

Lubuskie, immediately across the border from Brandenburg, 67.3 per cent of language learners opted for German in 2005. The significance of this figure is underlined when compared with the 55 per cent of language learners in the same region who took English – the most popular foreign language in Poland as a whole (Polish Ministry of Education 2005).

These are certainly interesting and revealing statistics, but, as Jaworska (this volume) so clearly explains, such quantitative data 'only scratch the surface' and if they are to be meaningful, they must be read in their social and political context: the reasons informing language choice must be investigated. Behind the asymmetry in language provision in the German–Polish borderland lie a multitude of attitudes and, indeed, prejudices towards the respective *Nachbarsprache* (neighbouring language). In their investigations into language attitudes in communities situated along the former Iron Curtain, Carli et al. (2003: 868) found that in interviews on both sides of the border:

> [l]inguistic issues as a 'hot' identity indicator [cf. Blommaert and Verschueren 1998: 192] are expressed through assertions that language – the term 'mother tongue' is often used – forms the 'way of thinking' of its speakers, and thus the different 'mentalities' and 'national characters' are connected with the use of different languages.

For some Poles, particularly the older generation, German thus remains the language of the oppressor, of the Nazis: a hard, ugly, cruel language that they would not want to learn. Their refusal to learn German, despite any practical benefits it might bring them, is an assertion of their Polish national identity and a form of continuing resistance against their former but still present enemy; the geographical proximity of the Germans and their language has the effect here of 'strengthening the national project' (cf. Donnan and Wilson 1998: 16). However, as evidenced by the learner statistics cited above, these associations are changing for younger generations.

Sue Wright (2002: 91) maintains that:

> [w]hen a group chooses to acquire another idiom, the choice is rooted in politics and in the cultural status of speakers of the new language. It is also related to the personal advantage learners hope to acquire by allying themselves with any prestige and with economic and political benefits enjoyed by that language community.

Regina Hessky (1995: 64) similarly underlines the role of linguistic prestige in decisions to learn a foreign language, arguing that individuals choose to learn languages that they see as being beneficial to their future careers and that these languages are normally those that play a leading role on the international stage, both politically and economically (see also Černá, Jaworska, Krzyżanowski and Schneider, this volume). For the younger generations in Poland, particularly in western Poland, German is perceived as a prestigious language, associated with economic advantage and with employment and education opportunities both at home and abroad; for the westward-looking Poles, German has considerable 'linguistic capital' (cf. Bourdieu 1991). The ability to speak German – be it as a native or foreign language – awards its speakers status or 'distinction' in various social 'fields' or 'markets'.

Bourdieu's (1991) concept of 'linguistic capital' refers specifically to forms or registers within one-language or diglossic communities, in which those who can master the standard, 'high' form of a given language have a considerable advantage over those, often less educated, members of the language community who speak only their regional dialect. However, the concept is also applicable to two-language borderlands, in which one language – in our case, German – dominates in most fields of transborder interaction. Indeed, Černá (this volume) also uses the term 'diglossic' to describe the similarly asymmetrical language situation in the German–Czech borderland. Not only is German a western language, but it is also, argues Ammon (1995: 25), an 'international language', 'used in international communication' both in situations involving native and non-native German speakers and, although less frequently, as a lingua franca between speakers of other languages. Furthermore, according to the Eurobarometer Special Report *Europeans and Their Languages* (2006), German has the most L1 speakers in the EU and is widely used as a working language within EU institutions, albeit less so than English and French. Native German speakers therefore already possess the prestige and linguistic capital necessary to succeed in the borderland and in Europe and it is to Poles' (and Czechs') advantage to acquire such capital by learning this prestigious western, international language. Admittedly, English is now the more popular language choice across Poland, as Jaworska (this volume) points out, but German remains strong in the border areas.

In contrast, the inhabitants of eastern German towns such as Frankfurt (Oder) and Görlitz, where unemployment remained at 16 percent and 22 per cent respectively in August 2007, see little advantage in learning Polish. They too look to the West and choose to learn other international languages such as English, French and Spanish, which they perceive to have a higher prestige or linguistic capital than Polish. They, like the Poles who learn German to improve their employment prospects, seek an 'instrumental bilingualism' (see Schneider, this volume) rather than a bilingualism based on a desire to identify with the two-language borderland space in which they live. Considering the persisting economic and political imbalance between Eastern and Western Europe, the depth of the 'socio-economic fault line' (Meinhof 2003b: 789), it is perhaps of little surprise that many more Polish inhabitants of the borderland show a willingness to learn and speak German than vice versa. More concerning – and perhaps more interesting for the purposes of this chapter – is the fact that Carli et al. (2003: 873) discovered in interviews conducted in Görlitz that German inhabitants of the border region excuse their lack of ability or interest in Polish by arguing the prestige of their own language: 'the Poles need to learn German to find a job, but we have no need to learn Polish'. I heard similar arguments repeated in interviews with cultural practitioners and policy-makers in Frankfurt (Oder) and Görlitz in 2007, even if apologetically or, in some cases, unintentionally. A representative of the town hall in Görlitz, for example, suggested that 'die Polen, die auch Deutsch können, können im Grenzgebiet mehr Geld verdienen. Deshalb macht es ihnen Sinn, Deutsch zu lernen' (Poles who can also speak German can earn more money in the border region. It therefore makes sense to learn German); while in Frankfurt (Oder) I was told that 'die Polen wollen ja Deutsch lernen, weil sie glauben, mit unserer Sprache in Europa weiterkommen zu können, und sie haben da Recht, glaube ich' (the Poles want to learn German because they believe that they will get further in Europe with our language; and I think they're right). These Germans see their own language as an entry ticket to employment and economic capital, and also as a key to the door of Europe.

   This 'attitude of dominance' could, following Ager et al. (1993: 208) be detrimental to German–Polish relations in the borderland: 'Attitudes of dominance, and the consequential feelings of marginalization and exclusion on the part of dominated groups, do not augur well for good inter-community relationships.' In her observations of a cross-border school exchange in the German–Czech borderland, Černá (this volume) certainly finds some evidence of Czech pupils – and to a lesser extent teachers – feeling 'marginalized and excluded' by the dominance of German in their interactions, and similar feelings were expressed to me in interviews conducted in Słubice and Zgorzelec. A Polish lecturer at the Collegium Polonicum in Słubice even used the same terminology as Ager et al. (1993) to explain that her colleagues who cannot speak German often feel marginalized or excluded because they are unable to make a full contribution to meetings and conferences with their German colleagues at the Europa Universität Viadrina; and this despite the utopian ideals of this pioneering cross-border university:

> Obwohl bei Vorträgen und Gesprächsrunden viel übersetzt und gedolmetscht wird, wird in den Pausen einfach erwartet, dass die Polen Deutsch können. Wenn nicht, bleiben sie untereinander und fühlen sich von den wichtigsten Gesprächen irgendwie ausgeschlossen.

> (Although there is a lot of translating and interpreting during lectures and discussion sessions, during the breaks it is simply expected that the Poles can speak German. If they can't, they stick together and feel somehow excluded from the most important conversations.)

A German teacher in Zgorzelec emphasized, somewhat reluctantly, the sense of inferiority which can also result from 'attitudes of dominance':

> Wir Polen fühlen uns schon minderwertig im Vergleich zu unseren deutschen Nachbarn, und wenn die Deutschen sich auch nicht bemühen, unsere Sprache zu lernen, wächst dieses Minderwertigkeitsgefühl.

> (We Poles do feel inferior to our German neighbours, and when the Germans don't even bother trying to learn our language, this feeling of inferiority increases.)

Making an effort to learn Polish and to use Polish in at least some cross-border communication is, therefore, an important move towards equalizing relations in the borderland. It should, however, be noted that both women cited above were more than happy to conduct their interviews with me – a foreigner 'who couldn't be expected to know Polish' – in German.

Choosing Polish as the language of production

As in most other areas, the borderland asymmetry in favour of German is reproduced and reinforced in the theatre. German is the dominant language of cultural production in the borderland, largely because most cultural institutions, including theatres, are to be found on the German side of the border. Frankfurt (Oder) has a publicly funded *Stadttheater* (municipal theatre) in the form of the *Kleist Forum*, which hosts visiting drama, cabaret, dance and opera productions from across Europe. There is also a small professional theatre group with its own performance space: the *Theater Frankfurt*. Görlitz similarly boasts its own *Stadttheater*, the *Theater Görlitz*, and also its own ensemble. This theatre specializes in musical and dance productions, but also collaborates with the *Gerhart Hauptmann Theater* in the nearby town of Zittau to bring its audience a regular repertoire of plays. In contrast, there is no theatre in either Słubice or Zgorzelec; only a *Dom Kultury* (house of culture), which is used for theatre, concerts, cinema, exhibitions, and also as a community centre, hosting, for example, after-school clubs and exercise classes. Inhabitants of Słubice and Zgorzelec who are interested in theatre must either travel to larger towns in Poland or cross the border to Frankfurt (Oder) or Görlitz.

Potentially, both the *Kleist Forum* and the *Theater Görlitz* could tap into an unfulfilled audience across the border, an audience which they claim to welcome but in reality rarely cater for, as almost all theatre productions are in German and thus accessible only to those Poles with a good level of German. It was therefore highly significant that the *Theater Görlitz* once chose to include a Polish-language repertoire in each season. Between 2001 and 2006 several Polish productions would be invited every year to perform in Görlitz. The aim of this programme was to attract a Polish audience from Zgorzelec on the other side of the Neiße river, an audience normally excluded from the theatre by the language barrier, and to make the *Theater Görlitz* into a cultural 'bridge' linking the two sides of the *Europastadt Görlitz-Zgorzelec*.[3] Indeed, in an interview conducted in April 2007, Michael Wieler, *Intendant* (artistic director) of the *Theater Görlitz*, directly echoed the border theorist Scartezzini (1998) in his assertion that 'der Kulturbereich ist nach wie vor ein Brückenbauer dazwischen' (culture still functions as a bridge-builder between [both sides of the border]). Scartezzini (1998: 261) argues for an understanding of post-Cold War European borders as 'bridges which unite rather than barriers which divide', across which borderland inhabitants can develop a 'feeling of belonging to a local (region) and a cosmopolitan (European) reality' (see also Wilkinson 2009).

Choosing Polish as the language of performance was an important gesture of inclusion and equality in Wieler's project to 'build bridges' between Görlitz and Zgorzelec, Germany and Poland, through the staging of shared cultural events. In many areas of transborder cooperation, however, Polish participants are expected to use German and thus to master a foreign language. As we have seen, this can create feelings of resentment and inferiority: the Germans assume that the Poles will be willing and able to speak their language, because it is western and thus more important, and they thereby imply that Polish is a less valued language (cf. Carli et al. 2003). Staging plays in Polish in a German theatre sent a message to the Polish audience that they were welcomed and valued in Görlitz and also that Polish was a viable language of cultural production in the borderland, even on the German side. Theatre plays a similar role in negotiating the status or cultural capital of a perceived 'minority' or 'inferior' language in the diglossia of German-speaking Switzerland. There, the 'official' language, used in administration and in much cultural (particularly literary) production is *Hochdeutsch* (high or standard German), but the vast majority of the population speaks a variety of *Schweizerdeutsch* (Swiss German). For Swiss Germans this is more than a dialect and more than a means of spoken communication as distinct from the written form: Swiss German is *their language*, the language which identifies them as Swiss and differentiates them from the – again dominant – Germans (see Watts 1999). It is, therefore, very important that many amateur (and some professional) theatre companies in German-speaking Switzerland choose to perform only in their local dialect and often to translate plays from standard German and other languages into dialect for performance. Elsewhere, I have argued that the positive decision to translate between the two languages of the diglossia imbues their performances with a distinct sense of 'Swissness' and helps to 'raise the status' (cf. Corbett 1999: 4) of their language to that of a valid language of cultural production, equal to standard German (Wilkinson 2005). Wieler's decision to stage plays in Polish in the two-language borderland in which his own language, German, dominates could have had a similar effect on the status of Polish.

The project was funded by the town of Görlitz, the *Kulturstiftung Sachsen* (Cultural Foundation of Saxony) and the *Deutsche Bühnenverein* (German Stage Association). This meant that tickets for the Polish-language productions could be offered at substantially reduced rates and costs could still be covered if the theatre was not filled – which often turned out to be the case. In 2005 and 2006, attempts were made to encourage the town of Zgorzelec to take over the funding of the project, as it was a project for a Polish rather than a German audience, and thus not officially in the area of responsibility of the municipality of Görlitz. However, the funding could not be found and in 2007 the Polish repertoire of the *Theater Görlitz* was cancelled.

Why was this project unsuccessful despite its good intentions? Why did the Poles show such a lack of interest? There are, in my opinion, two principal and related reasons. First, there is an often voiced feeling among the inhabitants of Zgorzelec that transborder projects are usually imposed on them by Germany or 'Europe', with little consideration of their interests, needs and wishes (cf. Meinhof and Galasiński 2002). A representative of the *Dom Kultury* explained to me:

> Weil die meisten grenzüberschreitenden Initiativen von der anderen Seite oder gar von Europa stammen, haben viele Zgorzelecer das Gefühl, dass sie, die Bewohner der Grenzregion, gar nicht in Betracht gezogen werden … dass sie gar nicht so wichtig sind.

> (Because most cross-border initiatives come from the other side or even from Europe, many people from Zgorzelec feel that they, the inhabitants of the border region, are not even taken into consideration … that they are not very important at all.)

These feelings of marginalization and inferiority mirror those related to language cited earlier. They also reflect a more general 'assumption of the non-symmetrical rights of Poles and Germans' (Meinhof and Galasiński 2002: 72) and reinforce the border's function as 'an axis of contemporary socio-economic inequality' (Meinhof 2003b: 781).

Second, and following on from this, is the fact that the theatre occupies a very different position in the cultural landscapes of Germany and Poland. In Germany the theatre receives generous state funding and most medium-sized towns have their own *Stadttheater*, which, in theory at least, offers a wide-ranging repertoire to suit a variety of tastes and social groups. Amateur theatre is also a widespread and popular phenomenon across the German-speaking world. In contrast, theatre in Poland is generally viewed as 'high' culture or, at least, culture for the educated classes in possession of considerable cultural, and often economic, capital. It is associated either with classical theatre in grand, traditional buildings, attended by the upper classes in formal dress, or with the internationally renowned, experimental director's theatre of personalities such as Jerzy Grotowski and groups such as *Teatr Piezn Kozla* (The Song of the Goat Theatre). The inhabitants of smaller towns without their own theatres, such as Zgorzelec, find it hard to picture themselves in a theatre; they have to overcome a considerable *Schwellenangst* (literally, threshold fear)[4] to go to a play. Understandably, this *Schwellenangst* is even greater if they have to cross the *Schwelle* (threshold) of the German border before they even reach the theatre. It could thus be argued that the German theatre in Görlitz was offering Polish-language plays to appeal to a Polish audience, but was imposing on that audience a German cultural form, of which they had little experience or knowledge and in which they had little interest. This could be seen as a kind of cultural imperialism, as the West again imposing itself on the East in a way that was viewed with trepidation at the dawn of EU expansion. The call from the Polish borderland communities is for grassroots cross-border activities, initiated, organized and attended by the inhabitants of that community.

The fact that the Polish-language programme was then cancelled following its mediocre success can only serve to exacerbate Polish feelings of resentment and inferiority. Rather than entering into discussions with cultural practitioners, policy-makers and audiences in Zgorzelec and working with them to find a new, more suitable programme, the *Theater Görlitz* simply withdrew its offering and re-established the border between the two towns. The message that this conveys, however unintentionally, is that the Polish-language repertoire and Polish audience are not worth fighting for and certainly not of equal status or importance to the German repertoire and German audience. The German language thus maintains its position of prestige and dominance in the border region.

Bilingual productions

An alternative way of dealing with the language question without excluding either language community is to stage bilingual productions in which each language is accorded equal status on stage. The youth theatre group *JuThe* (a branch of the *Theater Görlitz*), for example, offers young people in Görlitz and Zgorzelec the chance to act together on stage but in their own language. *JuThe*'s theatre group director, Peter Hanslik, is German but is fluent in Polish and can therefore run bilingual meetings and rehearsals and direct bilingual plays in which the young German actors speak German, the Polish actors speak Polish and the whole performance is accompanied by sur-titles projected onto a screen next to the stage. In May 2007 the group performed Shakespeare's *The Tempest* with the protagonist Prospero played by a young Polish actress, and his daughter Miranda by a young German actress.

This theatre group is, however, fairly low profile in the towns of Görlitz and Zgorzelec. On the evening that I attended *The Tempest* in May 2007, there were only eleven others in the audience, four of whom were parents of cast members, and two of whom were friends of the director. Bilingual theatre does not make it onto the main stage of the *Theater Görlitz* itself due to the lack of interest in Polish-language theatre, evidenced by the poor response to the Polish-language repertoire, and to the clumsiness of sur-titles, which many people find spoils their enjoyment of a performance.

However, using both languages on stage can potentially transform the theatre into a liminal space between languages and cultures; a space perhaps comparable to that of the Salsa clubs in Frankfurt/Main described by Schneider (this volume), in which code-switching between German and Spanish becomes 'a way to create a cosmopolitan, multilingual identity'. In other words, the stage could become a microcosm of the borderland itself, a 'proximate space of flows across the dividing line...where cultural identity, sheltered by the boundary, becomes blurred, mixed, creolized' (Morehouse 2004: 19); a space in which participants move across, or at least negotiate, the linguistic (and cultural) divide and thereby come a step closer to understanding, if not identifying with, each other. As the important research of Meinhof et al. found, and some of my own interviews have reaffirmed, the German–Polish borderland is not yet experienced by most as a 'blurred, mixed, creolized' space, but rather as divided and asymmetrical. Barbara Morehouse (2004: 30) argues that borderlands are always 'in between', but that, in situations where the inhabitants are granted, or indeed take for themselves, a degree of agency, they can also 'constitute liminal spaces of becoming, spaces for redefining "what is", and thinking about "what might be"'. Bilingual theatre, in which both groups are granted at least linguistic agency, could constitute such a 'liminal space' of transformation and 'fecund hybridity' (van Houtum et al. 2005: 8).

Avoiding the language issue: music, dance and alternative theatre

Considering the disappointing response to the *Theater Görlitz*'s Polish-language repertoire and the *JuThe*'s bilingual experiment, it is perhaps unsurprising that the main way in which German theatres in the border region seem to deal with the language issue is by avoiding it altogether. Rather than offering a Polish-language repertoire to a potentially very small audience or attempting to stage bilingual productions, most theatres and individuals opt for music, dance or alternative theatre when trying to organize a transborder event or to attract a Polish audience, thereby removing the language barrier and the question of language choice from the equation. Let us look now at some examples of non-language-specific theatre events.

Interface is a dance theatre project initiated by the new director of the *Tanztheater Görlitz*, Gundula Peuthert, in the summer of 2007. New to the town of Görlitz and to the border region, she wanted to bring German and Polish choreographers together to work on a dance production experimenting with the ideas of borders, boundaries, encounters – 'interfaces'. The production was staged in the disused offices of the old *Bombardier* plant in Görlitz, with the audience moving from room to room to watch four 20-minute dance performances inspired by the same piece of music and by the performance space. The themes of power, relationships, individuality and identity, expressed within and across boundaries, were explored entirely through music and movement – there were no language barriers to get in the way of communication or to exclude certain members of the audience (although the audience on the night I was there was almost entirely German-speaking). Interestingly, however, none of the choreographers localized these themes through reference to the German–Polish borderland context; thematically, the performances were placeless, universal, despite the inspiration for the project arising from the specificities of the border location. The universal relevance of the project was further emphasized by the choice of the English title *Interface*, which again avoided confrontation with the linguistic asymmetry between German and Polish by opting for neither.

The sequel, *Interface II* (2008), was developed into a more international dance theatre festival and included companies from Germany, Poland, Switzerland, Croatia and Israel, thereby entering into an 'intercultural dialogue' across multiple borders. It could be argued that in changing from a German–Polish to a European festival, *Interface* is becoming further displaced from the Neiße border between Görlitz and Zgorzelec, with which it purports to engage. Importantly, however, the 2008 event was staged in a number of 'unusual' performance spaces in Görlitz and Zgorzelec, which means that the supposedly inclusive, non-language-specific dance productions were being taken to audiences on both sides of the border, creating a temporary cultural symmetry in the borderland.

Similarly, the main cultural centre in Frankfurt (Oder), the *Kleist Forum*, stages only one regular Polish production in its programme each year, and that is a dance performance by the *Polski Teatr Tanca* from Poznan. In May 2007 the renowned Polish dance theatre staged *Tango mit Lady M*, a contemporary ballet based on the character of Lady Macbeth, to an almost full house in the *Kleist Forum*. Admittedly, the audience was, as is normal in the *Kleist Forum*, predominantly German, but there was a reasonable and enthusiastic Polish presence.

The point that I would like to underline here is that the only explicitly transborder or German–Polish productions in the 2006–7 repertoire of the public theatres in Görlitz and Frankfurt (Oder) were dance productions, chosen because dance allegedly has its own 'universal' language which transcends all normal linguistic boundaries. Frau Wolle, the *Bürgermeisterin für Kultur* (mayor responsible for culture) in Frankfurt (Oder), claims that 'Musik- und Tanztheater, ideal, ja, man versteht sich ohne Worte, also ganz prima' (musical and dance theatre, ideal, yes, we can understand each other without words, which is great). Arnold Bischinger, director of the *Kleist Forum* in Frankfurt (Oder), similarly maintains that:

> Im Musiktheater funktioniert das, weil da sind die Sprachbarrieren gering... Im Tanztheater haben wir eine ähnlich gute Erfahrung... Im Schauspiel funktioniert das gar nicht, da haben Sie die Sprachbarriere.
>
> (In musical theatre it works, because the language barriers are minimal... In dance theatre we have had similarly good experiences... With plays it doesn't work at all; there you have the language barrier.)

Of course, the universality of music and dance is strongly contested by many specialists, who argue that dance is as culturally specific as any other cultural form (see Desmond 1994; Thomas 1995). However, I would support my interviewees' contention that dance and music theatre are more accessible across cultures: even if audience members are not familiar with the specificities of particular cultural traditions, movement and music are open to interpretation (see also Schneider's discussion of Salsa in Germany, this volume), whereas a foreign language production puts up a solid barrier to understanding and enjoyment and thus to any form of cross-border communication. The *Tanztheater Görlitz* (2008) is thus surely justified in maintaining that 'die größtenteils sprachfreie Kunstform Tanz eignet sich besonders dafür, grenzüberschreitende Kommunikation zu initiieren' (the largely speech-/language-free art form of dance is particularly appropriate for initiating cross-border communication).

In Görlitz the only regular, explicitly cross-border theatre event is *ViaThea*, a street theatre festival which celebrated its fourteenth consecutive year in August 2008. The three-day summer event is the result of a long-running collaboration between the *Theater Görlitz* and the *Teatr Jeleniogórsko* in Jelenia Góra. Each year performers are invited from all over the world to bring the parks and squares of Görlitz to life. In 2007 performances ranged from a one-man 'gorilla' show, *Hans Affe*, to a British slapstick comedy in the style of a silent Charlie Chaplin film, to an elaborate French trapeze and tightrope spectacle. As with most street theatre, the performances at *ViaThea* rely on movement, gesture, music and costume, with only minimal spoken language, thus making them accessible to a wide audience and across languages.

Further key ingredients in the festival's accessibility are the fact that it takes place in the open air in recognized public spaces and is not ticketed. Together with the lack of language barrier, these factors help to break down the *Schwelle* typically associated with the theatre: there is no 'threshold' to cross into a, for some audience members, unfamiliar and intimidating theatre building, and there are no prohibitively expensive tickets to buy. Street theatre is democratic theatre (cf. Gooch 1984; Mason 1992), which, the organizers hope, will attract both German and Polish audiences otherwise uninterested in or unaccustomed to the theatre. Somewhat disappointingly, however, none of the performances actually take place on the Polish side of the border in Zgorzelec. The nearest the festival came to Poland in 2007 was a performance called the *Flower Fairies*, which was staged on the German side of the footbridge over the Neiße, in view of the border checkpoint and guards but never going past them. Yet again, the inhabitants of Zgorzelec are expected to cross the border to Görlitz if they want to experience any supposedly transborder cultural events.

The preference for non-verbal forms of theatrical expression in transborder events has two possible interpretations. On the one hand, we could see this as mere 'avoidance' of the language problem: a reluctance to take a stance on the sensitive issue of language choice either way by opting for German or Polish. Holly et al. (2003: 828) found that one of the ways in which the inhabitants of communities along the former Iron Curtain cope with the multiple asymmetries between East and West is by 'avoiding' confrontation with the problems, or even by avoiding contact with the people on the other side altogether. Germans are well aware of the linguistic asymmetry in the region: they are aware that many more Poles speak German than vice versa and that this is because their language is more prestigious; they also understand that this causes resentment on the Polish side. However, rather than making the effort to learn Polish and to use Polish as a language of performance, or risking upset by choosing their own language German, they simply opt for non-language-dependent forms of theatre; they avoid direct confrontation with the language barrier. In so doing, it could be argued that the organizers inadvertently make their projects less relevant to the borderland and thus less successful in breaking down the surviving boundaries between Germany and Poland, particularly where non-language-specific forms are coupled with 'global' texts (note the two instances of Shakespeare) and universal themes.

On the other hand, the use of music, movement, gesture and props to communicate with the audience could be seen as a sensible, even sensitive, democratic decision. The one-language option inevitably carries the risk of excluding part of the audience and reinforcing the linguistic divide, making it ultimately unsuited to cross-border projects. The *Theater Görlitz*'s Polish-language repertoire might have opened up the German theatre to a Polish audience, but its potential for bringing German and Polish inhabitants of the *Europastadt Görlitz-Zgorzelec* together across the border was limited because it was not accessible to most Germans. Removing language from the equation by adopting alternative theatrical forms means that the event is inclusive across languages and nationalities and it also accords neither language a higher status than the other. In a similar way to bilingual theatre, it creates an 'open', democratizing space.

Conclusions: (how) can theatre transcend the linguistic divide?

Transborder theatre events in Frankfurt (Oder) and Görlitz provide a liminal space for encounter and even interaction between German and Polish inhabitants of the border region, as audience members, organizers or even performers. However, the success of such events is dependent on effective negotiation of the linguistic divide that is 'Europe's hardest language boundary'. We have seen that there are three ways in which the German organizers attempt this: they choose Polish as the language of performance; they stage bilingual theatre; or they avoid the language issue by opting for musical, dance or street theatre. Each of these choices is reflective of a similar language ideology or similar 'set of beliefs' (cf. Silverstein 1979: 193) about the roles and positions of German and Polish in the borderland. Both Germans and Poles are acutely aware that German is perceived as the more prestigious, Western European language and is for this reason the more widely used language of cross-border communication. They are also aware that the prestige of German means that German speakers are reluctant to learn Polish and that Polish speakers consequently feel marginalized and inferior. In order not to exacerbate the linguistic asymmetry of the border region, German is rarely chosen as the sole language of performance.

But how successful are the other three options in transcending the linguistic divide that is both the cause and effect of so many problems in German–Polish relations in the borderland? Creating a separate Polish-language repertoire for the *Theater Görlitz* failed as a transborder event because it excluded the German audience and met with minimal interest on the Polish side. The language barrier was moved but not *re*moved. Music, dance and alternative theatre are the most popular forms for cross-border events because they do *re*move the language barrier: they are thought to 'transcend' the linguistic divide. Enjoyment might be dependent on familiarity with certain traditions or conventions, but it is not determined by linguistic ability, and is therefore attainable for Germans and Poles alike. It is, however, possible to argue that choosing music and dance is simply a way of sidestepping the language barrier and the problems it poses; that the theatre event is thereby universalized and detached from the specific borderland context with which it is supposed to engage.

Bilingual theatre so far has had only minimal success in the borderland because theatre practitioners believe it to be more difficult and time-consuming to produce than monolingual theatre, and also less accessible to audiences. I believe, however, that there is considerable potential for the creation of a liminal, European space in the German–Polish borderland through the staging of bilingual theatre. This space does not simply ignore differences between Germany and Poland, but incorporates two languages and thus two 'markers of identity' on stage, thereby facilitating at least encounters and at best interaction and negotiation between the two sides of the border. This is particularly important at a time when both Germans and Poles see their language being threatened by the global spread of English, the 'killer language' (Braselmann 2004: 101). Despite the perceived threat posed to their respective national identities by this 'lingua franca of the world' (Braselmann 2004: 100), cross-border communication is increasingly being conducted in English, a third language which is foreign to everyone in the area. While the use of a neutral foreign language does have certain benefits – no one is in the privileged position of being able to speak his/her mother tongue – learning each other's languages is a way for Germans and Poles to start understanding something of the culture and mentality of their neighbours. Bilingual theatre is a step in the right direction.

Notes

1. By 'divided communities' I mean the towns and villages situated immediately on the Oder and Neiße rivers that were entirely German until 1945, when they were divided by the new German–Polish border. A suburb of the German town Frankfurt an der Oder thus became the new Polish town of Słubice, while the parts of Görlitz on the eastern bank of the Neiße became the Polish town of Zgorzelec.
2. The Schengen Area includes all the EU member states that have signed up to the Schengen Agreement to abolish checks and controls at internal borders, thereby allowing free movement for all EU citizens and all others granted entry to the EU at the (now strictly controlled) external borders. The first Agreement was signed by France, Germany, Belgium, Luxembourg and the Netherlands in the eponymous town of Schengen, Luxembourg in 1985 and now includes most EU member states. The 'new' members, including Poland, were permitted to join only when they had demonstrated technological capabilities sufficient for integration into the Schengen Information System and adequate controls at their external borders.
3. On 5 May 1998, the mayors of Görlitz and Zgorzelec declared their towns to be two parts of one European city, the Europastadt Görlitz-Zgorzelec. This name reflected their desire to unite the two towns across the Neiße, to make them one again, and is now used on the official websites of both towns (www.goerlitz.de and www.zgorzelec.com), and in most tourism marketing.
4. Directly translated, the term *Schwellenangst* means 'threshold fear', and is used literally to describe a fear of entering a certain place, of stepping over a certain physical threshold, and figuratively to describe a fear of embarking on something new or crossing a metaphorical threshold. When used to describe an attitude towards the theatre, *Schwellenangst* embodies both fears: fear of physically entering a theatre building, and fear of the – usually unaccustomed or unfamiliar – activity of theatre-going.

References

Ager, D., Muskens, G. and Wright, S. (eds) (1993) *Language Education for Intercultural Communication* (Clevedon, Philadelphia and Adelaide: Multilingual Matters).

Ammon, U. (1995) 'To what extent is German an international language?', in Stevenson (1995), 25–54.

Artega, A. (1994) *An Other Tongue: Nation and Ethnicity in the Linguistic Borderlands* (Durham, NC and London: Duke University Press).

Bauman, Z. (2000) *Liquid Modernity* (Cambridge: Polity).

Berg, E. and van Houtum, H. (eds) (2003) *Routing Borders Between Territories, Discourses and Practices* (Aldershot: Ashgate).

Bhabha, H. (1994) *The Location of Culture* (London: Routledge).

Blommaert, J. (ed.) (1999) *Language Ideological Debates* (Berlin: Mouton de Gruyter).

Blommaert, J. and Verschueren, J. (1998) 'The role of language in European nationalist ideologies', in Schieffelin et al. (1999), 189–210.

Bourdieu, P. (1991) *Language and Symbolic Power* (Cambridge: Polity Press).

Brandenburgische Bildungsserver (2008) 'Polnisch-Unterricht', http://www.bildung-brandenburg.de/index.php?id=258. Accessed 1 July 2008.

Braselmann, P. (2004) 'Language policies in East and West: national language policies as a response to the pressures of globalization', in Gardt and Hüppauf (2004), 99–118.

Carli, A., Guardino, C., Kaučič-Baša, M., Sussi, E., Tessaroldo, M. and Ussau, M. (2003) 'Asserting ethnic identity and power through language', *Journal of Ethnic and Migration Studies* 29(5), 865–83.

Clyne, P., Hanks, W. and Hofbauer, C. (eds) (1979) *The Elements: A Parasession on Linguistic Units and Levels* (Chicago: Chicago Linguistic Society).

Corbett, J. (1999) *Written in the Language of the Scottish Nation: A History of Literary Translation into Scots* (Clevedon: Multilingual Matters).

Desmond, J. (1994) 'Embodying difference: issues in dance and cultural studies', *Cultural Critique* (Winter 1993–94), 33–63.

Donnan, H. and Wilson, T. (eds) (1998) *Border Identities: Nation and State at International Frontiers* (Cambridge: Cambridge University Press).

Ehlers, N., Buursnick, J. and Boekema, F. (2001) 'Introduction: binational cities and their regions: from diverging cases to a common research agenda', *GeoJournal* 54, 1–5.

Eurobarometer (2006) *Europeans and their Languages. Special Report 243* (Brussels: European Commission).

Gardt, A. and Hüppauf, B. (eds) (2004) *Globalization and the Future of German* (Berlin, New York: de Gruyter).

Glante, N. (2003) 'Europa bauen – die Chancen gemeinsam nutzen: Polen und Deutschland am Vorabend der EU-Erweiterung', http://www.glante.de/download/artikel_von_ng/0304_erweiterung.pdf. Accessed 1 July 2008.

Glass, K., Kranjc, J. and Luthar, O. (eds) (1998) *Grenzlandidentitäten im Zeitalter der Eurointegration* (Wien and Poznan: Österreichische Gesellschaft für Mitteleuropäische Studien Verlag).

Gooch, S. (1984) *All Together Now: An Alternative View of Theatre and the Community* (London: Methuen).

Gubbins, P. and Holt, M. (eds) (2002) *Beyond Boundaries: Language and Identity in Contemporary Europe* (Clevedon: Multilingual Matters).

Hessky, R. (1995) 'Die Rolle der großen Verkehrssprachen in Ostmitteleuropa am Beispiel Ungarn', in Wodak and de Cillia (1995), 63–74.

Holly, W., Nekvapil, J., Scherm, I. and Tišerová, P. (2003) 'Unequal neighbours: coping with asymmetries', *Journal of Ethnic and Migration Studies* 29(5), 819–34.

Krumm, H. (ed.) (1999) *Die Sprachen unserer Nachbarn – unsere Sprachen: Chancen zur Diversifizierung des Sprachenangebots im Zuge der EU-Erweiterung* (Wien: Eviva).

Laitinen, K. (2003) 'Post-Cold War security borders: a conceptual approach', in Berg and van Houtum (2003), 13–33.

Mason, B. (1992) *Street Theatre and Other Outdoor Performance* (London: Routledge).

Matthiesen, U. (2002) 'Härteste Sprachgrenze Europas', http://www.uwe-rada.de/themen/grenzregionen6.html. Accessed 1 July 2008.

Meinhof, U. (ed.) (2002) *Living (with) Borders: Identity Discourses on East–West Borders in Europe* (Aldershot: Ashgate).

Meinhof, U. (coordinator) (2003a) *Border Discourse: Changing Identities, Changing Nations, Changing Stories in European Border Communities*, http://www.borderidentities.com.

Meinhof, U. (2003b) 'Migrating borders: an introduction to European identity construction in process', *Journal of Ethnic and Migration Studies* 29(5), 781–96.

Meinhof, U. and Galasiński, D. (2002) 'Reconfiguring East–West identities: cross-generational discourses in German and Polish border communities', *Journal of Ethnic and Migration Studies* 28(1), 63–82.

Morehouse, B. (2004) 'Theoretical approaches to border spaces and identities', in Pavlakovich-Kochi et al. (2004), 19–39.

Oppermann, D. (ed.) (2002a) *Sprachen und Grenzräume: Partnersprachen und interkulturelle Kommunikation in europäischen Grenzräumen* (St. Ingbert: Röhrig Universitätsverlag).

Oppermann, D. (2002b) 'Partnersprachen und interkulturelle Kommunikation in europäischen Grenzräumen: Orientierende und einführende Bemerkungen', in Oppermann (2002a), 7–24.

Paasi, A. (2001) 'Europe as social process and discourse: considerations of place, boundaries and identity', *European Urban and Regional Studies* 8(1), 7–28.

Pavlakovich-Kochi, V., Morehouse, B. and Wastl-Walter, D. (eds) (2004) *Challenged Borderlands: Transcending Political and Cultural Boundaries* (Aldershot: Ashgate).

Polish Ministry of Education (2005) 'Edukacja językowa w Polsce, http://www.men.gov.pl/wspolpraca/rada_europy/country_profile.php. Accessed 26 June 2008.

Prescott, J. (1987) *Political Frontiers and Boundaries* (London: Allen & Unwin).

Scartezzini, R. (1998) 'Social representations of northeast Italian border regions', in Glass et al. (1998), 257–72.

Schieffelin, B., Woolard, K. and Kroskrity, P. (eds) (1998) *Language Ideologies: Practice and Theory* (Oxford and New York: Oxford University Press).

Silverstein, M. (1979) 'Language structure and linguistic ideology', in Clyne et al. (1979), 193–247.

Statistik Berlin-Brandenburg (2007–8) 'Allgemein bildende Schulen des Landes Brandenburg: Verzeichnis Schuljahr 2007/2008' (Potsdam: Amt für Statistik Berlin-Brandenburg), http://www.statistik-berlin-brandenburg.de/Publikationen/VeroeffVerzeich/Schulverz_A-07-08_www.pdf. Accessed 30 June 2008.

Statistik Sachsen (2007–8) 'Schüler im Fremdsprachenunterricht an allgemein bildenden Schulen im Schuljahr 2007/08 nach Fremdsprache und Schulart, http://www.statistik.sachsen.de/appsl1/Bildung/index2.html?suche/suche.html. Accessed 30 June 2008.

Stevenson, P. (ed.) (1995) *The German Language and the Real World: Sociolinguistic, Cultural, and Pragmatic Perspectives on Contemporary German* (Oxford: Clarendon Press).

Tanztheater Görlitz (2008), 'TanzArtFestival Görlitz-Zgorzelec: Künstler und Companies aus Deutschland, Israel, Kroatien, Polen, Schweiz', http://www.theater-goerlitz.de/ballett0.0.html. Accessed 1 July 2008.

Thomas, H. (1995) *Dance, Modernity and Culture: Explorations in the Sociology of Dance* (London and New York: Routledge).

Turner, V. (1982) *From Ritual to Theatre: The Human Seriousness of Play* (New York: P. A. J. Publications).

van Houtum, H., Kramsch, O. and Zierhofer, O. (eds) (2005) *B/Ordering Space* (Aldershot: Ashgate).

Watts, R. (1999) 'The ideology of dialect in Switzerland', in Blommaert (1999), 67–103.

Wilkinson, J. (2005) 'Staging "Swissness": inter- and intracultural theatre translation', in *Language and Intercultural Communication* 5(1), 72–85.

Wilkinson, J. (2009) 'Building literary bridges across the Oder', in *Seminar* 45(4) (forthcoming).

Wodak, R. and de Cillia, R. (eds) (1995) *Sprachenpolitik in Mittel- und Osteuropa* (Wien: Passagen Verlag).

Wojciechowski, K. (2002) 'Der deutsch-polnische Grenzraum als Brücke nach Osten: Die Rolle des Deutschen und des Polnischen entlang der Oder und ihre Bedeutung für eine neue europäische Kultur', in Oppermann (2002a), 81–96.

Wright, S. (2002) 'Fixing national borders: language and loyalty in Nice', in Gubbins and Holt (2002), 91–100.

5
Czech–German Relationships and Identity in a Cross-border Region

Kateřina Černá

Introduction

In this chapter, I discuss some of the findings from a research project on bilingual, binational teaching in a Czech–German border area. In this study, I have adopted ethnographic and ethnomethodological approaches, the common object of which is to reconstruct social reality from the perspective of speakers themselves (Emerson and Pollner 2007). On the one hand, language functions as an image of existing social structures, on the other, it plays an active role in creating certain social structures. For example, as I show below, insufficient competence in a partner language can bring about problems in the relations between members of two partner nations.

In my choice of approaches I have also taken into account that there has been a shift from studies in bilingualism focused on knowledge of language(s) to investigations of multilingualism focused on language function (Nelde 2001; Franceschini 2006). Franceschini (2006: 38), for example, defines multilingualism as 'die Fähigkeit von Gesellschaften, Institutionen, Gruppen und Individuen, in Raum und Zeit einen regelmäßigen Umgang mit mehr als einer Sprache im Alltag zu haben' (the capacity of societies, institutions, groups and individuals in time and space to have regular contact with more than one language in everyday life), and from this perspective she views multilingualism as a necessary force for European integration, multilingual individuals being potential bearers of a European communicative competence and thus mediators of a European plural identity. Nekvapil and Sherman (this volume) examine multilingualism within multinational companies in the Czech Republic, analysing the specific functions of English, German and Czech. In my study I focus on the function of Czech and German in cross-national education projects. In particular, I trace the function of language in conceptualizing social identities and how competence in a 'partner language' influences the relationship between members of two cooperating partner nations.

Language has long been considered an element in the constitution of national identity. Recently, however, the relationship between language and nation in Europe has been recontextualized and reformulated as a relationship between language and citizenship (see Stevenson, this volume). European language policies – as formulated, for example, by the Council of Europe – regard language as an instrument that can help create a sense of belonging to the same community, as well as a basis for democratic citizenship: a shared repertoire of languages is seen as an element of democratic citizenship (Language Policy Division 2007: 70-2).

Any transformation of both the language situation and the shaping of identity typically takes place first in border regions, where people are faced most frequently with a neighbouring culture and language (see also Wilkinson, this volume). For this reason, border areas have become an important focus of sociolinguistic research in Europe over the last 20 years (see, for example, Krumm 1998; Nelde 2001; Meinhof 2003; Raasch 2005; Franceschini 2006). With rising internationalization the importance of national frontiers as dividing lines has declined: Nelde (2001) has written of them as being merely symbolic, while Franceschini (2006: 36) refers in this connection to 'fuzzy concepts' and 'blurred boundaries'. Raasch (2005: 122) pinpoints the function of newly emerging cross-border regions and specifies 'cross-border competence' (*Grenzkompetenz*) as part of a newly emerging cross-border identity (*grenzüberschreitende Identität*).[1]

Geopolitical changes bring with them language conflict (Nelde 1997; Meinhof 2003). Nelde makes much of the fact that language contact and conflict make sense only between individual speakers and language communities, not between the languages themselves. With the merger of originally separate national regions into a common Euroregion comes a transformation of two monolingual communities into a single multilingual community. Nelde (1997: 294) notes in this connection that:

> Symmetric multilingualism, in which equal numbers of speakers are invested with equal rights, and in which both language prestige and linguistic identities are congruent, is impossible, since one of the language groups will always be subject to stigmatization and/or discrimination, with conflict the inevitable result.

Both Nelde (1997) and Meinhof (2003) consider the primary sources of conflict to be difference in social status, difference between socio-economic structures, and historical tensions. Meinhof (2003) adds that the construction of one's own identity depends on constant comparison with the 'others' on the other side. Specific domains of asymmetry in the Czech–German border area have been enumerated by Holly et al. (2003), who ascribe feelings of superiority or inferiority in the Czech–German border area above all to differences in wealth and the overall economy, linguistic competence, the state of development and also crime. In my study, I focus on the asymmetry in linguistic competence (understood as knowledge and use of both languages, Czech and German) and its consequences for the relationship between members of both partner nations as well as for their experience of their own identities. For two ethnicities to be brought closer together these asymmetries have to be handled institutionally, hence the support for so many projects of cross-border cooperation. The present study concerns a project on cross-border bilingual teaching, where the school should be seen as a crucial institution in which new concepts are developed and applied and new language standards and social identities are produced (cf. Heller 2006: 11, 16-17). The analysis focuses on the micro-level as the only one that allows of the observation of specific linguistic and social practices.

Objectives, data and methodology

In this chapter, my principal question is: Are cross-border initiatives in bilingual education effective in replacing the conception of 'borders as barriers' with a more constructive conception of transnational communities based on multilingual competence? I am primarily interested in the identities of Czech and German participants and their attitudes towards each other, as well as any possible a/symmetry in the use of the two partner languages. In the next section, I seek to discover whether 'Euro-citizenship' and a cross-border identity, as proclaimed by the EU, are becoming a lived reality for my respondents, or whether the historically and economically conditioned separation of the two nations has persisted, that is, whether in monitored discourse the ethnic distinction is still apparent. I then try to establish what attitudes members of the two nationalities express to one another, and the reasons they give for possible separation along ethnic lines. It seems that symmetrical language competence (the knowledge and use of both partner languages) is a necessary condition for closer relations between members of both nations, since seeing both partner languages as having equal status implies equal status of the speakers of the two language/ethnic communities. Finally, I explore the functioning of German as a working language and as a language of instruction. In order to investigate identity conceptions and mutual relations I focus in particular on the speech production of members of the youngest generation (school pupils), because they are indicative of the relationships of future generations. Moreover, I also consider the teachers' speech production, because I see teachers as local authority figures who can exert a fundamental influence on their pupils' socialization, and as experts who manage the linguistic practices of their pupils (see, for example, Macbeth 1991; Gajo and Mondada 2000: 157)

A project for the joint bilingual teaching of pupils at Czech and German primary schools has been running in the German-Czech-Polish Neisse-Nisa-Nysa Euroregion since 1999 as a component in the development of cross-border cooperation. The project is not the outcome of state policies, but of civic commitment. The Civic Society in Zittau (in the German *Land* of Saxony) had aspired to intercultural tuition since 1993, but at the time, the attitudes of supranational, national and local politicians to the project differed. While it is an aim of EU policy to create cross-border regions and identities, the Czech and Saxon education ministries repeatedly raised objections to the bilingual teaching project on the grounds that they lacked the necessary funds. The German side was putting money into supporting new partnerships with Italy, France, Britain and the United States, while on the Czech side the experience of a history spent alongside a politically and economically stronger partner leading to Germanization led to a reluctance to commit funds to cooperation of this kind. However, in 1998 the German primary school of Hartau situated near the Czech border was threatened with closure and the idea of bilingual tuition became a suitable innovatory method by which to keep the school open.

It would perhaps help at this point to explain the geography in more detail. The town with the German school is called *Hartau* in German and *Hartava* in Czech; the Hartau/Hartava primary school drew up a cooperation agreement with a primary school across the border in the Czech Republic called *Hrádek* (nad Nisou) in Czech and *Grottau* in German. They lie less than one kilometre apart. The management teams of both schools drew up a draft project, in which they set out their views: 'Dabei geht es nicht um kulturelle Anpassung, Kopie oder Vermischung, sondern um nationale Identität, um Stolz und um Akzeptanz und Wissen über "die Anderen"' ('The project is not about cultural adaptation, copying or mixing, but rather about national identity, about pride and about acceptance and knowledge of the other') (Neue Konzeption für die Grenzlose deutsch-tschechische Schule Hartau/Hrádek – Freie Grundschule, 1998). The primary school in Hartau was saved by this initiative, but ceased to be a state school and became a private school. Since 1999, pupils of the two schools have been meeting once a week, alternately on the Czech and German sides, for joint lessons. Outings together and other leisure activities have also been organized.

My analysis is based on data gathered during a week-long school trip for fourth-graders. At the time, the pupils had been learning the partner language (German or Czech) for four years. I recorded ordinary conversations among pupils and teachers during walks or games, or in rooms they shared. I transcribed the recorded texts using the conventions of conversation analysis (see, for example, Psathas, 1995; the notation I used is given at the end of the chapter). The conversations recorded were neither initiated nor steered by the researcher, but occurred spontaneously and, among the pupils, often with no adult present. Thus, following Gumperz's declaration that

> interpretive analysis of conversational exchanges in key, naturally organized situations can yield significant insights into the communicative processes that underlie categorization, intergroup stereotyping, evaluation of verbal performance
>
> (Gumperz 1988: VII)

I am not restricted to investigating the identities produced institutionally by the school, but can observe the natural practices of the pupils (cf. Heller 2006: 17).

My analysis uses the methods of the ethnography of communication and ethnomethodology, specifically, membership categorization analysis. Both methods follow the interpretive tradition, both examine natural interaction and set out interpretatively from the emic ('insider') perspective. However, integrating the two approaches can achieve greater methodological sensitivity (Emerson and Pollner: 2007): ethnography provides a basic knowledge of the area under investigation, while ethnomethodology adds depth to this knowledge.

To observe a/symmetry in the use of the two partner languages I apply ethnographic methods, 'that is, a close look at language practices in a specific setting' (Heller 2006: 13). Multilingual teaching in borderland regions is a fairly specific, recent phenomenon, which is only just beginning to lead to specialist publications (e.g. Schröder and Bahr 1998; Halink et al. 2003; Abel et al. 2006).[2]

Ethnomethodology is well suited to observing identity formation and how it is experienced by members of the observed community, since its object is to 'identify and describe how members of society *make use* of social identity in their talk and action', in other words, the investigation of social identity as a members' phenomenon (Hester and Housley 2002: 4–12). Following this principle, I focus on the facts that are apparent from the data (Francis and Hester 2004: 28), and follow how identity is reflected in the teachers' and pupils' exchanges. The school discourse has been chosen here as the object of analysis because institutions function as a powerful instrument in the construction of identities (Hester and Housley 2002: 2). I start from the concept of membership categorization analysis (Sacks 1992; Lepper 2000; Fitzgerald and Housley: 2002; Schegloff 2007), since social categorization helps an individual define his/her place in society; the manner of categorization reflects attitudes to others, and social inclusion or exclusion. These concepts are discussed in more detail in the next section.

Identity as a members' phenomenon

My first research question focused on people's identities which I regard as experiences which are constructed by the participants in a given discourse. Each of us attaches a number of identities to ourselves and prioritizes the use of one or another according to the type of interaction or discourse we are engaging in. Thus, speaker X may describe himself in school as someone's fellow-pupil, at home as a son and among a group of Italians as a foreigner or specifically as a Czech. The speaker will select a designation according to which identity she/he sees as relevant to the situation. In this context, Sacks (1992) writes of a 'Member's activities of categorizing Members' and calls such designations as 'pupil', 'son', 'Czech' *membership categories*. By using a membership category an individual defines his/her place in society, since a membership category expresses both a social identity and social relations (Sacks 1992). Not only does membership categorization reflect local social structures, it also assists in their creation and is involved in the process of standardizing them. Membership categorization analysis (MCA), originally devised for the purpose of categorizing persons, was subsequently elaborated for non-personal categories (Lepper 2000; McHoul and Watson 1984; Eglin and Hester 1992; and others). The present study notes, in addition to personal membership categories ('pupil', 'Czech'), the use of location categories ('at home', 'Bohemia'), that is, 'members' practices

of "formulating place" through the use of "location formulations"'
(Schegloff 1972: 85).

In using a particular category in a particular setting a speaker prioritizes one identity over others that are available to them. In the examples
of interethnic communication that I analyse ethnic categories and ethnically modified categories are frequently used. A category not only
designates someone's identity, it also expresses relationships to other
categories (for example, the category 'pupil' expresses an existing relationship to a teacher or fellow-pupils) and the speaker's relations and
attitudes to what is being categorized (for example, the category 'at
home' expresses the speaker's relationship to where she or he lives, be
that a country, town or building). Each category is associated with certain typical features or activities (for example, a child is playful, a pupil
studies). A category is said to have tied to it *categorial predicates*, which
are category-bound and/or category-constitutive features and activities.
A category-bound feature or activity is a predicate that implies a given
category (identity) and is tied to a given category by convention (cf.
Sacks 1992): for example, a 'crying baby' – the activity of crying is tied
conventionally to 'baby'. By contrast, a category-constitutive predicate
is not merely one that is category-relevant, but is category-required (see
Jayyusi 1984; Eglin and Hester 1992). A constitutive predicate constitutes the relevant category, which means that it is embedded in each
category member. Thus, for example, tied to the category 'basketball
player' is the activity of dribbling. Because it holds that every basketball
player knows how to dribble, this is a category-constitutive activity, the
point being that anyone who does not know how to dribble cannot be
a basketball player (cf. the necessary condition in mathematical logic)
(Stetson 1999: 98).

Membership categories may be interlinked and so make up a category collection, for example American/Canadian/Danish/French. The
category collection and some rules of application have been called by
Sacks a *membership categorization device* (MCD) (see Schegloff 2007). For
example, the collection or MCD 'family' embraces the membership categories of 'mother', 'father', 'child', and so on. A special instance of a
membership categorization device is the standardized relational pair,
defined by Lepper (2000: 17) as 'a pairing of Members such that the
relation between them constitutes a locus for rights and obligations':
for example, husband and wife, mother and baby, lecturer and student,
neighbour and neighbour.

In observing members' category work in situ, it is crucial to consider
the context. I use the pragmatic concept of deixis, which refers to the

dependence of the meaning of a given expression on the extralinguistic context, and on how it varies with the context. I distinguish between personal (for example, we–you), local (for example, here–there), temporal (for example, now–tomorrow) and social deixis (for example, the use of 'tu' over 'vous' in French; 'du' over 'Sie' in German; 'ty' over 'Vy' in Czech). The use of the personal pronoun 'we' and the constitution of 'we' and 'they' groups within a bilingual setting is especially significant.

Using the conceptual framework outlined above, I next discuss five extracts to explore what kinds of identity (relation) are constructed in school discourse in Hrádek and Hartau. The first two are evidence of the category work of teachers, the other three reveal the categories used typically in pupils' discourse.

One afternoon, the teachers devised a competition, the aim of which was to stimulate the pupils to use the partner language. Two teams were drawn up on the basis of language affinity, one of Czech-speaking pupils and teachers (from the Hrádek school) and the other of German-speakers (from the Hartau school). Each pupil and teacher was given five cards. The pupils were to put any question they liked to the members of the partner school. If the person replied 'yes' (*ano/ja*), s/he had to hand one of his/her cards to the questioner. The winning team was the one that held most cards after a given time. About 20 minutes into the game all the children in the Czech group had handed over their own cards to a single Czech child and, likewise, all the German children had given their cards to a single German child. Speaker LA is a Czech teacher, working at the time at the German primary school in Hartau. In extract 1, LA informs the children about the new situation that only one child in each group was holding all the cards and explains the rules of the game first to the German pupils and then to the Czech pupils.

Extract 1 Competition Czechs v. Germans

LA: *OK, die tschechischen kinder haben jetzt alle karten zusammen. das heißt, wenn ihr jemanden ausredt (2) wen jemand. aus den tschechischen, von den tschechischen kindern habt ihr habt ihr anspruch auf eine karte. ted' sem jim to ještě řekl jednou (.) versteht ihr?*

   (OK, the Czech children have all their cards together. this means that when you ask someone (2) when someone. from the Czech, of the Czech children, you are you are entitled to one card. now I've told them once more (.) do you understand?)
   (1)
N1: *je?*
   (je?)
N2: *noch mal.*
   (once more).

   ((In the following 29 seconds LA explains the rules to the German children again. Then he turns to the Czech children and gives them the explanation.))

LA: *e děcka, (.) německý děti to maj úplně stejně, taky mají karty společně takže jakmile někoho napálíte z německejch dětí, dostáváte kartičku. ~T~ je správkyně karet.*

(er kids, (.) the German children are doing the same thing, they too have all the cards together so as soon as you outwit one of the German children you will receive a card. ~T~ is the custodian of the cards.)

LA speaks first in German. He employs the ethnically modified category: *die tschechischen kinder* (the Czech children), which is one that the teachers in these utterances use regularly. The expression *die tschechischen kinder* implies the pronoun 'they'. The personal pronoun 'you' (*ihr*), that is, the group of German children whom the teacher is addressing, then designates a different group in the competition from the group *die tschechischen kinder*. The distinction 'you'–'they' speaks of the existence of two different groups, of the German children and of the Czech children. LA included himself in neither group. Then he turns to the Czech children and speaks in Czech: *teď jsem jim to řekl ještě jednou* (now I've told them once more). The personal pronoun *jim* (them) in this case defines the group of German children as the 'they–group'. The next sentence – *versteht ihr?* (do you understand?) – is addressed to the German children, this time designated as the 'you-group'. After 29 seconds LA addresses the Czech children: *e děcka německý děti to maj úplně stejně* (er kids, (.) it is the same for the German children). And this time he designates the Czech children as the 'you-group' and the German children as the 'they-group'. Teacher LA, therefore, alternates deictic expressions according to the group he happens to be addressing.

So LA addresses his utterance to two groups, which he calls the group of 'Czech children' (*die tschechischen kinder*) and the group of 'German children' (*německý děti*). He uses both languages in his explanation; addressing the group of 'Czech children' he speaks Czech, to the group of 'German children' he switches to German. On the basis of language competence, two groups are created and designated by ethnically modified categories. In this instance, therefore, language is a category-constitutive feature.

The division of the pupils into 'Czech children' and 'German children' is typical of the teachers' discourse. Alternatively, one could have referred to the school (Hrádek children, Hartau children), their classes ('the A's', 'the teddy bears') or by random division of the children into teams (by, for example, a counting-out process) in order to avoid making a distinction based on the children's nationalities.

When explaining the rules of the game in extract 1, LA did not identify himself with either ethnic group, probably identifying himself more with his managerial position. In extract 2 we see that preservation of his 'ethnic immunity' is a posture that is neither adopted deliberately nor sustained consistently. During the game, a situation arose when LA did reply 'yes' to one question, but declined to give the Czech girl his card, explaining that the German group had different rules.

Extract 2 We Germans have different rules of the game

UD: *ale asi by měly bejt na to jasný pravidla, nó*
    (but there should be clear rules, shouldn't there)
LA: *já nevim. my máme prostě že se musí odpovědět na otázku. (.) a na otázku prostě (.)*
    (I don't know. we have simply the rule that the question must be answered. (.) the
    question simply (.))
K: *odpověděl si*
    (you replied)

Here LA uses the deictic expression *my* (we) to denote the German group, thus including himself in it. The teams were made up on the basis of the children's linguistic competence (the aim of the game was to practise the partner language). LA is Czech, but because he is fluent in German, he had been employed at the German school; in this instance he was playing with the German team. A necessary condition for identifying LA as a member of the German group is his very good knowledge of German, so his language competence is a constitutive feature of the category 'German'. A bound feature is LA's affiliation to the German primary school. In the following turn LA's belonging to the German group is expressed as well, but this time implicitly, through the use of social deixis. The Czech girl K addresses teacher LA as 'du' (informal 'you'). (Addressing the teachers as 'du' is common practice at the German school, though Czech children address their teachers as 'Sie'/'Vy' (formal 'you').) So K treats LA as a teacher of the German school, and thus she too treats as relevant the category-bound feature of where teacher LA's workplace is situated, not his real nationality.

The exchange in extract 2 shows that the ethnic Czech teacher LA has come to be considered as a member of the German community in this interaction. This shift in perception of his identity from his original Czech to German can be seen as a consequence of the linguistic competence he has acquired.

In the next three extracts I concentrate on the production of categories typical of the children in the study. Two of the extracts analysed come from conversations held in mixed Czech–German rooms, where two Czech and two German children lived together. Extract 3 comes from a boys' room. Teacher LB is reprimanding boy D; both speakers are from the German school and both are ethnic Germans.

Extract 3 Not me, it's the Czechs' fault

LB: *klid ~D~*
    (calm down ~D~)
D: *xxxx die tschechen hier meckern, weil sie immer nie die tür zumachen. (.) meckern mal sie an. (.) TÜR ZU ZAVŘETE DVEŘE.*
    (the Czechs here are moaning/whingeing because they never close the door. have a go at them. CLOSE THE DOOR!)

LB tells D to calm down. D accuses his Czech room-mates: *die tschechen hier meckern* (the Czechs here are moaning/whingeing) and explains that they are the cause of his misbehaviour: *weil sie immer nie die tür zumachen* (because they never close the door). He wants the teacher to reprimand the Czech pupils: *meckern mal sie an* (Have a go at them). Again in this turn the ethnic category *die tschechen* (the Czechs) is employed, to which the deictic expression *sie* (they) cross-refers in both grammatical forms (nominative and accusative). The designation of the 'they – the Czechs' group – implies the existence of a 'we – the Germans' group. D ties the activity *immer nie die tür zumachen* (never close the door) to the category 'Czechs'. Note too the code-switching and voice-raising aimed at achieving maximum effect, that is, that the command *ZAVŘETE DVEŘE* (close the door) be indeed carried out.

Extract 3 demonstrates that two separate ethnic groups are created in the mixed rooms as well. Extract 4 reveals what the significant feature is when it comes to dividing the room-mates into two groups. It is from an interaction in a boys' mixed room; D is an ethnic German from the German school, A and M are ethnic Czechs from the Czech school.

Extract 4 I to-be Czech, I not to-be German

D: *leckt mir am a:rsch* ((with edgy voice)) *xxxxxxxxxx*
    (fuck off)
A: *was ist das? (.) noch einmal.* ((short laugh))
    (what's that? (.) say it] again)
M: *ještě jednou (.) já být čechem, ne být němec (.) ja bydlet na haradechově. já bydlet v hrádek. ich wohne in hrádek.*
    (once more (.) I to be Czech, I not to be German (.) I to-live in Haradechov. I to-live in Hrádek. I live in Hrádek.)

In the first turn we can observe German boy D's forcing activity (see Kallmeyer and Schmitt 1996). The utterance is formulated in German.

Czech boy A switches to German in order to ask what the sentence means and for it to be repeated: *was ist das? noch einmal.* (what's that? (.) [say it] again) Then Czech boy M asks for it to be said again: *ještě jednou* (once more) and refers to his ethnic background: *já být čechem, ne být němec.* (I to-be Czech, not to-be German). In doing so, he designates two ethnic groups, Czechs and Germans. The constitutive feature of the relevant ethnic category is again language in the sense that the elementary distinctive feature of the categories 'Czech' and 'German', as A expressed it, was the lack of understanding of the first German sentence. At the same time, the ethnic category 'Czech' has bound to it the local category 'Hrádek': *já bydlet v hrádek ich wohne in hrádek* (I to-live in Hrádek. I live in Hrádek). Once again note the code-switching in order to achieve maximum communicative effect, that is understanding. In his turn, the Czech boy M is partially accommodating: he speaks more slowly and uses infinitives, also avoiding the case-ending in adapting the name of the town.

In discussing extracts 1–4 I focus on what personal categories are relevant in this kind of school discourse and show that the preferential use of ethnic categories and the use of personal deixis are aimed at distinguishing two ethnic groups. Extract 5 makes the distinction of location categories evident. In the same way as personal categories, location categories can provide inferences, generate distinctions, and so on so that 'the common sense geography employed by interactants may be used for a variety of sense-making purposes' (Lepper 2000: 26). Unless you are 'local', you will have a different common-sense geography and may run up against problems similar to those encountered by the teacher-outsider UD (McHoul and Watson 1984).

In extract 5, UD is chatting to some Czech children during a ramble.

Extract 5 So we can't be in one and the same country

1 UD: *hrádek.(.) a ~A~ vadí že německé hartau nazývám hrádek*
   (Hrádek. (.) and it bothers ~A~ if I call the German Hartau Hrádek)
2 L: *paní učitelko my tam pojedeme autobusem*
                 (miss, we'll go there by bus)
3 X: *no to mně taký*
    (well, me too)
4 N: *mně taký*
    (me too)
5 UD: *aha?*
    (aha?)
6 L: *paní učitelko*
   (miss)

7   UD: *a próč?*
        (and why?)
8   I: *no vadí nam to protože voni?*
        (well, it bothers us because they?)
9   N: *protože češi a němcííí*
        (because Czechs and Germans::)
10 UD: *achi*
        (oh dear)
11 N: *prostě to je něco*
        (simply it is something)
12 K: *protože každej mluví jinym jazykem tak nemůžem bejt v jedný zemi*
        (because everyone speaks a different language so we can't be in one and the
        same country)
13 UD: *aha.*
        (aha)

In her first turn UD mentions the problem of the consistent use of a location formulation: '*~A~ vadí že německé hartau nazývám hrádek*' (It bothers ~A~ if I call the German Hartau Hrádek). The other children also express the need to distinguish between the Czech Hrádek and the German Hartau (turns 3, 4, 8). UD would like to discover why the children find it so necessary to separate them geographically: '*a próč?*' (and why?) (turn 7). A Czech girl, I, confirms the need for the geographical separation of the two towns and explains it by the existence of two distinct groups, 'we' and 'they': *nam, voni* (us, they) (turn 8). She doesn't specify who is included in the 'we' group and the 'they' group, but the other participants understand it automatically. In the next turn (9) the two groups are named explicitly by means of two distinct ethnic categories: *češi a němci* (Czechs and Germans). The place categories 'Hrádek' and 'Hartau' are, then, predicates bound to the ethnic categories 'Czechs' and 'Germans'. However, up to this point no reason has been given for why the two ethnic groups are distinguished. Turns 8, 9 and 11 are interrupted at the point where a distinctive feature of the two ethnicities is to be given. The non-enunciation of the reason for the division, together with the utterances *vadí nám to* (it bothers us) (8) and a *achi* (oh dear) (10) hint at some problem between the two nations which everyone knows well, but no one wants to put into words.

Speaker K winds up the evasive replies with the diplomatic formulation '*protože každej mluví jiným jazykem*' (Because each speaks a different language) (12). K is appealing to language as a constitutive element of ethnic identity and a reason for the geographical distinction of the two countries: '*tak nemůžeme bejt v jedný zemi*' (so we can't be in one and the same country). This argument is accepted as sufficient and the question is deemed answered by *aha* (aha) and the conversation is wound up. Once again, this extract reveals the ethnic distinction as the primary division, with language in the role of the category-constitutive predicate for the ethnic categories and the location formulation in the role of bound predicate.

In this section, I have investigated the category work of members of a bilingual setting that is made up of two schools participating in the project of bilingual education. Observing the use of both personal and local categories the existence of two exclusive groups, a 'we-group/here' and a 'they-group/there', is evident. In allocating themselves and/or other participants to these groups the speakers employ the ethnic distinction preferentially over age, social status, gender or any other distinction. While it is typical for the pupils' discourse to operate with the single ethnic categories *Čech* and *Němec*, the teachers, as local authorities, make an effort to mitigate the ethnic distinction by employing ethnically modified categories – *české děti* (Czech children), *německé děti* (German children). The two ethnic groups are defined on the basis of their language competence and geographical affiliation, language competence being a category-constitutive feature and local affiliation a bound feature of the relevant ethnic category. Similarly, Nekvapil (2000: 37) notes that 'on the territory of the Czech Republic the relation between ethnic category and language is category-constitutive'. That is why the acquisition of a new language led to the shift in ethnic categorization and so to the new perception of one's own identity (see extracts 1 and 2).

Moreover, this section has demonstrated the relationship between practical action (category work), local production of social order and the process of standardization. The discourse in question sees the relational category pair Czech–German as being constituted as a standardized relational pair which is constructed within the social discourse that has been analysed (see beginning of this section and Lepper 2000). The relation between paired categories (in this case 'Czech' – 'German'), which consists of standardized rights and obligations, is inherent in a bilingual setting that depends on language exchange and partnership between two neighbouring nations. Thus the collection of interlinked categories as Czech–German, Czech children–German children, Czech teacher–German teacher in the given bilingual setting could be seen as MCD.

Attitudes: reflections on the connection between commonly used ethnic categories and language competence

Category work in situ showed ethnicity to be the fundamental distinctive feature of two groups cooperating on a single project. These groups have been constituted on the basis of their language competence and are bound to local affiliation. In extract 5 there was a hint of a problem between the two groups, but the speakers were loath to make it explicit. In order to make the reason for the ethnic distinction apparent, I shall look at the attitudes of one group to the other as expressed by the participants in the discourse.

Extracts 6 and 7 represent two typical views held by Germans as expressed by members of the middle generation of Czechs. Both were voiced by the Czech teacher UC in a reflection on Czech–German relations. In extract 6 he compares relations between French- and German-Swiss in Switzerland and relations between Czechs and Germans.

Extract 6 We're so far apart

UC: . . . *k sobě mají, daleko míň antipatií než my a němci. my a němci máme k sobě tak*
daleko už, (.) já to řeknu kolik sedm set osm set let? dlouhodobě . . . .
(. . . they ((meaning the Swiss)) have fewer antipathies to each other than we and the Germans. we and the Germans have been so far apart for, (.) I will say it, how many seven hundred eight hundred years? very long-term . . . .)

In extract 7 UC describes the typical use of partner languages in the situation of German citizens making a purchase in a Czech shop.

Extract 7 They don't speak Czech

UD: *no a to potom voni trošku mluví česky nebo ty prodavači německy?*
(yes and then do they speak a bit of Czech or the salespeople German?)
UC: *něme- prodavači německy přizpůsobujou se, my se přizpůsobujeme jim. a to mě*
zlobí . . . ať se naučí česky dyž chce se mnou mluvit. . . . .
(. . . we adjust to them. and that annoys me. . . . . let him/them learn Czech if he wants to speak to me. . . .)

In extracts 6 and 7 the speaker acknowledges the existence of two separate ethnic groups: a 'we-group' denoting the group of Czechs and a 'they-group' denoting the group of Germans. UC points up the problematic nature of the relationship between the two (antipathies) as a longstanding phenomenon: *'sedm set osm set let? dlouhodobě'* (seven hundred eight hundred years? very long-term). In extract 7 UC describes how, when a German citizen is making a purchase in a Czech shop, the Czech salesperson addresses him/her in German. UC explicitly points out the greater accommodation the Czech population shows in the course of inter-ethnic communication: *'my se přizpůsobujeme jim'* (we adjust to them). Asymmetry in the use of the partner languages is assessed negatively by this speaker: *'a to mě zlobí'* (and that annoys me). UC further mentions the problem of German incompetence in Czech: '*at' se naučí česky*' (let them/him learn Czech). Thus it is evident that relations between members of the Czech and German ethnic groups are impacted negatively by the asymmetry of language use.

Extract 8 demonstrates typical views held by Czech children and arising from their experience in using the partner languages in interethnic communication. This extract was recorded when the Czech and German children were taking a walk together; only UD is an adult.

Extract 8 (In) Czech, not a hope! And that's just what's so silly

1 K: *jenže, naši řeč: neumí, vůbec ji nezvládá. (3) kdežto my, my jejich řeč musíme zvládat úplně perfekt. my tam musíme mluvit německy, a voni tam musej mluvit německy. ČESky ani nápad.*
(but they can't speak our language, they can't handle it at all. (3) but we, we have to speak their language excellently. We have to speak German there and they have to speak German there. CZEch not a hope.)
....

2 UD: *no ale já sem myslela že dyž děláte ve skupině takže voni prostě taky musí mluvit česky*
(but I thought that when you work in groups they simply have to speak Czech as well)

3 K: *ne, voni na nás mluvěj německy*
(no, they speak to us in German)

4 UD: *hm*
(hm)

5 K: *a to je právě že blbý*
(and that's just what's so silly)

6 I: *a my na ně musíme taky mluvit německy*
(and we also have to speak to them in German)

In this extract too, two ethnic groups are designated: the 'we-group' is the group of Czech pupils from the Czech school, and the 'they-group' German children from the German school (turns 1, 3, 6). The deictic expressions *naši* (our) and *jejich* (their) indicate language as each ethnic group's constitutive feature: *naši řeč, jejich řeč* (our language, their language) (turn 1). Both ethnic groups are associated with a specific speech activity: '*naši řeč neumí, vůbec ji nezvládaj, my jejich řeč musíme zvládat*' (they can't speak our language, they can't handle it at all. but we, we have to speak their language excellently) (turn 1), '*voni na nás mluvěj německy*' (they speak to us in German) (turn 3), '*my musíme mluvit německy*' (we have to speak in German) (turns 1 and 6). Knowing and using German are ascribed to both ethnic groups, in the German case as voluntary, in the Czech case as obligatory, as expressed by the

modality of the verbs used: *my musíme* (we have to) (turns 1 and 6).
The asymmetry in language competencies (knowledge and use of both
partner languages) is expressed in turn 1, confirmed in turn 3 and evaluated negatively in turn 5: '*a to je právě že blbý*' (and that's what's just so
silly). The lower status of Czech is expressed explicitly in turn 1: '*ČESky
ani nápad*' (CZEch not a hope). Extract 8 again demonstrates the negative impact of linguistic asymmetry on relations between the two ethnic
groups.

Both the Czech children and their teachers give a negative assess-
ment of the asymmetry in language competence and the higher rate
of accommodation on the Czech side: '*a to je právě že blbý*' (and that's
just what's so silly) (extract 8), '*a to mě zlobí*' (and that annoys me)
(extract 7). Unfamiliarity with and non-use of Czech by the German
side is seen as a problem between the two ethnic groups. A similar situation is mentioned by Albert Raasch, who studied the language situation
in the Saar–Lor–Lux Euroregion and noted that 'Individual bilingualism is found on the French side but not (or very little) on the German
side.' (2002: 16). Gass and Varonis (1991) have described non-activity
in a language as a fundamental problem in inter-ethnic communication. Moreover, Nelde (1997) draws attention to the difficulties in the
relations between two nations when there is accommodation on the
part of speakers of the language that enjoys lower status. According
to a Eurobarometer study (see European Commission 2005), German
is the second most widely used language in the EU, while Czech is
merely one language out of 23. It is obvious that non-competence
in a partner language leads to asymmetry in interethnic communication, which reinforces the ethnic exclusivity of the interested
communities.

With a higher level of language competence we would expect a more
symmetrical language situation and better relations between two ethnic
groups. An example of this is the room shared by two Czech boys, L and
T, and two German boys, D and M. D understands Czech better than
is usual among German speakers, because his father is Czech. He is not
good at forming whole Czech sentences, but he does use Czech more
often than the other German children. Note the relevance of the use of
ethnic categories among the boys in this mixed room.

Extract 9

L: *neumíš ~D~, (.) ~D~ kuk mal*
   (can't you ~D~,(.) ~D~ have a look)

Extract 10

M: ~*T*~ *e* <<*Nemecko Niederlands*>> *null null,*
   (~T~ er Germany: Netherlands nil nil)
T: >>*jo*<<
   (>>yes<<)

Extract 9 shows clearly that the boys, members of both ethnic groups, cooperate. The Czech boy L explains to the German boy D how to play diabolo, using both partner languages in the process. He calls D by his first name: ~*D*~. The German boy M in extract 10 also calls his Czech room-mate by his first name: ~*T*~. He is telling him the football results. Note his preservation of ethnic neutrality in identifying the teams when he says *Nemecko* (Germany (in Czech)) *Niederlands*, and not 'we and the Netherlands', and the use of both partner languages. The ethnic distinction, typical in the other children's discourse, does not occur in these extracts.

Extract 11

D: *budeme tady něco dělat?*
   (will we do something here?)
L: *e puč si tady to, puč si tady to*
   (er borrow this, borrow this)

The personal deixis in extract 11 shows that the German boy D includes himself *and* the Czech boy L within the same 'we-group'. This is exceptional, because neither ethnic exclusivity nor two ethnically distinct groups – a 'we-group' and a 'they-group' – occur here.

In section 3 the exclusivity of two cooperating ethnic groups (Czech and German) was evident and the language has been found to be the constitutive feature of these ethnic groups. In section 4, then, the reason for ethnic distinction has been investigated. It has been shown that language asymmetry (the asymmetry in language competence) causes problems in the relationship between members of two interacting ethnicities.The incompetence in the respective partner language, that is the unfamiliarity with and especially the non-use of the Czech language, is the motivating element for the ethnic distinction. On the other hand, the competence in the partner languages stimulates ethnic inclusion (extract 9–11).

Asymmetrical language use

In the previous section I have discussed the problem of the asymmetrical language use of both partner languages, Czech and German. On this Winford (2003: 14) adds that, within multicultural communities, the use of language codes in particular domains and functions of communication becomes, over time, specified, giving rise to diglossia or polyglossia. A prerequisite for this, however, is a higher-level knowledge of the partner language than is the case with our fourth-grade pupils, who are not able to use a foreign language in a targeted way in certain domains of communication, and so to specify each code functionally. However, in the teachers' discourse it is possible to trace the functionally differentiated use of German and Czech. Moreover, as they represent authority on the ground, the teachers manage the present and future speech activity of their pupils (see section 2 above). For that reason I focus in this section on the speech activity of the teachers.

The asymmetry in the language behaviour of the community of teachers may be described by the formula: '3 Czechs + 1 German = German'. On the school outing four teachers were present. UD and UC are from the Czech school; both are Czech. LA and LB are from the German school; LA is Czech, LB German. Although by ethnicity the Czech teachers are in the majority, thanks to their competence in German they create conditions for the symmetrical use of both languages. Three teachers speak Czech (the three Czechs: UD, UC, LA), and three speak German (one German: LB, and two Czechs: UD, LA). Figure 5.1 shows what language they use when speaking together.

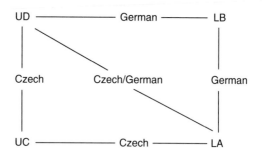

Figure 5.1   Language use among teachers

It follows that the two teachers, UC and LB, who can only speak their respective native language, do not speak together and are thus deprived of one relation in comparison to the others. Note also the peculiarity of the use of German between the two Czechs UD and LA.

Extract 12 illustrates how the teachers speak when all four are present. We might logically assume the dominant use of the ethnic majority language and a tendency to assimilate among the ethnic minority. So, in a situation where there are three Czechs and one German, we assume that Czech would be used. This extract was recorded in a situation where all four teachers were present. On the ramble, they are jointly consulting the map as to which way to proceed.

Extract 12 How Czechs don't speak Czech, or: inverse asymmetry

1   LB: *jetz.gehen wir aber doch <u>ein bach über</u>*
       (but now we do have to get across a stream)

2   LA: *<u>ach ne doch wir</u> müssen.ein bisschen <u>hoch</u>*
       (ah no OK we have to go a bit further up)

3   UD: *<u>wir</u> müssen da*
                                       (there we have
       to)

4   LB: *ja*
       (yes)

5   LA: *ja, weil hier ist es, der damm*
       (yes because here it is the dam)

6   LB: *da gehen wir aber jetzt.(auch an den) so lang.*
       (but we now have to go. along (that thing))

7   LA: *ja*
       (yes)

8   LB: *ja*
       (yes)

9   LA: *bis, also bis zu mariánské boudy <u>(.)</u> mariahütten*
       (until, well until mariánské boudy (.) mariahütten)

10   LB: *<u>hhh,</u>*

11   LA: *und jetzt sind wir von hier gekommen.*
       (and now we have come this way)

12   UD: *und jetzt sind wir von hier her gekommen? oder? <u>(.)</u> wir sind jetzt im na ja mariánská hora*
       (and now we have come this way? haven't we? (.) now we are, well, in mariánská hora)

13   LB: *<u>ja.</u>*
                            (yes)

14   LA: *na ja. also es ist mir nur.ein stück((xxx hier))*
       (well then it is only. a short way (here))

15   UD: *na genau glaube ich auch das ((short laugh))*
       (well exactly I believe so too)

16   LA: *na ja . . . . doch wir müssen*
       (well . . . . yes we have to)

17   LB: *da haben wir auch nicht tempo dran* <u>xxxx wird es</u> *anstrengen (sind wir) eine*
      (scheisse)
         (we don't go fast enough either xxx will find it hard (we are) a (shit))

Contrary to expectation, the only language used is German. Two of
the Czech teachers are fully accommodating, speaking German even
when discussing something between themselves (turns 11, 12, 14, 15,
16). The third Czech is excluded from the shared conversation, having
only a limited knowledge of German. Only one teacher, LB, is speaking
his native tongue. The use of German as the working language is typical
of the teachers' meetings. One consequence is the absence of UD from
the regular evening meetings, as his spoken German is inadequate for
the purpose.

We have seen how the teachers speak when together. Let us now turn
to the language in which they instruct their pupils. Only two teachers, the Czechs UD and LA, have adequate language competence to give
instruction to children of both ethnic groups in their respective mother
tongues. Indeed, they do employ as the language of instruction the
mother tongue of the ethnic group they are addressing (see extract 1).
The German LB and the Czech UC are competent only in their respective mother tongues. LB knows a few basic phrases in Czech and UC
did learn German once but has not used it for a long time. German
teacher LB mostly uses German as the language of instruction for both
ethnic groups, which causes problems of communication (for example,
he did not understand the Czech children when they needed help, so
he failed to assist them). Czech UC, on the other hand, respects the
use of German when instructing German children and gives them short
instructions in German. Where longer instructions are required, he asks
UD or LA to translate, placing the Czechs in the role of interpreter. This
confirms once more that the Czech participants show a higher measure
of accommodation.

Having examined the speech activity of the teachers, we have witnessed greater accommodation in the ethnically Czech teachers. UD
and LA exhibit a high level of competence in both partner languages.
They thus create the kind of situation described by Georges Lüdi as
'situation bilingues-endolingues',[3] which is typical of diglossic communities, where two languages are used according to specific domains
and functions (Matthey and Py 1995: 16). Extract 12 reveals the use
of German in the function of working language, despite the preva-
lence of ethnically Czech teachers (3:1). Given this language asymmetry,

UC, whose German is inadequate, is excluded from the management process – teachers' meetings. German is also dominant as a language of instruction, the German pupils receiving instruction in German and the Czech pupils in both languages. The teachers, as authority figures, may be said to have initiated a situation of diglossia within the bilingual setting.

Conclusions

In this chapter I have explored the dynamic relationship between language and identity as reflected in everyday conversations. I have clarified the causal dependence between category work and language competence (knowledge and use of language) in interethnic interaction. The original question of whether people acquire cross-border competencies or whether the border remains a barrier in their perceptions of members of the respective other nation may be answered to the effect that in the discourse under investigation the existing ethnic distinction between the two cooperating groups is very evident. The constitutive element of ethnic identity in this case is language. A change in language competence brings about a change in the experience of identity. In this context we have noticed a tendency towards assimilation, a shift in the use of personal categories as a consequence of the bilingualism of Czech teacher LA (extracts 1 and 2). We also recorded the exceptional case where children in a mixed room created a more symmetrical language situation and did not replicate the ethnic distinction (extracts 9–11). There are grounds for believing that an increase in competence in a partner language leads to a reduction of the ethnic distinction, and in general a change of category-constitutive predicate causes a shift in membership categorization.

I have also observed the attitudes of the two ethnic groups towards each other. Inadequate competence in the partner language is the main feature viewed negatively. As regards the speech activity of the teachers, I identified an asymmetry in the knowledge and use of the two languages and found that German serves the function of a working language and is dominant in the function of language of instruction. To support good relations between two ethnic groups, it is important to create a symmetrical language situation based on the equal status of both partner languages, which implies equal status of both neighbouring nations. In short, the overcoming of language barriers stimulates the overcoming of national barriers.

Transcription conventions

(.)	pause, short
(3)	pause, elapsed time in silence in seconds
:	prolongation of the immediately prior sound
xxxx	unintelligible word
xxxxxxxxxx	unintelligible passage
~F~	first initial of participant's name (omitted)
(but)	words and phrases difficult to hear but presumed
((laugh))	comments from the author of the transcription
underlining	overlapping talk
MAX	sounds especially loud relative to the surrounding talk
>>já nevim<<	faster speech
<<nevim>>	slower speech
?	rising intonation
.	falling intonation
,	slightly rising intonation indicating the continuation of the turn
*	markedly rising intonation
....	omitted passage of the transcript

Direct speech is written in italics, the English translation in normal style.

Acknowledgement

I am extremely grateful to Jenny Carl and Patrick Stevenson for their valuable comments and clarifications on earlier drafts of this chapter as well as for their support with the translation of my chapter.

Notes

1. This cross-border competence is made up of five core competencies, namely *landeskundliche Kompetenz, kontrastiv-landeskundliche Kompetenz, Empathie-Kompetenz, interkulturelle Kompetenz* and *intra-kulturelle Kompetenz*, which Raasch argues are essential for acquiring cross-border identities.
2. The original objective of the bilingual school project was the integration of migrant, non-native speakers in the classroom, where pressure to assimilate is exerted on the minority group. Bilingual teaching involving two neighbouring nations, for example in Euroregions, ought, conversely, to pursue the objective of the symmetrical teaching of two languages having equal status, which implies the equal status of members of both groups. The symmetry principle in teaching seeks, however, to underpin a system of dual language education, using the model of a two-way immersion programme (Lindholm-Leary 2001/2002; Collier and Thomas 2004; García 2005). Dual

education means teaching native and non-native speakers together in both partner languages, and, provided the numbers of native and non-native speakers are balanced, we can indeed speak of a two-way (bilingual) immersion programme.
3. Matthey and Py (1995) refer to Lüdi's (1989) typology of communicative situation and define the 'bilingual-endolingual' situation as 'une conversation entre des bilingues qui ont une maîtrise égale des deux codes de la communication et qui les utilisent tous les deux' (a conversation between bilinguals who have equal competence in the two codes of communication and who use both of them).

References

Abel, A., Stuflesser, M. and Putz, M. (eds) (2006) *Mehrsprachigkeit in Europa* (Bozen: Eurac).

Atkinson, P., Coffey, A., Delamont, S., Lofland, J. and Lofland, L. (eds) (2007) *Handbook of Ethnography* (London: Sage).

Collier, V. P. and Thomas, W. P. (2004) 'The astounding effectiveness of dual language education for all', *NABE Journal of Research and Practice* 2(1), 1–20.

Coulmas, F. (ed.) (1997) *The Handbook of Sociolinguistics* (Oxford: Blackwell).

Coupland, N., Giles, H. and Weimann, J. (eds) (1991) *Miscommunication and Problematic Talk* (Newbury Park, CA: Sage).

Denk, R. (ed.) (2005) *Nach Europa unterwegs* (Herbolzheim: Centaurus).

Eglin, P. and Hester, S. (1992) 'Category, predicate and task: the pragmatics of practical action', *Semiotica* 88, 243–68.

Emerson, R. M. and Pollner, M. (2007) 'Ethnomethodology and Ethnography', in Atkinson et al. (2007), 118–35.

European Commission (2005) Europeans and Languages: Special Eurobarometer 237 Wave 63.4, http://ec.europa.eu/public_opinion/archives/ebs/ebs_237.en. pdf. Accessed 14.03.2006.

Franceschini R. (2006) 'Mehrsprachigkeit: das Lernpotential von Grenzregionen', in Abel et al. (2006), 33–41.

Fitzgerald, R. and Housley, W. (2002) 'The reconsidered model of membership categorization analysis', *Qualitative Research* 2(1), 59–83.

Francis, D. and Hester, S. (2004) *An Invitation to Ethnomethodology* (London: Sage).

Gajo, L. and Mondada, L. (2000) *Interactions et acquisitions en contexte* (Fribourg: Éditions Universitaires Fribourg Suisse).

García, E. (2005) *Teaching and Learning in Two Languages: Bilingualism and Schooling in the United States* (New York and London: Teachers College Press).

Gass, S. and Varonis, E. (1991) 'Miscommunication in nonnative speaker discourse', in Coupland et al. (1991), 121–45.

Gumperz, J. J. (ed.) (1988) *Language and Social Identity* (Cambridge: Cambridge University Press).

Halink, R., Raasch, A., Schmitz-Schwamborn, G. and Schwarz, U. (eds) (2003) *Neighbouring Languages in Border Regions/La langue du voisin en région frontalière*, CD-ROM (Strasbourg: Conseil de l'Europe).

Heller, M. (2006) *Linguistic Minorities and Modernity: A Sociolinguistic Ethnography* (London: Continuum).

Hester, S. and Housley, W. (eds) (2002) *Language, Interaction and National Identity* (Aldershot: Ashgate).

Holly, W., Nekvapil, J., Scherm, I. and Tišerová, P. (2003) 'Unequal neighbours: coping with asymmetries', *Journal of Ethnic and Migration Studies* 29(5), 819–34.

Jalbert, P. L. (ed.) (1999) *Media Studies: Ethnomethodological Approaches* (Lanham, MD, New York and Oxford: University Press of America).

Jayyusi, L. (1984) *Categorisation and the Moral Order* (London: Routledge & Kegan Paul).

Kallmeyer, W. (ed.) (1996) *Gesprächsrhetorik* (Tübingen: Gunter Narr Verlag).

Kallmeyer, W. and Schmitt, R. (1996) 'Forcieren oder: Die verschärfte Gangart', in Kallmeyer (1996), 19–118.

Kremer, D. (ed.) (1989) *Actes du XVIIIe Congrès International de Linguistique et Philologie Romanes. Université de Trèves (Trier)* (Tübingen: Niemeyer).

Krumm, H.-J. (ed.) (1998) *Die Sprachen unserer Nachbarn - unsere Sprachen* (Wien: Eviva).

Language Policy Division (2007) *From Linguistic Diversity to Plurilingual Education: Guide for the Development of Language Education Policies in Europe* (Strassbourg: Council of Europe). http://www.coe. int/t/dg4/linguistic/Source/ Guide_Main_Beacco2007_EN.doc. Accessed 25 July 2008.

Lepper, G. (2000) *Categories in Text and Talk: A Practical Introduction to Categorization Analysis* (London: Sage).

Lindholm-Leary, K. J. (2001/2) *Dual Language Education* (Clevedon: Multilingual Matters).

Lüdi, G. (1989) 'Aspects de la conversation exolingue entre Suisses romands et alémaniques', in Kremer (1989), 405–24.

Lüdi, G. and Py, B. (1995) *Changement de langage et langage du changement* (Lausanne: L'Age d'Homme).

Macbeth, D. (1991) 'Teacher authority as practical action', *Linguistics and Education* 3, 281-314.

Matthey, M. and Py, B. (1995) 'Introduction', in Lüdi and Py (1995), 9–28.

McHoul, A. W. and Watson, D. R. (1984) 'Two axes for the analysis of "common sense" and "formal" geographical knowledge in classroom talk', *British Journal of Sociology of Education* 5, 281-302.

Meinhof, U. H. (2003) 'Migrating borders: an introduction to European identity construction in process', *Journal of Ethnic and Migration Studies* 29(5), 781–96.

Nekvapil, J. (2000) 'On non-self evident relationships between language and ethnicity: how Germans do not speak German, and Czechs do not speak Czech', *Multilingua* 19(1–2), 37–53.

Nelde, P. H. (1997) 'Language conflict', in Coulmas (1997), 285–300.

Nelde, P. H. (2001) *Neue Mehrsprachigkeit: Perspektiven für eine europäische Sprachpolitik* (Hagen: EuroCom) http://www.fernuni-hagen.de/sprachen/kongress/ Abstracts/NeldeDE.pdf. Accessed 15 September 2005.

Neue Konzeption für die grenzenlose deutsch-tschechische Schule Hartau / Hrádek – Freie Grundschule (1998) (Hartau: PEZ Schulträgerverein e.V.) http://www. schkola.de/de/download/konzept_grundschule_hartau.8pdf. Accessed 2 May 2007.

Psathas, G. (1995) *Conversation Analysis. The Study of Talk-in-Interaction* (London: Sage).

Raasch, A. (ed.) (1998) *Grenzenlos – durch Sprachen. Dossier 'Beispiele guter Praxis'. Zum Kongreß 'Die Sprachen unserer Nachbarn – unsere Sprachen', Wien 1998* (Saarbrücken: Universität des Saarlandes).

Raasch, A. (2002) *Europe, Frontiers and Languages* (Strasbourg: Council of Europe).

Raasch, A. (2005) 'Grenzkompetenz – ein Weg nach Europa', in Denk (2005), 119–29.

Sacks, H. (1992) *Lectures on Conversation*, 2 vols (Oxford: Blackwell).

Schegloff, E. A. (1972) 'Notes on a conversational practice: formulating place', in Sudnov (1972), 75–119.

Schegloff, E. A. (2007) 'A tutorial on membership categorization', *Journal of Pragmatics* 39, 462–82.

Schröder, H. and Bahr, A. (1998) 'Fremdsprachenlernen in einer deutsch-polnischen Grenzregion', in Raasch (1998), 46–52.

Stetson, J. (1999) 'Victim, offender and witness in the emplotment of news stories', in Jalbert (1999), 77–110.

Winford, D. (2003) *An Introduction to Contact Linguistics* (Oxford: Blackwell).

6
Czech, German and English: Finding Their Place in Multinational Companies in the Czech Republic

Jiří Nekvapil and Tamah Sherman

Introduction

Large multinational companies/corporations (multinationals) operate in several countries and are characteristic of the exchange of know-how, people and products which takes place between parent and daughter companies (subsidiaries). An important common feature of such businesses is that several operational languages are involved. This chapter examines the changing roles of three languages, Czech, German and English, in the everyday functioning of Czech-located subsidiaries/branches of companies based in Germany. It identifies some of the past and present language problems in the multinationals and how these problems are managed, particularly in relation to the local conditions and practices and the socio-economic structure, with respect to the relationship between the old and new EU member states. The chapter is based on long-term research of such companies operating in the Czech Republic (see Nekula et al. 2005; Nekvapil and Nekula 2006a, 2006b), but it extends this research, drawing on more recent fieldwork and new conceptualizations.[1] We focus on the situation in one multinational, but view this multinational against the background of other companies.

Framework for analysis

Parent companies decide to establish subsidiaries in particular places for various reasons, many of which may have to do with language considerations, not only with regard to the selected country (for example, the Czech Republic), but also to the selected region. Local companies, local educational institutions (secondary schools, universities, language schools) and authorities may play a great role in this. Local conditions affect the professional skills and knowledge of languages of the local employees of the subsidiary. At the same time, language skills of the local employees influence their positions in the company and in the regional job market in general. The volume of foreign direct investment (FDI) is also largely region-dependent. Of the total FDI in the Czech Republic, amounting to $60.7 billion, more than half has been invested in the capital, Prague (CNB 2007). Yet this is not the whole story; it is important to consider the 'regional innovation systems' which may be in operation (Williams 2006; Braczyk et al. 1998; Cooke et al. 2004). Localized or regionally-based sources of knowledge and learning sustain innovative capabilities in the new economy because tacit knowledge is more easily and inexpensively transferred within a region or locality. Social capital may also be conditioned by regional culture – regions can display a distinct system of innovation which differs from both the state norm and the systems operating in other regions.

Both the companies and their subsidiaries constitute 'communities of practice' (Wenger 1998; Barton and Tusting 2005). Having common goals, the employees work together over an extended period to share ideas, find solutions and develop innovations. In this framework, there is a distinct difference between 'codified' and 'tacit' knowledge. In our research, we are interested in how these two types of knowledge may be connected to competence in various languages – the local language (in this case Czech), the language of the company headquarters (in this case German) and the 'international language of business', English – how the knowledge of these languages is acquired at the various stages of a career, and what functions the various languages have in the exchange of information and knowledge among colleagues, or conversely, how they prevent such transfer. Also of interest is how and to what extent issues of power influence the building of communities of practice of varying complexity.

In the context of the regional character of the subsidiary and the practices that occur within it, it is necessary to ask how these practices, particularly communication, are managed. This includes the extent to which management takes place on the level of individual discourses as well as that of company structures of varying scope, and the interplay between these levels. There are also relationships between language, communicative and socio-economic management in the company. All these issues are explored by Language Management Theory (LMT) (Jernudd and Neustupný 1987). LMT presumes the existence of norms or 'expectations' for linguistic behaviour which different participants possess in different situations. Drawing on these norms, participants may generate their discourses without paying any attention to the language they use, with language serving 'as a mere means of expression'. The management process starts only when they begin paying attention to the language – when they *note* a language phenomenon, to use LMT terminology. More importantly, the participants may not only *note*, but also *evaluate* a language phenomenon – and if they *evaluate* the phenomenon negatively they face a *language problem*. Yet, management includes further phases as the participants (or particular institutions) may also deal with the problems, be it only *designing* solutions to the problems or even actually *implementing* them. For example, the following post-interaction management strategy (Nekvapil and Sherman forthcoming) was applied in a German-based multinational several years ago: after a meeting held in German with German expatriates working in the company some Czech participants asked their Czech colleagues who had a good command of German about the outcome of a particular phase of the meeting.

In the everyday operation of subsidiaries of German companies in the Czech Republic, three languages (Czech, German, and English) are used, and they are used in certain domains. Yet this does not apply to all employees and all domains – only some groups of employees speak these languages, and with varying degrees of competence. This leads to the main question which is posed in this chapter: How and to what extent do the languages spoken fulfil varying functions?

The data

The data for this chapter are mixed. Their primary component consists of visits to subsidiaries of foreign companies in the Czech Republic. The ultimate goal was to capture naturally occurring interactions, such as meetings, telephone conferences and other work situations in which a foreign language was used; and on the occasion of such interactions, follow-up interviews were subsequently conducted. Semi-structured interviews were also held, covering the following areas: the composition of the company, its employees, their job descriptions and knowledge of languages; languages in the company, translation and interpretation, communication in a foreign language, company support for language and cultural competence; communication with the parent company, the local system of teaching foreign languages, the communicative climate and potential problems in the area of communication and/or collaborative work. These interviews were conducted above all with the members of the company's senior management, both locals and expatriates, but some administrative and support staff members were also included. Other types of data include written materials which reflect company policy (brochures, business cards, annual reports) and observations of the 'linguistic landscape', or signs and labels inside and around the company buildings.

Languages taught in the country

Knowledge of foreign languages represents an important condition for the successful functioning of regional innovation systems in general and of multinationals in particular. The Czech Republic is a country in which historical and political conditions, especially those of the twentieth century, are significantly reflected in the languages which are taught and used. In this former Soviet bloc country (as well as in others; see Maitz and Sándor, this volume; Jaworska, this volume), Russian became a mandatory subject in all schools when the regime of state socialism was established. However, German was commonly taught during that period as well, and the number of pupils learning English and French was also considerable. Following the political changes of 1989, Russian ceased to be a compulsory subject in the Czech education system and the principle of free choice in language learning was declared. Most students (98 per cent in 1997–8) chose German or English. Being the current 'neighbouring' language and historically a language spoken in the Czech lands for many centuries, German was the choice of more pupils in the early 1990s. During the 1997–8 school year, however, English overtook German in terms of the total number of learners and the gap between them continues to grow (see tables 6.1 and 6.2; Nekvapil 2007).

Currently, the choice between English and German is largely region-dependent. The percentage of pupils learning German is higher in the areas bordering Germany and Austria. This choice also correlates with career ambitions: German tends to be offered to and/or chosen by those who prefer more practically-oriented careers, and English tends to be offered to and/or chosen by students pursuing academic secondary (and university) education.

The management of foreign language selection in the Czech Republic also takes an organized form at the level of governmental intervention. In 2006, the Czech Ministry of Education implemented the National Plan for the Teaching of Foreign Languages, which stipulates the mandatory teaching of two foreign languages, with the implication that the

Table 6.1   Pupils learning foreign languages at primary schools between 2000/1 and 2005/6

	2000/1	2001/2	2002/3	2003/4	2004/5	2005/6
English	435,918	456,265	477,071	492,727	497,391	503,215
German	300,563	274,522	246,787	218,033	187,285	166,808
French	7,971	8,287	7,277	7,082	9,056	7,250
Russian	1,046	1,683	1,953	2,896	3,952	5,657
Spanish	553	610	685	725	1,036	1,235
Italian	22	19	46	43	49	44
Latin	–	–	–	–	–	–
Classical Greek	–	–	–	–	–	–
Other European languages	–	–	34	205	194	29
Other languages	737	201	296	113	46	48

Sources: The Yearbook of the Development of the Educational System – Education in the Czech Republic in 2000/01–2005/06, Tab. B6.2.1.

Table 6.2   Students learning foreign languages at secondary schools between 2000/1 and 2005/6

	2000/1	2001/2	2002/3	2003/4	2004/5	2005/6
English	334,672	345,752	360,043	376,294	388,747	399,351
German	319,423	313,791	310,253	308,210	298,563	287,799
French	29,062	29,908	31,826	33,758	38,966	40,370
Russian	7,556	7,813	8,918	10,820	12,472	14,329
Spanish	7,592	8,093	9,888	11,367	12,723	14,904
Italian	1,320	1,534	1,576	1,456	1,570	1,358
Latin	15,917	15,598	15,037	15,327	13,508	12,570
Classical Greek	124	111	141	112	113	112
Other European languages	105	156	57	121	116	112
Other languages	170	172	189	178	290	304

Sources: The Yearbook of the Development of the Educational System – Education in the Czech Republic in 2000/01–2005/06, Tab. B6.2.3.

most commonly taught language is to be English. One potential result of this policy is that the gap between English and German will continue to widen. Trends from the previous era, however, remain highly visible and relevant in a large part of the adult employable population. One case in point is that in multinational companies operating in the Czech Republic we find many 'white-collar' employees over 40 years of age who did not start learning English until later in life, and thus find themselves at a disadvantage in the job market and in negotiations with senior management in multinationals.

Types of multinationals operating in the Czech Republic

Before we turn to multinationals with headquarters in Germany, it will be useful to consider multinationals in the Czech Republic in general. Overall, there are almost 4,000 foreign-owned companies operating in the country (see CNB 2007). Of the total FDI in the Czech Republic, amounting to $60.7 billion as of December 2005, the largest share comes from the Netherlands (29 per cent), followed by Germany (20 per cent), Austria (10.9 per cent), France (6 per cent), Spain (5.9 per cent), United States (4.6 per cent), Belgium (3.5 per cent), United Kingdom (3.1 per cent) and Switzerland (2.2 per cent). Other countries contribute a combined total of 15.9 per cent. Though these numbers cannot be taken as absolute because some foreign investors from the US and Japan invest in the Czech Republic through third countries (which partly explains the high share coming from the Netherlands) they are nevertheless a good starting point for selecting the types of multinationals worth researching. However, with respect to the topic of our study, these types should be established not only on the basis of the volume of FDI in the Czech Republic but also by the position of the parent company language in the education system of the Czech Republic (with a clear distinction, for example, between the position of Japanese and French). The position of English in a multinational (with a clear distinction, for example, between the position of English in an American firm and in a German firm) could be another criterion. Given these criteria, the research should focus particularly on the following types of multinationals:

- branches of German/Austrian/Swiss companies (Germany/Austria/ Switzerland = 33 per cent of FDI as of the end of 2005);
- branches of American/British/South African companies (US/UK = 7.7 per cent of FDI as of end of 2005);
- branches of French/Belgian companies (France/Belgium = 9.5 per cent of FDI as of the end of 2005);
- branches of Spanish companies (Spain = 5.9 per cent of FDI as of the end of 2005);
- branches of Dutch companies (Netherlands = 29 per cent of FDI as of the end of 2005);

- branches of Japanese/Korean companies (though the FDI is not significant in comparison, these countries' contributions include many high-profile companies such as Toyota and Hyundai. Both these countries and Russia come under the category 'other' in the data, which collectively accounted for 15.9 per cent of FDI);
- branches of Russian companies.

Given this distribution of multinational companies and the languages taught in the schools, a number of points need to be considered. One is that a reasonable percentage of foreign investment in the Czech Republic comes from German-speaking countries. Yet the number of pupils learning German is declining, which raises the question of whether an expectation is developing that it will eventually no longer be necessary to speak German with German native speakers. Another is that although the proportion of investment that comes from 'English-speaking countries' is lower, there is a significant percentage that comes from countries whose inhabitants are typically very proficient in English (particularly the Netherlands), or where English may be expected as the medium of conversation due to the distance between the languages and cultures (such as Japan and Korea). Given the growing rate of English teaching in the Czech Republic, it is probably presumed that most of the English the pupils learn will not be used with native speakers, but rather will serve as a lingua franca.

There are several other countries whose investments and languages, while not high ranking in the statistics, should be taken into consideration. There is investment from other countries (for example, France and Spain) whose 'national' languages are becoming increasingly economically relevant. The teaching of French and Spanish is on the increase, although French has many more learners than Spanish. Also, though the share of FDI flowing from Russia is currently relatively low, there are reasons why Russian companies should be considered in this context as well. On the one hand, there are some regions where the presence of the Russian economic element in the Czech Republic is salient enough to be the focus of attention of both the Czech populace and media (the well-known spa town Karlovy Vary/Carlsbad in particular). On the other hand, it is important to observe the situation of Russian in the economic domain: previously an obligatory foreign language in the Czech education system, Russian was largely abandoned after 1989 but is currently on the increase once again. Moreover, Russia represents an important destination for 'outward flow', that is, the FDI of Czech firms, with

Czech-based multinationals having headquarters in the Czech Republic and subsidiaries in Russia.[2]

As the data on FDI in the Czech Republic demonstrate, geographical proximity is still relevant with respect to the investment of foreign capital, and German-speaking countries remain the major investors. It is also relevant to ask whether German companies expect their Czech employees to speak German or whether they prefer to conduct all their business in English, and how such decisions are explained by those making them. We address these questions in the following sections.

The example of multinational Company X

Company X is a German company manufacturing car components, with branches and clients all over the world. The branch of Company X that is the subject of our research is located in eastern Moravia (Czech Republic) and production began here in 1996. The parent company chose this region due to its long-standing industrial tradition, the presence of high-performing secondary technical schools and a relatively high unemployment rate in the mid-1990s. As of June 2007, the branch had 2,182 employees, most of whom were Czech, but some Slovak, Polish or of other origin. All ten 'expatriates' or 'delegates' (German and Austrian nationals sent by the parent company to the subsidiary) working in the branch occupied senior management positions.

Company X has established an official corporate language, English. However, this does not mean that all employees at the subsidiary are required to speak English in all work situations, but rather that English serves as the medium of communication in certain functional domains. And although English has been declared the official corporate language, German is used in this branch as well and is the subject of organized management (language courses). This is due to a number of factors, the most important being that some customers, most of them originating from the neighbouring German-speaking countries, prefer to speak German. Another factor is that most of the expatriates come from Germany and Austria and, moreover, the subsidiary has numerous visits from the German headquarters. Foreign employees at the subsidiary can if they choose take classes in the local language (Czech) financed by the company. Both English and German are taught in the subsidiary only to those who need it for their work. Currently, this translates to ten English classes, each class comprising about ten learners, three German classes, various sessions of individual instruction and Czech classes for expatriates. Also, advertisements for many management jobs in the subsidiary state that English is 'required' and German 'an advantage'.

For Company X, the management of the 'official corporate language' may be reflected in the discourse in meetings or telephone conferences, where certain speakers may find it difficult to express themselves in English and will switch to German or Czech depending on the course of communication. This is illustrated in the following section.

A meeting

In order to contrast the information gathered using the various types of statistics with actual practices in the subsidiary, it is necessary to capture instances of spontaneous talk. One type of talk available for analysis is that which occurs during meetings. We now examine an excerpt from a meeting in Company X which was held so that the various project and product managers could inform senior management of the progress of numerous manufacturing projects, and to draw attention to situations or problems in which senior management support or intervention was needed. The meeting lasted 5–6 hours, only the first hour of which was recorded. Approximately 20 individuals participated, nearly all of whom were Czech. The exceptions were one German senior manager and one Austrian senior manager who joined the meeting after the first hour. In addition two German managers based in the German headquarters participated by telephone and online.

The participants were seated in a room at tables arranged in a square. A series of presentations was made by project managers, who made their individual contributions standing in front of a screen onto which a PowerPoint presentation was projected. Each presenter introduced a series of approximately 5–10 different projects. The format for the presentation was standardized, approximately five slides per project. With each slide, the other participants had the opportunity to comment or ask questions, but usually their comments or questions were made at the end of the total presentation of an individual project. After each project manager's presentation, there was a short break (lasting about five minutes) during which the next speaker's presentation was set up, and the participants talked among themselves.

The meeting followed company policy and was held in the 'official corporate language', English. However, we now look at one excerpt in which all three languages were spoken.

Extract 1 The meeting

Participants

MM: Employee sitting at computer, directing meeting, in control of PowerPoint, Czech
P1: First presenter at the meeting, a project manager, Czech
S: Senior manager in the subsidiary, German
R1: Parent company manager on telephone, German
R2: Parent company manager on telephone, German

```
 1  MM: OK next one (.) Nissan t one d
 2  P1: ((to MM)) (budeme muset se na to podívat já tomu nevěřím víš?[3]) OK next is c
 3      sixty one b uh description we have new we have new uh version ( ) it's f ninety
 4      one a which will be the Nissan (torrent) and the new person in the department is
 5      (tomas) (.) uh new variant u f ninety one these uh will be implemented in july
 6      in about about a month uh one milestones is the same (…) there is the setting
 7      the setting ( ) newly implemented () is not finished the prior (from nissan)
 8  S: does it mean we are using already (type already)
 9  P1: yeah we are using already but we are (at delivery) with the with the specialists
10      (.) we don't need management support (..) ((computer sound)) so renault b c m
11      ninety one
12  R1: sorry can you start it again I guess we lost the line
13  MM: I heard
14  P1: ( )
15  ((pause, reconnection with speakers at headquarters))
16  R1: ( ) merenda we can
17  ((pause reconnection w/speakers at headquarters, Czech heard in the background))
18  R1: OK let's say
19  R2: (hello) alphonse speaking hello
20  MM: hello alphonse
21  R2: I'm trying also just with (direct meeting) but uh
22  R1: wrong number
23  R2: oh it's another number
24  R1: ( ) nine one one four four
25  R2: one four four
26  R1: one four five
27  R2: one four five
28  R1: one four one
29  R2: sorry uh eins vier vier[4]
30  R1: eins vier fünf eins vier eins[5]
31  R2: eins vier eins[6]
32  R1: eins eins sechs[7]
33  R2: OK six ()
34  ((pause, connecting))
35  R2: (eins eins  )[8]
36  ((pause))
37  MM: so can we continue? it's feasible for you?
38  R2: it's it's (going) it's
39  (..)
40  P1: so we are on d c ninety one description…
```

P1 is a project manager presenting a particular job case. MM is the employee chairing the meeting, sitting at the computer, not far from P1. Both are Czech. S is a German senior manager who is sitting on the other side of the room. R1 and R2 are German managers located in Company X's main headquarters (but are not in the same room there). Both are connected to the meeting by phone and have the PowerPoint presentation in front of them as well.

This excerpt captures two episodes in the meeting. The first is the progression of the standard format for presentations, as done by P1, and the subsequent questions posed by the other participants (lines 1–11). The other begins at the point during the meeting immediately after the conclusion of the presentation of one project and the beginning of another (line 10), when the parent company participants become disconnected, that is, they lose the line to the computer presentation but can still speak to the participants by phone. What follows is that R1 and R2 are gradually reconnected (lines 16–38), and the meeting then resumes in standard format (line 40).

As can be observed, the meeting is held almost exclusively in English but Czech is used twice. In the first instance, P1 comments in Czech to the Czech colleagues sitting nearest him, including MM (line 2). These comments concern the presentation of the previous project: P1 expresses some doubt about some of its details and notes that he will have to confirm them. This information, then, is not relevant to the whole group or to the 'official' course of the meeting. The second instance occurs at line 17, during a longer pause while the parent company participants were being reconnected. At this point, some of the Czech participants talk among themselves.

German is used only once, during the attempt to reconnect the parent company participants. In line 10, a computer sound is heard and in lines 12–13, R1 and MM indicate that the sound indicates that the connection to the computer screen has been lost by the German headquarters participants. In lines 16–21, R1, R2 and MM work together to re-establish the connection. However, beginning at line 22, when R2 indicates that he had dialled the 'wrong number', R1 and R2 communicate and confirm the correct telephone number primarily among themselves, with R1 dictating the number and R2 repeating it after him. It may be supposed that once it becomes clear to them that they are the only relevant participants at this point, they switch to German so that they can clearly dictate the number to one another (line 29). The use of German between native speakers for matters relevant exclusively to them was also reported by the native German-speaking senior managers in the semi-structured interviews.

To summarize, we have observed that English is used for official, 'on-record' or 'topical' meeting content, including PowerPoint presentation content. German and Czech are used for 'side-sequence' or 'off-record' content, often of a practical/technical nature concerning the production of the meeting (phone connection information) or commentary on a minor aspect of the meeting, exclusively between native speakers of the given language, usually between two speakers and not addressed to the whole group.

One hour after the meeting, a follow-up interview was conducted with the CEO, who participated in the meeting (he did not speak in the fragment above). Overall, he expressed satisfaction with how the meeting had gone, with the readiness of the Czech participants to communicate and the level of understanding achieved, though he admitted problems with the language proficiency of some of the Czech white-collar employees in a more general sense.

Extract 2 Follow-up interview

Participants

P = Czech CEO of Company X subsidiary
T = native English-speaking researcher

```
 1  T: And do you think the meeting would be different if it were held in–
 2     Czech?
 3  P: Mm, maybe more more words,
 4  T: Mm hmm
 5  P: More sentences.
 6  T: mm hmm
 7  P: But I am telling you, I am very known, uh now, here in this factory. That I – I am
 8     very content-oriented, I am very –
 9  T: Mm.
10  P: I – I like – if there is a time, if we are sitting outdoor,
11  T: Yeah, yeah.
12  P: Barbecue,
13  T: ((laughs))
14  P: I told you already.
15  T: Yeah, yeah, yeah.
16  P: But here, guys, really, we are in business.
17  T: Yeah.
18  P: We are profit-oriented.
19  T: Yes.
20  P: Time is money, and life is short.
21  T: Mm hmm, right, right, yes.
22  P: It means this is – for sure, it still can be better.
23  T: Mm
24  P: But currently not too bad, I would say.
25  T: Mm
26  P: And – and what is important, they don't have problems with this language.
27  T: Mm hmm.
```

28 P: For such a level of communication.
29 T: Yes.
30 P: It would be even – we allow, if there is somebody that, uh, new,
31 T: Yeah.
32 P: (If he is) a good expert,
33 T: Yes.
34 P: And he still, uh, needs to learn really English,
35 T: Mm hmm.
36 P: We let him speak Czech ( ), and afterwards –
37 T: Uh huh.
38 P: Yes, because this is important, please, you are responsible, you are
39   (process owner), tell us.
40 T: Mm hmm.
41 P: And we will, afterwards, really, but this is very uh seldom, like I don't even
42   remember –
43 T: Mm.
44 P: Here you could see everybody was able –
45 T: To speak, yeah, mm.
46 P: OK.

There are two points to emphasize here. One is the CEO's focus on the 'content-orientation' of the meeting held in English (lines 7–8), that is, speaking Czech would be less economical as it uses more words and sentences (lines 3–5). In other words, speaking Czech would lead to the less effective management of projects, the subsequent consumption of time and, accordingly, the loss of money.

The other point is the CEO's insistence that all meeting participants understand everything that is said in the meeting. As P says in lines 26–42, he does not expect perfect English proficiency from his employees when they first join the company. Rather, employees who have good technical expertise are given an adjustment period, during which they can make their presentations in Czech until their competence in English is sufficient. This adjustment period, with time allotted for learning or improving English competence, was also mentioned in the interviews with the senior managers.

The role of Czech, German and English

On the basis of our observations and interviews conducted in the branch of Company X and in some other German-based multinationals, it is possible to describe the varying distribution of Czech, German and English as the conflict of four particular functions: language for communication vs. language as a symbol; language for communication vs. language for social purposes; language for communication vs. language for emotion; and language for communication vs. language for privacy. We now examine each in more detail.

Language for communication vs. language as a symbol

One important distinction is that between the language of a parent company, which symbolizes economic power, and the language of most of the employees in the subsidiary, particularly when the two languages belong respectively to an older EU state and an EU new member state. To add to this, contact between the Czech and German languages is marked by hundreds of years of history, not free from conflicts, involving the two nations (see Carl and Stevenson, this volume). The Czech and German languages both symbolize national identity, and their use in German-based multinational companies is no exception to this. The establishment of English as the official corporate language and its subsequent actual use weakens the symbolic position of Czech and German in the company, and aims to contribute to the creation of transnational identities. This is noted by both the German-speaking and Czech senior managers.

Extract 3 'Everybody has to learn English'

Participants

M = Austrian senior manager in Company X
T = native English speaking researcher

```
 1  M: But it's definitely not easy, the situation, in that in this company not all are
 2      speaking the same language
 3  T:  Mm hmm,
 4  M: This is definitely one of our challenges I would say.
 5  T:  Mm hmm, and how do you think it could be uh changed?
 6  M: Easy.
 7  T:  The situation, yeah
 8  M: Everybody has to learn English.
 9  T:  Yeah
10  M: For me, for me it's a must and I – I do not – I do not understand, I get really angry
11      with people for example um also in the German area,
12  T:  Mm hmm.
13  M: Refusing to learn English.
14  T:  Mm hmm.
15  M: For me it's – it's really something, um, it has maybe something to do with
16      proudness or something like that.
17  T:  Mm hmm.
18  M: Some people really refuse English.
```

19 T: Mm.
20 M: But for me, English is, is one kind of possibility to speak with nearly the whole
21   world.

Czech and German have in the past formed a 'dominated–dominant' dichotomy in the Czech lands, with each language playing each role at various points in history (see Nekvapil 2000). English, ideally, gets round this dichotomy. However, there are other relationships between languages, and the refusal to learn English, as noted by M, who is an Austrian manager, is also perceived as a question of 'proudness'.

In Company X, there is one area in which the knowledge of languages other than English is to one's advantage in the subsidiary and where the use of German, above all, is officially recommended. This is the area of logistics, which often involves direct contact with clients. All the senior managers noted that knowledge of German, as well as knowledge of other languages such as French and Italian, was necessary when communicating with clients, because the clients insisted on speaking their own language. As one Czech senior manager noted, 'our German customers are very proud of their German language'. This was also a subject of discussion in the meeting and the follow-up interview: the project manager assigned to a job involving a German car company was replaced by another manager who had German language skills.

In the subsidiary, situations are created in which nobody is speaking his or her native language, and, theoretically, neither side has an advantage over the other. The use of English as opposed to German by Czechs reflects neutrality in power relations: the Czechs are 'freeing' themselves from German (and, in effect, the Germans). However, these two facts still do not create a level playing field. It is easier for some local employees to 'free' themselves from German than it is for others, and the knowledge of English on both sides may not be equal.

Extract 4 'Neutral territory'

Participants

T2 = Czech CEO of subsidiary of Company X
T1 = Czech researcher

T2: A už třeba jenom- jsme německá firma, ale v komunikaci s Němcem, když máte na
    stole angličtinu, nikdo nemá výhodu, protože jste na neutrální půdě, že jo.
T1: Mhm mhm.

T2: I když říkám, že pro Němce ee naučit se anglicky je jako pro nás naučit se rusky, jo?
(T2: And maybe just – we're a German company, but in communication with a German, when you have English on the table, nobody has an advantage because you're on neutral territory, right.
T1: Mhm mhm.
T2: Even though I say that for Germans eh to learn English is like for us to learn Russian, right?)

English is, from the perspective of the closeness between languages, easier for Germans than for Czechs. Also, as observed earlier in this chapter, the teaching of English in the Czech Republic is currently in what we might call a 'catching up' phase, in which national language policy is attempting to ensure that every citizen is taught English beginning in elementary school. As a result older Czech employees may be at a disadvantage when learning and using English (see Nekvapil and Nekula 2006a, 2006b).

Language for communication vs. language for social purposes

In the workplace, there are many types of communication, not all of which are directly work-related and which occur exclusively between speakers of the same language (Czech or German). For example, meetings and other work events occur in which only Czech employees are present. More commonly, there are meetings at which there are a majority of Czech speakers and a minority of foreign language speakers (for example, the meeting analysed in this chapter, in which 16 Czechs and four German speakers participated). In the subsidiary of Company X, it was both observed and reported in interviews that English as opposed to Czech was regularly used in meetings where nearly everyone is a native speaker of Czech. The main explanation for this was the following: when nearly all employees are speaking a foreign language (English), in particular when the native speakers of Czech are in the majority, they are less likely to chat and waste time. As observed above, it is hypothesized by senior management that the native speakers of Czech or German will 'use fewer words' in English than in Czech or German, and they must get to the point and stick to it.

Extract 5 'Three times less chatty'

Participants

T2 = Czech CEO of subsidiary of Company X
T1 = Czech researcher

```
 1   T1: Pociťujete nějaký rozdíl když ta komunikace probíhá v češtině?
 2   T2: Ano.
 3   T1: V němčině? V angličtině?
 4   T2: Ano, ano.
 5   T1: Jo.
 6   T2: Když je to v cizím jazyce, je to mnohem katalyzujíčtější. To znamená, když
 7       někteří, e páni inženýři začnou rozpravu v českém jazyce, protože nesedí žádný
 8       zahraniční kolega kolem stolu, tak- tak mám někdy tendenci bouchnout do
 9       stolu a říct a dost. A půjdeme do angličtiny, protože to bude třikrát méně ukecané.
10   T1: Mhm.
11   T2: To je ten rozdíl, jo?
12   T1: Mhm.
13   T2: Protože skutečně, češtinu miluju a jsem na ni pyšný, ale je jiná věc, když sedíte
14       někde na kávičce a máte čas a a můžeme si s tím jazykem hrát.
15   T1: Mhm.
16   T2: A nebo potřebujete sdělovat a vyměňovat
17   T1: ( )
18   T2: si infor- ne: rychle, ale věcně.
19   T1: Mhm.
20   T2: Jo? Bez ňákých e zbytečných příkras a přívlastků. A to je opravdu problém.
```

```
 1   (T1: Do you feel a difference when the communication takes place in Czech?
 2   T2: Yes.
 3   T1: In German? In English?
 4   T2: Yes, yes.
 5   T1: Yeah.
 6   T2: When it's in a foreign language, it's more of a catalyst. That means that when
 7       some, eh engineers begin talking in Czech, because there's no colleague from abroad
 8       sitting at the table, so – so I sometimes have the tendency to bang my fist against the
 9       table and say enough. And let's switch to English, because it'll be three times less
10       chatty.
11   T1: Mhm.
12   T2: That is the difference. Right?
13   T1: Mhm
14   T2: Because really, I love Czech, and I take pride in it, but it's another thing when
15       you're sitting somewhere in a café, and you have time, and, and we can play with
16       the language.
17   T1: Mhm,
18   T2: Or you need to give some information, and exchange
19   T1: ( )
20   T2: Infor- not quickly, but to the point.
21   T1: Mhm.
22   T2: Yeah, without any, eh, extra embellishment or attributes. And that's really a
23       problem.)
```

A final result of the emphasis on content as opposed to form means that the English used in 'transnational' interactions need not be grammatically perfect. This is explored in the next section.

Language for communication vs. language for emotion

In this research we are examining not only who speaks what to whom, when and where, but also *how well* they do so. As has been observed, the English language competence of non-native speakers is centred on certain genres and communicative situations; and, as has been demonstrated in the examples thus far (particularly from the meeting), the competence of the non-native speakers of English, particularly the Czechs, is far from perfect in a grammatical or other sense. This may or may not be noted as a problem by the participants in the communication. At certain moments, then, this competence may not be sufficient to express everything that needs to be expressed or to deal with all situations on an emotional level, as the following excerpt reveals.

Extract 6 'Emotions are very high'
Participants

C = Czech senior manager in Company X
T = native-English-speaking researcher

```
 1  T: And what about situations where you are speaking Czech where there are
 2     foreigners present? Do – are – do these situations ever occur where there's a
 3     foreigner who won't understand?
 4  C: Yes, sometimes it happened because there is this (emotion high too high), yes.
 5  T: Yeah.
 6  C: We usually switch to Czech because it's for us better.
 7  T: With the emotion high?
 8  C: ( ) some – some hard discussion, yes.
 9  T: Yeah.
10  C: And the emotions are very high and –
11  T: Uh huh.
12  C: And if, uh, we want to explain with uh with some Czech colleagues,
13  T: Mm hmm
14  C: We usually switch to Czech.
15  T: Uh huh.
16  C: After – after we explain with this emotively.
17  T: Yeah
18  C: We – we calm down and uh – to explain what we – we uh speak about.
```

In this excerpt, the Czech senior manager C points out that the selection of Czech as the temporary language of negotiation may not reflect a problem with conveying content in English, but rather, in certain emotionally charged situations, Czech is chosen. Once, as C puts it, emotions have 'calmed down' (line 18), the details of the interaction are explained to anyone who may not have understood (presumably their German-speaking colleagues).

This description was motivated by the interviewer's question regarding situations in which a language is being spoken which may not be understood by some participants in an interaction (that is, German not understood by Czechs; Czech not understood by Germans). Such situations are explored in a final set of relationships in the next section.

Language for communication vs. language for privacy

When considering which language to use in basic workplace communications – bearing in mind the goal that everyone should be able to understand and express themselves appropriately (something that was expressed repeatedly in interviews with the Czech CEO) – one of the three languages, Czech, was quickly ruled out, or rather, not even considered. As Czech is not widely taught in Germany and Austria, expatriates sent from those countries have little or no background in it prior to their arrival at the subsidiary (with a few exceptions). Furthermore, they do not intend to stay in the Czech Republic for more than a few years (also with some exceptions). Their economic or other motivation for learning Czech is thus quite low, and although they attend Czech language classes at the subsidiary, they report that the time they can devote to studying is minimal and that they find the language difficult. The classes often serve functions other than to enable expatriates to learn Czech for use in actual work communication. One such function is a phatic one (in Malinowski's or Jakobson's sense) – using a few words of a local language contributes to establishing or maintaining social contacts and, moreover, it is considered polite to be able to use a few basic phrases in the language of the subsidiary's local employees. Another function will be discussed below.

There are several noted language problems which result from these conditions. The most general is that not every employee in the subsidiary is able to speak with every other employee. Expatriates in senior management often cannot communicate with local employees in production, though this is a problem of varying relevance in different departments. For some departments (for example, Information Technology), this may not be relevant at all because employees in production do not use these networks. The expatriates also do not communicate with local authorities (the municipality, local schools, media, and so on).

Another, more significant language problem is what we call the 'secretive function' of Czech. That is, talk that occurs in Czech is accessible almost exclusively to local employees and the transfer of information and tacit knowledge which takes place during exchanges in Czech is not available to non-Czech speakers. Similar usage of a particular language was witnessed by Vaara et al. (2005), who observed the secret function of Finnish in a Swedish-Finnish merger, and concluded that this contributed to the Finnish speakers' reclamation of power after Swedish was declared the official corporate language. Assuming this function, Czech can serve as a means of protecting national social networks. These networks do not go unnoticed by 'outsiders', however, as the following excerpt indicates.

Extract 7 Social networks

Participants

K = German researcher
I = German manager of subsidiary of Company Y

```
 1  K: Wie würden Sie die tschechische Kommunikationsart charakterisieren?
 2  I: ...und da die Kommunikation eher formell und netzwerkgesteuert. Also ich glaube
 3      man muss um hier gut funktionieren zu können sehr großes Netzwerk haben. Also die
 4      informelle Kommunikation muss glaube ich stärker ausgeprägt sein als die formelle.
 5  K: Bringt diese Art der Kommunikation Probleme mit sich?
 6  I: Bringt sie für Aussenstehende. Für die die an dieser informellen Gruppe nicht
 7      teilhaben bringt sie zum Teil sogar größere Probleme mit sich.
 8  K: Und Vorteile?
 9  I: Vorteile für die die in diesem Netzwerk tätig sind. Vorteile für die die nicht drinn
10      sind sehe ich keine.
11  K: Welche Vorteile sind das?
12  I: Dinge schnell erledigt zu bekommen. Über Dinge Bescheid zu wissen die zum Teil
13      nicht kommuniziert werden dürfen. Das ist eine Sache die ich immer wieder feststelle,
14      dass eigentlich Sache die gar nicht bekannt sein können dürfen, trotzdem bekannt
15      sind. Ja das sind dann Vorteile.
```

```
 1  K: How would you characterize the Czech manner of communication?
 2  I: ...there the communication is rather formal and controlled by networks. So I
 3      think you have to have a large network to function well. The informal
 4      communication has to, I think, be more developed than the formal one.
 5  K: Does this form of communication lead to problems?
 6  I: It does for outsiders. For those who don't participate in this informal group it
 7      sometimes creates quite major problems.
 8  K: And advantages?
 9  I: Advantages for those who are active in this network. I see no advantages for those
10      who aren't in it.
11  K: What are the advantages?
12  I: Things which can be done quickly. To be in the know about things which to some
13      extent are not allowed to be communicated. That's one thing I'm finding more and
14      more, that things that cannot be allowed to be known, are known in spite of this.
15      Those are the advantages.
```

The researcher's ability to gain information on the 'secret function' of language is highly dependent on having a common language or ethnicity with the interview subject. That is, it is important to consider the fact that statements regarding advantages of local social networks (lines 12–15) and problems for those outside them (lines 6–7) were made by a German expatriate interviewed by a German researcher. Conversely, in interviews conducted in Company X in English by an American researcher, Czech employees said that they considered it impolite to speak Czech in the presence of an expatriate who did not understand. German employees interviewed by the same researcher, on the other hand, often assumed that talk occurring in Czech concerned subjects which were irrelevant to them, for example, the employees' personal affairs, and which, in fact, they would rather not to hear.

One adjustment design for the perceived 'secretive function' of language is the implementation of Czech language classes for expatriates. Note that all the German and Austrian managers in Company X stated that they were attending these classes or had attended them at some point in the past. Currently, Czech may be the only one of the three languages analysed in this study which can function in this manner. However, it is important to realize that German could also be used as a secret language by the German-speaking expatriates at some point in the future if the trend to abandon the learning of German increases among the Czech population.

Conclusions

Effective communication among the inhabitants of the old and new EU member states does not merely concern finding a common communicative code. Rather, it is complicated by the fact that languages can symbolize national identity and are used to fulfil particular communicative tasks. Our research in the German-based multinationals operating in Central Europe has demonstrated that the varying distribution of Czech, German and English can be described as the conflict particularly between the following functions:

- language for communication vs. language as a symbol;
- language for communication vs. language for social purposes;

- language for communication vs. language for emotion;
- language for communication vs. language for privacy.

Obviously, profit-oriented multinationals are interested in finding the most effective medium of communication, suitable for most participants involved in the economic process. We have observed that this function is often assumed by English. In the branches of the multinationals based in Germany, given the absence of native English speakers, English is perceived as a language unencumbered by national identity symbolism, as the language of business communication, an emotionally neutral language which is transparent and accessible to everybody. These basic functional features of English complement the functional allocation of Czech and German. Both Czech and German symbolize corresponding national identities (which have often found themselves in conflict), both are used for social purposes and for expression of emotions among the employees of the same ethnicity and both can potentially be used as a secret language (assuming that the Other does not know the other language). On the other hand, beyond the boundaries of the enterprise, and to some extent even within it, it is the customer who determines which language will be used in many areas of company communication. This is why German is still highly regarded in the German-based multinationals. Also, due to this socio-economic factor, the position of Czech can be elevated. Several informants from a branch of another German company operating in Prague reported that the communicative value of Czech is increasing as the number of Czech customers grows.

It is evident that the relationship between individual communication situations and official language policy is influenced by the changing economic and social climate in Central Europe, and this also determines the functions of the individual languages used. These findings lend themselves to several considerations for organized language management, both by the companies themselves and by higher organs at the national and European-wide level. The companies may examine more closely the strategies their employees use to deal with language problems in order to constantly seek new communicative innovations which can be codified as (written) company policy (see Nekvapil and Sherman forthcoming). The companies may seek (or be required by higher organs) to remove inequalities in language competence, either by relaxing the conditions for the origin of asymmetrical language adaptation of the local employees or by establishing compensational strategies (see also Nekula et al.

2005). This may be realized, on the one hand, by strong support for the teaching of local languages (for example, Czech) to parent company employees (for example, German), and on the other hand, at least in part, through the creation of situations in which no group of speakers is at a disadvantage. This means at least passive knowledge of the other's language, and the continued use of a lingua franca, most likely English. The further elaboration of processes through which these situations and policies operate is an appropriate subject for future research.

Transcription conventions

[ ]	the onset and ending of simultaneous talk of two speakers (overlap)
?	rising intonation
.	falling intonation
,	continuing intonation
:	lengthening of the preceding syllable
=	sudden insertion of the following expression or turn, without pause (latching on)
(.)	short pause
(..)	longer pause
(…)	long pause
( )	unintelligible point
(but)	presumed, but not completely intelligible expression
((laughs))	comment by the transcriber
-	sudden interruption of construction or flow of speech
never	strong emphasis on a syllable or word
…	omitted portion of the transcript

Notes

1. The new research was supported by the LINEE project co-funded by the European Commission (contract nr FP6-2004-CIT4-28388). While writing this chapter, we were also supported by the grant MSM 0021620825 awarded by the Czech Ministry of Education.
2. According to CNB (2007) as of December 2005, Czech direct investment abroad, amounting to $3.6 billion, was as follows (by target country): Slovakia (25.1 per cent), Netherlands (20.5 per cent), United Arab Emirates (8.9 per cent), Russia (5.5 per cent), Liechtenstein (5.0 per cent), Portugal (4.6 per cent), Bulgaria (4.0 per cent), British Virgin Islands (3.6 per cent), other countries (22.8 per cent).

3. This Czech sentence means 'we're going to have to look at it, I don't believe it, you know?'
4. 'one four four' in German.
5. 'one four five one four one' in German.
6. 'one four one' in German.
7. 'one one six' in German.
8. 'one one' in German.

References

Barton, D. and Tusting, K. (eds) (2005) *Beyond Communities of Practice. Language, Power, and Social Context* (Cambridge: Cambridge University Press).

Braczyk, H-J., Cooke, P. and Heidenreich, M. (eds) (1998) *Regional Innovation Systems* (London: UCL Press).

CNB (Czech National Bank/Česká národní banka) (2007) *2005 Foreign Direct Investment*, http://www.cnb.cz/www.cnb.cz/en/statistics/bop_stat/bop_publications/pzi_books/PZI_2005_EN.pdf

Cooke, P., Heidenreich, M. and Braczyk, H-J. (eds) (2004) *Regional Innovation Systems. The Role of Governance in a Globalized World*, second edition (London and New York: Routledge).

Jernudd, B.H. and Neustupný, J. V. (1987) 'Language planning: for whom?' in Laforge (1987), 69–84.

Laforge, L. (ed.) (1987) *Proceedings of the International Colloquium on Language Planning May 25-29, 1986 / Ottawa* (Québec: Les Presses de L'Université Laval).

Nekula, M., Nekvapil, J. and Šichová, K. (2005) *Sprachen in multinationalen Unternehmen auf dem Gebiet der Tschechischen Republik* (München: Forschungsverbund Ost- und Südosteuropa).

Nekvapil, J. (2000) 'On non-self-evident relationships between language and ethnicity: How Germans do not speak German, and Czechs do not speak Czech', *Multilingua* 19, 37–53.

Nekvapil, J. (2007) 'On the language situation in the Czech Republic: what has (not) happened after the accession of the country to the EU', *Sociolinguistica* 21, 36–54.

Nekvapil, J. and Nekula, M. (2006a) 'On language management in multinational companies in the Czech Republic', *Current Issues in Language Planning* 7, 307–27. Reprinted in R. B. Baldauf and A. Liddicoat (eds) (2008) *Language Planning in Local Contexts* (Clevedon, Buffalo and Toronto: Multilingual Matters), 268–87.

Nekvapil, J. and Nekula, M. (2006b) 'K jazykové situaci v nadnárodních podnicích působících v České republice', *Slovo a slovesnost* 67, 83–95.

Nekvapil, J. and Sherman, T. (forthcoming) 'Pre-interaction management in multinational companies in Central Europe', *Current Issues in Language Planning* 10.

Vaara, E., Tienari, J., Piekkari, R. and Säntti, R. (2005) 'Language and the circuits of power in a merging multinational corporation', *Journal of Management Studies* 42(3), 595–623.

Wenger, E. (1998) *Communities of Practice. Learning, Meaning, and Identity* (Cambridge: Cambridge University Press).

Williams, G. (2006) 'Regional innovation systems and communities of practice: Two themes in search of knowledge', *Sociolinguistica* 19, 168–84.

Part III

Migrations Past and Present

7
Changes in the Linguistic Marketplace: The Case of German in Hungary[1]

Péter Maitz and Klára Sándor

Introductory remarks

For centuries, the German language has occupied a significant place on Hungary's linguistic map. It has been present as a mother tongue and minority language in the wake of the migration processes that have taken place since the Middle Ages, while as a foreign language it has played and continues to play a role as a result of Hungary's close ties with German-speaking countries. However, over the centuries, its social status, prestige and use have undergone considerable changes as a function of the changing power relations and political, economic and cultural interests of the time. Our aim in this chapter is to provide an overview of these changes in status and the reasons for them from a macro-sociolinguistic perspective (for a micro-sociolinguistic analysis of the present situation, see Knipf-Komlósi 2008: 265–327; Carl and Stevenson, this volume). We begin the (necessarily) sketchy review of the social history of the German language in Hungary with the eighteenth century,[2] as it was at the end of that century that the question of the status of the German language – or rather, the question of the German speech communities – first emerged. This was the time when, in Hungary, as in other European countries, language became the main carrier and symbol of national identity (cf. Gal 2006: 14f.). The Herderian concept of 'one language – one nation' established a close link between nation and language, and it cast language as a source of conflict, a mobilizing force in order to gain power and achieve political goals. It was this concept, then, that made it possible for the German language to become the political-ideological means of power, and, by the same token, its victim, in nineteenth- and twentieth-century Hungary (cf. Stevenson

2000: 109f.), crucially determining the status of the German speech community and the German language.

In the next section we introduce the historical and social layers of German speech communities in Hungary. We then outline and explain the fundamental changes in the status of German during the nineteenth century, which in turn determined the sociolinguistic events in the twentieth century. This is followed by a reconstruction of the process and the socio-political and ideological antecedents of the decline of German as a minority language in the twentieth century, and we conclude with a general survey of recent changes in the status of German as a foreign language in Hungary.

The historical and social layers of German speech communities in Hungary

At the turn of the eighteenth and nineteenth centuries we can see two layers of German speech communities in Hungary, clearly separable in historical and sociological terms:

1 The bourgeois layer which was concentrated in towns. It was literate, and, for this reason, standard-oriented in terms of language use. Its members had migrated during the Middle Ages mainly from the German Empire and in eighteenth and nineteenth centuries from the Austrian parts of the Habsburg Empire.
2 The other layer was concentrated in villages. Its members were peasants, who had a predominantly oral culture and a dialectal background. At that time its members lived in mainly monolingual German villages in the western regions of the country, creating closed communities in isolated settlements. These communities arrived at the end of the seventeenth and mainly during the eighteenth centuries, through organized settlement policies, the aim of which was to populate the areas which had been deserted during the Ottoman occupation.

These two layers and the language varieties spoken by the inhabitants show markedly different patterns, reflecting the political and related linguistic ideologies of the nineteenth and twentieth centuries. In time both were caught in the crossfire of power exactly because of the instrumentalization of language, an ethnic and national symbol, as a means of attaining and exercising power. As we shall see in the next section, nineteenth-century Hungarian linguistic nationalism proved fatal for the first layer, and with it, for standard German. The second layer succeeded in securing ethnic survival, albeit at the cost of enormous losses and tragedies. Linguistic survival, however, as we shall see in section 4, was beyond their reach. We are witnessing this layer's language shift and the extinction of the German dialects in present-day Hungary.

Language, nation and identity: the nineteenth century

The multiethnic and multilingual Hungary of the eighteenth and nineteenth centuries was dominated by the Habsburg Empire and, later, a dependent part of the Austro-Hungarian Monarchy, both exercising an assimilatory (that is, Germanizing) language policy. Hungarian remained a subordinated language until 1844. The official language of the country was Latin, and later German. The German language, for this reason, gained symbolic significance from the eighteenth century and became the symbol of the oppressive power standing in the way of national independence and prosperity. Most of the country's bourgeois public as well as the mainstream language cultivation movement of the period came to consider German as a dangerous force, blocking a unified national language, and, through this, in preventing national unity as well (cf. Maitz 2008). Therefore, in the nineteenth century German-Hungarian societal bilingualism, which had evolved naturally and which had presented no serious conflicts in earlier centuries, became a source of deviance. German contact phenomena began to be seen as harmful and dangerous. At the same time, German as a mother tongue became an obstacle standing in the way of the social integration of German speech communities.

The adoption of the monolingual Herderian ideal and the factual multilingualism of the monarchy certainly resulted in ethnolinguistic conflicts. Through the newborn ideology of the 'national language' a basic means of power and a source of conflict developed, around which a widespread public discourse emerged. Herder became one of the main references of this discourse, especially in Hungary, since he projected the nightmare of the death of the Hungarian language in his main historical-philosophical work (*Ideen zur Philosophie der Geschichte der Menschheit*) to his bourgeois readers, who were highly sensitive to national questions at that time (cf. Gal 2001: 30f.). Herder predicted that:

> Das einzige Volk, das aus diesem Stamm [das heisst, dem 'finnischen Völkerstamm'] sich unter die Eroberer gedrängt hat, sind

die Ungern oder Madscharen.... Da sind sie jetzt unter Slawen, Deutschen, Wlachen und andern Völkern der geringere Teil der Landeseinwohner, und *nach Jahrhunderten wird man vielleicht ihre Sprache kaum finden.*

(The only people from this tribe [that is the 'Finnish tribe'] who managed to get to the rank of conquerors are the Hungarians or Magyars.... They are now among Slavs, Germans, Vlachs and other peoples the minor part of their country's population and *in centuries to come even their language will probably be lost.*)

(Herder 1989: 688, emphasis added)

Contemporary Hungarian language cultivation, institutionalized at the time through the periodical *Magyar Nyelvőr* ('The Hungarian Language Guardian'), joined this national linguistic discourse. The main source of legitimation for language cultivation was provided by the creation of a unified national linguistic norm. Based on the concepts of the 'purity of language' and 'linguistic homogeneity', its main objective was to eradicate German-Hungarian societal bilingualism. According to their argument, the century-old contact-induced changes stemming from bilingualism were destroying the genealogical purity of the Hungarian language and endangering the native speakers' 'national language instinct', and so, it was claimed, were hindering the dissemination of a cultivated, unified national linguistic standard. As a result, contemporary language cultivation and public opinion influenced by language cultivation considered bilingual linguistic socialization harmful, and it was condemned, like most contact-induced phenomena (cf. Maitz 2008). The purist language cultivation project, not knowing, or rather, not acknowledging, the phenomenon of the bilingual norm stigmatized almost all forms of contact phenomena and labelled them 'Germanisms'. This notion became one of the most important topics of language cultivation, an influential means of linguistic stigmatization for decades. The struggle against 'Germanisms', referring to the national language as the main national value, represented the most emphasized thesis of contemporary language cultivation.

However, it is important to realize that the stigmatization of German based on the above argument did not affect all aspects of the presence of German in Hungary, or every scene of its usage. In spite of the fact that natural bilingualism and contact phenomena in the national language were considered dangerous and were condemned, the status and prestige of certain forms of the usage of German remained the same.

This can be attributed to three main factors. First, the contemporary official Hungarian state language policy was predominantly pluralist rather than assimilative, especially after the end of Habsburg oppression and the attainment of (partial) political autonomy in 1867 – in spite of some indisputable assimilative elements. The National Minority Law of 1868, which regulated the language rights of the country's ethnicities and remained in force until the end of the nineteenth century, is considered to be one of the most liberal regulations of its kind in contemporary Europe (for the text of the law, cf. Maitz 2005: 201ff.). Second, German remained the most important foreign language in Hungary throughout the nineteenth century until the recent past. The primary reason for this was certainly the political and economic interest of the Hungarian state and the native Hungarian population. Knowledge of German constituted considerable political, economic and cultural capital in contemporary Hungary forming a part of the Habsburg Empire with a large native German population. And third, the grounds for German as a minority language were not questioned, whether in politics or in public life. The national and linguistic rights of the Hungarian minorities were enshrined in law. Since the German language was claimed to be dangerous to the creation of a unified and purified national language, its usage became undesirable among the literate, standard-oriented speakers, namely, the German and Jewish bourgeois population. However, language use of the predominantly monolingual German dialectal speech communities with their peasant lifestyle was not a core issue in political or language cultivation debates. These speech communities were much less representative of the linguistic ideology of linguistic nationalism represented mainly by the bourgeois layer. For this reason, language maintenance remained much more characteristic of these communities than language shift until well into the middle of the twentieth century.

Therefore, it is the German-speaking (German and Jewish) bourgeois populations of Hungary that may be regarded as the 'real linguistic losers' of Hungarian linguistic nationalism. According to contemporary sources, these communities professed a definite Hungarian national identity, as a result of the continuation of their Hungarus identity, that is, their language- and ethnicity-independent state patriotism stemming from the Middle Ages. As a result of this and of the social pressure these communities were subjected to, they started to adopt the values of Hungarian linguistic nationalism; moreover, many of their members became the leaders of the Hungarian national movement of the time. As a consequence, in spite of the awakening national minority movements among

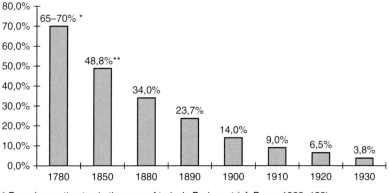

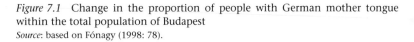

* Based on estimates in the area of today's Budapest (cf. Berza 1993: 182)
** Proportion of the German nationality

Figure 7.1   Change in the proportion of people with German mother tongue within the total population of Budapest
Source: based on Fónagy (1998: 78).

other minority groups in Hungary during the nineteenth century, those initiated by the German population in Hungary were neither substantial nor successful. Therefore, the bourgeois German speech communities in the towns, as shown by Budapest's example (see Figure 7.1), through their Hungarian national identity, social mobility and individual economic and cultural interests, had undergone a language shift by the end of the nineteenth century. Consequently, standard German as a native language had become extinct in Hungary by the beginning of the twentieth century and since then has existed only as a foreign language. German as a mother tongue is present only in the form of non-standard vernaculars in the rural speech communities of modern times. Thus, in the following section, when referring to German minorities and their language use, we mean the mostly rural speech communities and the use of their vernaculars.

German as a minority language in twentieth-century Hungary

In the twentieth century, the split in the history of native vs. standard German in Hungary has been completed. However, in the last decades of the century, their histories interfered again, causing unhappy consequences for the use of Hungarian German as a vernacular.

In the first decades of the century, the language policy of the Hungarian state towards the German minority was supportive in the sense that the state financed German primary education. On the other hand, there were no German high schools except in Transylvania, where the German-speaking minority had access to secondary education in their mother tongue. From the beginning of the century, bilingualism became a requirement for Hungarian German children. According to a law introduced in 1907, by the end of the fourth year all pupils were supposed to be able to read, write and speak fluently in Hungarian. Although the number of German primary schools decreased dramatically between 1880 and 1900, from 867 to 383, a slow increase began in the following years, and by 1917 there were as many as 447 German primary schools in Hungary.

In 1920, the Treaty of Trianon caused a dramatic turn not only in Hungarian history but also in the history of the Hungarian German minority. Hungary lost more than two-thirds of its territory and more than half of its inhabitants. Losing the main groups of its former minorities, Hungary became a largely monolingual and almost a mono-ethnic country. Its 1.9 million strong German-speaking population shrank to 550,000 as large German groups remained in Transylvania, Romania, Serbia, Czechoslovakia and Burgenland, Austria. Even with their remarkably decreased population, Germans became the largest ethnic minority in Hungary.

The Trianon Treaty strengthened the nationalistic ideology and this in turn had an impact on Hungarian minority educational policy. In 1923, three types of minority schools were established replacing the earlier practice by which the language of instruction had been the minority language. In type one, the language of instruction remained German; in type two, it was German and Hungarian, and in type three, the language of instruction was Hungarian, and German was taught as a compulsory subject. The development of types two and three shows a shift towards an assimilationist language policy. The change of conditions was also reflected in the minority parents' attitudes towards their native language: 75 per cent of them chose the second or third type of minority education.

During the Second World War and the preceding years some leaders of the Hungarian Germans played fateful roles, for their Nazi-friendly politics had disastrous consequences for the future of the Hungarian German population as a whole. During the war, Hungarian Germans were able to enlist in both the Hungarian and the German armies, and many of them were successfully recruited into the *Waffen SS*. In the last phase of the war, about 50,000 Germans left the country and many of those who remained were deported to labour camps by Soviet troops. After the war, as a 'penalty' for what was called 'collective guilt', large groups of ethnic Germans were expelled. About 170,000 were transported to the American Zone in West Germany, and about 50,000 to the Soviet Zone in East Germany (cf. Tilkovszky 1989).

The basis for the deportations was the data of the 1941 census when people were forced to make a categorical statement about their one and only national identity. Those who declared themselves to be Germans were entered on the list of people to be deported. This tragic event had grave, irreversible effects on both the status and the prestige of the German vernaculars. German national identity became a political stigma associated with the danger of being discriminated against, and in the German communities, strongly negative attitudes have evolved towards their own vernacular dialects. Language shift has therefore developed rapidly as a result of a conscious assimilation strategy.

The rejection of German and the fear of declaring it as a mother tongue are reflected in the fact that in 1949 only 22,455 people out of the 220,000 Hungarian Germans who remained in Hungary after the war identified, or rather, dared to identify, German as their mother tongue (see Table 7.1). As part of the accelerating language shift, another typical assimilation strategy emerged. Many members of the Hungarian German minority have changed their German surnames to Hungarian ones. The reason for this 'nominal assimilation', too, was the public rejection and renunciation of linguistic, and through this, ethnic affiliation in the hope of being spared expulsion or deportation. According to Kozma's (2002: 45) data, in the period between 1945 and 1948, by filing 24,000 applications, 50,000 people with a German background attempted to acquire Hungarian surnames.[3]

Table 7.1   Changes in the size of the Hungarian population of German nationality and German mother tongue as reflected in census data

Year of census	German nationality	German mother tongue
1941	302,198	475,491
1949	2,617	22,455
1980	11,310	31,231
1990	30,824	37,511
2001	62,233	33,792

After a long decade, in the middle of the 1950s the extremely strong political pressure on the German speech communities started to ease. The German minority, who had not previously enjoyed collective rights, were officially recognized by law as a minority, along with other national minorities. In 1955 the focus of the minority policy shifted to the cultivation of cultural traditions, mainly of folk music and folk dance. At the same time, the state started to train teachers for minority education, a German magazine and a radio programme were established, and in 1960 three high schools started to teach some subjects in German. In the following decades, there was a remarkable increase in the number of German minority primary schools, especially in the late 1980s. In spite of the improving conditions, many parents, having experienced the political pressure in the communist era, consciously chose Hungarian as their children's first language.

The political conditions improved considerably after 1989. The Constitution was amended to include paragraphs on minority rights, and in 1993 the Act on the Rights of National and Ethnic Minorities was ratified by Parliament. The Act established individual and collective minority rights for autochthonous minority groups who have been living in Hungary for at least a century. The unification of Germany as well as the collapse of the communist regimes in Central Europe recontextualized attitudes towards German as a minority native language (cf. Gal 1995). Although the Hungarian German communities differ linguistically, ideologically and socio-economically, and the language shift processes are not uniform, the German minority are unique in that the self-declared ethnic and mother tongue population of the Hungarian German minority is increasing (Bartha and Borbély 2006: 346).

There is also a remarkable increase in the number of minority schools. In 1985 182 schools had adopted the German minority programme, and this number had grown to 284 by 1999. This increase, however, is partly the result of the fact that non-ethnic German Hungarian citizens also send their children to German schools in order to ensure their access to high quality foreign language education as the language of instruction in minority German schools is standard German (cf. Nelde 2000).

This practice has become one of the most powerful factors accelerating the language shift of the Hungarian German minority groups. For ethnic Germans, standard German is obviously inappropriate to express their Hungarian German ethnic and cultural identity, which is connected to the vernacular varieties (cf. Gerner 2006: 168). Compared to the overwhelming prestige of standard German strengthened by the authority of school, and to the prestige of Hungarian, the state language, the non-standard German vernacular for youngsters seems increasingly redundant and not worth speaking (cf. Gal 2006: 27).[4] Therefore, the process of language shift seems irreversible, as sociolinguistic observations and surveys suggest (see, for example, Bindorffer 1998). In the German minority groups, only the elderly have native competence in the vernacular; the younger generations, as in many other language-shifting communities, use their dialects in fewer domains or only understand but do not speak it.

The 'mother tongue' data of the censuses show a rising tendency until 1990 (see Table 7.1). Although this seems to contradict what we have said above, the increase is only an illusion. In 1949, due to extremely strong political pressure, far fewer people than the actual number dared to identify German as their mother tongue. Thus the rising tendency observable in recent years is not a sign of an increase in the number of native speakers of German, but reflects the greater tolerance in the political climate. The fact that declaring German as a mother tongue reached its peak in 1990 is due primarily to the collapse of the communist era, the birth of the democratic state order and the restoration and establishment of familial, economic and cultural relations with Germany (e.g. twinned towns) (Bindorffer, 2003: 258).

The linguistic data of the 2001 census show a decreasing tendency and is an unambiguous indicator of language shift. The 2001 census, for the first time in the history of Hungarian censuses, allowed the informants to choose nationality, origin and mother tongue anonymously. The negative trend reflected by the data of the 2001 census shows the (f)actual processes signalled by the aforementioned sociolinguistic surveys and suggests language shift. In the background of the linguistic regression we can also see that the last, by now older, generations to acquire a German dialect as their first language and received primary school education in German are dying out (Bindorffer 2003: 258).

The census data also signal interesting trends in terms of the relationship between language and ethnic identity as it contains information about affinity to cultural values, traditions and the language used with family members and friends as well as about national identity and mother tongue (see Table 7.2).

The data show that in 2001 twice as many people identified themselves as Germans as in 1990 (see Table 7.1). The reason for this is only partly due to the anonymity offered; the positive changes in the socio-political environment are also definitely reflected in the numbers.

The other significant change mirrored in the 2001 data is the reversal of the relationship between the mother tongue and the nationality numbers. Previously, more people had identified German as their

Table 7.2 Linguistic and nationality data of the 2001 census

German nationality	Affinity to German cultural values, traditions	German mother tongue	Speaking German with family members or friends
62,233	88,416	33,792	53,040

mother tongue than as their nationality. In 2001, for the first time, significantly more (almost twice as many) people identified themselves as having German nationality than having German as their mother tongue. This clearly shows that the close link between German ethnic identity and the German mother tongue has been loosened. Many of those who claim Hungarian as their mother tongue identify themselves as members of the German minority. They are characteristically members of the younger generations. It seems that for them native language is not a marker of minority ethnic identity; this role has been taken over by cultural traditions (dances, songs, folk customs), and by awareness of German origin. This interpretation is supported by the large number of those who identified themselves as having an affinity to German cultural values and traditions, an even larger number than those who identified themselves as ethnic Germans (see Table 7.2). As Bindorffer (2003: 265f.) also highlights, this proves that language shift is not indicative of the extinction of a minority. The young generation's cultural affinity and the existential opportunities opening up for them thanks to the political and economic conditions create new perspectives for ethnic survival (cf. Gerner 2006). With the passing of the older generations, the traditional German dialects seem to be gradually disappearing from Hungary's linguistic map. However, there are signs that the younger generation's affinity to cultural values and traditions may replace this cohesion deficit brought about by the now apparently irreversible language shift (cf. Bindorffer 2003: 266). At the same time, while this may not be of significance for the (standing of the) indigenous German minority population, the prestige of standard German as a foreign language remains high, as it was throughout the twentieth century.

German as a foreign language in twentieth-century Hungary

Before the Second World War German was unquestionably the first foreign language in Hungary as a result of the cultural traditions and the history of the urban bourgeoisie, and because it had been the lingua franca in Central Europe. This function originated from the Habsburg period in several countries (Hungary, Czechoslovakia, Yugoslavia) and the cultural role of the German language in Poland.

Even though learning Russian became obligatory after the war, and even though German acquired negative connotations during the war, it seems that German kept its leading position on the prestige list until the mid-1980s. In addition to its role as a lingua franca, the main factors that stabilized the top position of German were the following: first, both Russian and German opened up the possibility for people to study or work in the Soviet Union and in the GDR; but in contrast with Russian, English and French, German was also useful to the overwhelming majority in the sense that it could be practised in real situations at Lake Balaton, which was not only the favourite holiday resort for Hungarians but also a meeting point for German families and friends separated by the German border. Other languages remained more or less classroom languages. Second, in the western part of the country, knowing German ensured advantages in finding well-paid jobs, as the Austrian restaurant and medical tourist industries expanded (in the 1980s). Furthermore, in the last decade of the communist era, retail tourism to Austria became fashionable, establishing another domain in which German was useful. Third, even if Hungarians mostly had direct contact only with East Germans, German was regarded as a Western language, which added to its prestige.

There were also negative feelings towards German, but they obviously did not outweigh the positive factors: for many people, it was associated with Nazi Germany, and according to a widespread folk linguistic judgement: German sounds 'unpleasant', 'too hard' and is 'harsh-sounding'.

However useful German was during this period, since the 1960s the most desired foreign language among young people is English. The yearning for the 'American dream', the spread of popular culture and, above all, the enthusiasm for pop music created a desire among young people to know English. When it turned out that English had actually become the new world lingua franca, it also increased its already high prestige. Access to the internet in this regard was the icing on the cake.

Today, the leading position of English has become unquestionable. Recent data on foreign language learning in Hungary (see Table 7.3) may be somewhat misleading, suggesting that German is still almost as strong as English. The data on foreign language learning do not reflect the real preferences of students. Once the obligatory teaching of Russian

Table 7.3 Changes in language learning between 1991 and 1999 (numbers of students)

	Russian			German			English		
	Primary	High school	Vocational	Primary	High school	Vocational	Primary	High school	Vocational
1991	485,000	76,000	3,500	186,000	54,000	14,000	130,000	71,000	6,000
1999	22,000	17,000	2,000	354,000	82,000	24,000	318,000	106,000	7,000

Source: The Ministry of Education.

was abolished after 1990, teachers of Russian were offered the opportunity to retrain in another language. German was a popular choice, so there are many teachers of German in the country. As a result, even if the pupils' preference is English, they are offered German, partly because of the lack of teachers of English and partly because it means that teachers of German can keep their jobs.

Nevertheless, trends in language choice and language policy clearly show that English will almost entirely overtake all other languages as the first foreign language in the near future. In high schools – the most prestigious form of public schooling – English had overtaken German as the language of choice by 1999. According to the law on public education (LXXIX/1993,133.§ (2)), from 2010 onwards, schools will be required to offer English classes. Although learning English is not compulsory, teaching English will become a legal obligation. It is therefore likely that German will lose its position as the first foreign language taught in Hungary; however, it will probably continue to be first choice as a second foreign language.

Concluding remarks

German has played a role in the history of the Hungarian-speaking community ever since the Hungarian kingdom was established in the Carpathian Basin. The intensity of language contact changed over time, as did the status of German as a native and second, or foreign, language. German seems to have achieved its greatest prestige during the Habsburg era, supported by the strong political and economic power it symbolized; but it was this very association that led to a significant change in the attitudes towards German when the ideology of 'one nation, one language, one culture' evolved in the early nineteenth century. However, the nineteenth century brought another important change as well. The German-speaking population of the Hungarian towns – especially of Buda and Pest, assimilated by the end of the century – sporadically settled in the country, and German as a native language became a minority language largely confined to a few villages. In the minority communities, German kept its symbolic function of signalling minority identity until recently but as the 2001 census shows, for the younger generation of Hungarian Germans this role is being overtaken by the traditional culture of the community. Even after the collapse of the Austro-Hungarian monarchy, German remained the foreign language of choice in Hungary until almost the end of the twentieth century; but since the 1960s English has taken over this position in line with the global tendency and strengthened by the collapse of the communist order in Eastern Europe in which German was seen as a 'friendly' but at the same time 'Western' foreign language and functioned as a lingua franca. Today the leading position of English is unquestionable, and although German is still the second foreign language in Hungary, it is far from being the lingua franca of the region: English seems to dominate all other languages in this function.

Notes

1. Peter Maitz's work was supported by the Alexander von Humboldt Foundation. We would also like to thank Kristine Horner (Leeds) for improving our English.
2. For previous centuries, see Maitz (2005); Manherz (1998).
3. Only 63.3 per cent of the petitions submitted were approved. With a few exceptions, the petitions of those who had declared themselves German in the 1941 census were denied. Petitions of Hungarians with a German mother tongue were approved only if the applicant's left-wing, anti-fascist record was authorized by influential patrons. Furthermore, immediate rejection awaited the petitions of those who had already been registered on the list of deportees (cf. Kozma 2002: 45, 56).
4. The German minority groups living primarily on the western border, next to Austria, in the vicinity of the towns of Sopron and Kőszeg are perhaps an exception. The German (Bavarian) vernaculars they speak are practically identical with the vernaculars spoken in the neighbouring Austrian provinces. Thus the Hungarian German dialects, rather than representing the past and the traditions, actually represent important economic capital – one of the prerequisites of employment in Austria offering serious economic advantages.

References

Bartha, C. and Borbély, A. (2006) 'Dimensions of linguistic otherness: Prospects of minority language maintenance in Hungary', *Language Policy* 5, 335–63.

Berend, N. and Knipf-Komlósi, E. (eds) (2006) *Sprachinselwelten – The World of Language Islands* (Frankfurt/M: Peter Lang).

Berza, L. (ed.) (1993) *Budapest Lexikon*, vol. 2, 2nd edition (Budapest: Akadémiai Kiadó).

Bindorffer, G. (1998) 'No language, no ethnicity? Ethnic identity, language and cultural representation among Hungarian Germans', *Review of Sociology of the Hungarian Sociological Association*. Special Issue 3(4), 143–157

Bindorffer, G. (2003) 'Németek a népszámlálások tükrében – 1980, 1990, 2001', in Kovács and Szarka (2003), 253–66.

Eichinger, L. M., Plewnia, A. and Riehl, C. M. (eds) (2008) *Handbuch der deutschen Sprachminderheiten in Mittel- und Osteuropa* (Tübingen: Narr).

Fónagy, Z. (1998) 'A budapesti németek lélekszáma', in Hambuch (1998), 76–80.

Gal, S. (1995) 'Cultural bases of language use among German-speakers in Hungary', *International Journal of the Sociology of Language* 111, 93–102.

Gal, S. (2001) 'Linguistic theories and national images in nineteenth-century Hungary', in Gal and Woolard (2001), 30–45.

Gal, S. (2006) 'Migration, minorities and multilingualism: Language ideologies in Europe', in Mar-Molinero and Stevenson (2006), 13–27.

Gal, S. and Woolard, K. A. (eds) (2001) *Languages and Publics: The Making of Authority* (Manchester: St. Jerome).

Gerner, Z. (2006) 'Identität – soziales Netzwerk – nationale Stereotype. Zur Identitätsbildung und Identitätsforschung in den deutschen Sprachinseln in Ungarn', in Berend and Knipf-Komlósi (2006), 149–73.

Government of Hungary (1993) *A közoktatásról szóló 1993. évi LXXIX. törvény* [1993 Law on the Education System].

Hambuch (ed.) (1998) *Németek Budapesten* (Budapest: Fővárosi Német Kisebbségi Önkormányzat).

Herder, J. G. (1989) *Ideen zur Philosophie der Geschichte der Menschheit*, vol. 6, ed. Martin Bollacher (Frankfurt/M: Deutscher Klassiker Verlag).

Knipf-Komlósi, E. (2008) 'Ungarn', in Eichinger et al. (2008), 265–327.

Kovács, N. and Szarka, L. (eds) (2003) *Tér és terep. Tanulmányok az etnicitás és az identitás kérdésköréből II* (Budapest: Akadémiai Kiadó).

Kozma, I. (2002) 'Névmagyarosítási mozgalom és kisebbségpolitika a koalíciós korszakban (1945–1948)', in Kovács and Szarka (2002), 41–73.

Maitz, P. (2005) *Sozialpsychologie des Sprachverhaltens. Der deutsch-ungarische Sprachkonflikt in der Habsburgermonarchie* (Tübingen: Niemeyer).

Maitz, P. (2008) 'Linguistic nationalism in nineteenth-century Hungary: reconstructing a linguistic ideology', in *Journal of Historical Pragmatics* 9(1), 20–47.

Manherz, K. (ed.) (1998) *Die Ungarndeutschen* (Budapest: Útmutató).

Mar-Molinero, C. and Stevenson, P. (eds) (2006) *Language Ideologies, Policies and Practices: Language and the Future of Europe* (Basingstoke: Palgrave Macmillan).

Nelde, P. H. (2000) 'Bilingualism among ethnic Germans in Hungary', in Wolff (2000), 125–33.

Stevenson, P. (2000) 'The ethnolinguistic vitality of German-speaking communities in Central Europe', in Wolff (2000), 109–24.

Tilkovszky, L. (1989) *Hét évtized a magyarországi németek történetéből, 1919–1989* (Budapest: Kossuth).

Wolff, S. (ed.) (2000) *German Minorities in Europe: Ethnic Identity and Cultural Belonging* (New York and Oxford: Berghahn).

8
Central European Time: Memories of Language – Lost and Found – in the Life Stories of German-speakers

Jenny Carl and Patrick Stevenson

Introduction: theoretical perspectives on temporality and the experience of loss

References to time are integral both to the substance and to the structure of narratives, but the conception of time that underlies these references and the role it plays in organizing accounts of processes, events and experiences are both variable and central to the interpretation of the narratives. For example, Blommaert (2005: 127–8) refers to the work of the French historian Fernand Braudel (1958/1969), who distinguishes between different 'layers' of time or time-scales, each of which necessarily contributes to our understanding and interpretation of the past:

> Braudel distinguished between three such layered time-scales: slow time or structural time (the 'longue durée'); intermediate time, or conjunctural time (the time of long cyclical patterns, e.g. the time of particular political regimes or the cycle of growth and crisis in capitalism); and the *événement*, event-time.

A similarly multi-stranded conception of time is subsumed in Schutz and Luckmann's (1974) notion of 'lifeworldly time', which, according to Baynham (2006: 189), is 'created by the intersections between the subjective time of inner consciousness (inner duration), the rhythms of the body which constitute "biological time", the seasons of the year which constitute "world time" and those of the calendar "social time"' (to which Baynham adds the category of 'historical time', more or less equivalent to Braudel's *événement*).

Braudel's stratification of time seems to imply both simultaneity (or 'nesting', or embedding) and sequentiality in our relationship with and understanding of the past. In their discussion of nostalgia and autobiography, however, Dickinson and Erben (2006: 224) suggest that our relationship with the past is determined by the socio-historical conditions in which we live and, drawing on Shaw and Chase (1989b), they contrast a cyclical concept of time 'in which change is part of a repeating circle of events, where change is not absolute, and in which the past is not lost forever', with a linear concept of time, which is characteristic of industrial societies 'with their continual social change, future orientation, tendency to secularization, and reactive systems of planning'. They go on to argue that neither of these conceptions is adequate to account for the complex temporal patterns in individual life stories, for which Brockmeier has coined the term 'autobiographical time', 'the process by which an individual, reflecting on and living through his or her life course, "constantly links the past with the present ... in the light of present events and future expectations"' (Brockmeier 2000: 55).

The link between time as lived (the narrated event) and time as narrated (the narrative event) is problematized by Mishler (2006) using the rhetorical image of the 'double arrow of time' to characterize the contradictory 'temporal orders' of 'clock or chronological time' and 'narrative or experiential time'. Mishler's argument turns on its head the 'common-sense view' of a narrative as a 'chronological sequence where events that precede others are independent, and potential causes or explanations of those that follow' in favour of a teleological conception that takes account of the ways narrators select, organize and present experiences as an exercise in 'reinterpreting the meaning of past events in terms of later consequences, through which they redefine who they are and revise the plots of their life stories' (Mishler 2006: 33, 36; see also Brockmeier 2001 on 'retrospective teleology' in autobiography).

This organizational principle seems to underlie the individual life stories of German speakers in Hungary and the Czech Republic that we discuss in this chapter,[1] in which life events are generally recounted as a developmental sequence, not a repeating cycle, although the narratives are episodic, discontinuous and oriented around recurring themes. Typically incorporating the experience of several generations of a family, the narratives are framed in terms of long-term historical processes but punctuated and given their momentum by reference to moments of change in 'event-time' (or rather, perhaps, to change *recalled as* momentary, such as starting school or a new job, or the transition from one political order to another). Changes in language use and linguistic practices are charted against these reference points, and a central topos, unsurprisingly, is the experience of loss, specifically the loss of those speech varieties traditionally considered constitutive of German ethnicity (see also Maitz and Sándor, this volume).

However, loss is also not a unitary phenomenon – it may, for example, be a result of censorship imposed by a hostile state authority, or a more or less voluntary relinquishing of a speech form seen as a concomitant of an undesirable lifestyle – and similarly experience of loss, and reactions to it, vary. Furthermore, while loss, in the sense of the displacement of a particular linguistic variety from the active speech repertoire of individuals, is more likely to be gradual than instantaneous, accounts of loss are generally framed in terms of outcomes rather than processes, and as both consequences and evidence of social change. In our narratives, the theme of language loss functions as one means of structuring the individual life course, and other life events are made relevant to the extent that they contribute to the recollection of loss, or the resistance to it, or in some cases to the regaining of what had been lost. This contingent relationship between time and language (loss) is captured in Gal's concept of a 'culturally coded temporality' derived from the temporal indexicality of linguistic practices and linguistic forms (and place):

> Not only do linguistic practices occur *in* time, linguistic forms and geographical regions come to index cultural categories *of* time: some point to modernity or the future; others become indexes of tradition and the past.
>
> (Gal 2006: 14)

To modify Gal's terms, language loss (and the loss of those things that are put in jeopardy as a result), therefore, not only occurs *in* time, but also constitutes a means of giving shape to the individual experience *of* time.

The salience of 'loss' in our narratives is not surprising, since all our informants share – either at first hand or through the recollections of older family members – the experience of assimilation into a society in which a previously defining feature of their sense of self (a linguistic variety) was not validated or legitimized. The 'authenticity' of traditional, local speech forms indexical of the past is outweighed by the 'authority' of standardized, national speech forms (both German and either Hungarian or Czech) indexical of the present and the future (see

Gal and Woolard 2001b; Gal 2006). But what exactly has been lost, how is this loss felt, and what does it represent in people's lives? Is it necessarily experienced as an irredeemable deficit, or may it sometimes be constructed retrospectively as a temporary suspension, or simply accepted as an absence of a former presence?

Of course, changes in social conditions impose some form of adjustment on those affected, but how do they incorporate this into their personal perspectives on their lives? How do they use the shifting compositions of their linguistic repertoires to structure their accounts of their experience of change? And how do these accounts serve to give meaning to the narrators' lives? Our narratives suggest a range of different responses to the experience of loss: from mourning and regret, through acceptance and resignation, to resistance and rediscovery. In the next section, we offer some brief examples of how people organize their accounts of loss and their reactions to it as one way of constructing a meaningful and personal sense of temporality, of establishing the 'past' and the 'present' in their lives. (For a more detailed analysis, see Stevenson and Carl forthcoming; further aspects of this research are discussed in Carl and Stevenson 2007; Stevenson and Carl 2008.)

The idea of 'language loss' and the temporal organization of life stories

In this section we examine aspects of the stories of six individuals of ethnic German origin from Hungary and the Czech Republic in order to see how they narrate the loss of the German language in their families and wider communities. In particular, we show how the (threat of) loss has been framed by stories of unexpected and chance circumstances, of a sometimes melancholic search for their identities, and of defiance, which they have chosen in order to represent their lives.

In extract 1, Mrs A, a 68-year old woman from Plzeň (Czech Republic), relates how her leisure activity of motor sport helped her keep in touch with her first language (German). Earlier in the interview she had told the researcher that her own mother was bilingual in Czech and German, that her mother spoke only German with her in her early life, but then spoke only Czech with her after the end of the Second World War in order to help her with her schoolwork and also make her life in the then Czechoslovakia easier. So she had virtually lost contact with the German language in her youth, but she managed to reconnect with it through her motor sport involvement.

1 Mrs A from Plzeň/CZ, 68 years old: motor sport and language maintenance

1 JA was mich . bisher gehalten hat . bei der deutsche Sprache war Sport/ . mein Mann ist
2 ein . Mechaniker fuer Speedway und der hat mich immer mitgenommen von Anfang.
3 und als wir- . mir haben viel mit DDR . damals ((xx)) gemacht/ . nach alle
4 verschiedene- . alle verschiedene Staedte in DDR/ . und ich hab . versucht.
5 gedolmetscht und ich hab gemerkt dass mir etwas doch in den Kopf geblieben ist von
6 der deutsche Sprache . und es war . eh SEHR . interessant mit denen zu machen .
7 mitmachen/ wegen dem dass ich eigentlich wieder . n – die Erinnerungen erwache und-
8 und dass ich wieder rede/

1 Well, what kept up my link with the German language until now was sport. My
2 husband is a speedway mechanic and he always took me along from the start, and when
3 we – we did a lot in the GDR in those days … and I tried, I interpreted, and I noticed
4 that something of the German language had stuck in my mind after all, and it was very
5 interesting to do things with them because I bring memories back to life and because I
6 talk again.

In this short sequence, Mrs A conjoins references to a place (the GDR) and a time (in those days) in connection with a specific activity (motor sport) to open up a social space in which she was able to regain a degree of control over her social actions, a space in which the use of an otherwise stigmatized and politically compromising language (in terms of its past associations) was legitimated through its role in facilitating working relationships with citizens of a sister socialist state. The double historical specification through both spatial and temporal deixis would have been tautological were it not for the fact that 'in those days' (i.e. pre-1989) the practice of speaking German in public would not have been sanctioned or positively evaluated for her other than in this particular context. However, the significance of this episode in her life story is not confined to a closed period in the past, but appears to extend into the present of the time of narration. The activity of interpreting provided the occasion for her to discover that she had, apparently unexpectedly, not completely lost her knowledge of German, but the shift from past to present tense in lines 5–6[2] extends the narrative trajectory beyond the temporal confines of the past events, and the two causal clauses ('because I bring memories back to life' and 'because I talk again') suggest that the revelation for her was not so much her surprising linguistic proficiency as her rediscovered ability to access closed-off parts of her life and finding a voice again with which to articulate them.

In contrast to Mrs A, Mrs B from Sopron (Hungary) constructs a very different story world (De Fina et al. 2006). She is a teacher of German and thus has been able to convert the cultural capital of her family 'legacy' (knowledge of German) into economic capital. She even portrays her profession as a birthright handed down to her through her bloodline (see Extract 2a).

2a Mrs B from Sopron/HU, 45 years old: linguistic legacies

```
 1 sie war WIENerin die Oma/ und der Grossvater war eben ein Soproner Handwerker/
 2 und so haben sie hier ((raeuspert sich)) hier gelebt/ und auch meine Mutter entstammt
 3 einer Ruster Familie/ Rust ist am Neusiedler See . ehm . ((raeuspert sich)) und jetzt
 4 gehoert . Rust zu Oesterreich/ und . und h- in diesen Familien ist es absolut egal ob
 5 Deutsch oder Ungarisch gesprochen wird/ soGAR die Grossmutter hat kein einziges
 6 ungarisches Wort gesprochen sondern nur Deutsch/ und . und so haben wir Deut-
 7 Deutsch gelernt/ und wenn wir Jungen waeren . ich hab auch eine SCHWESter dann
 8 waeren wir wahrscheinlich im Handwerk taetig wie alle in der Familie/ und . und dass
 9 wir eben das nicht weitergefuehrt haben dafuer haben wir aber die SPRA.che und so-
10 ich sag immer ,das Diplom in die Wiege gelegt bekommen'/
```

```
1 She was from Vienna, my grandma, and grandfather was a craftsman from Sopron. And
2 so they lived here, and my mother came from a family in Rust, Rust is on the
3 Neusiedler See, and Rust belongs to Austria now, and in these families it makes no
4 difference at all whether you speak German or Hungarian. Even my grandmother didn't
5 speak a single word of Hungarian, only German. And that's how we learnt German.
6 And if we were boys, I also have a sister, we would be craftsmen like everyone else in
7 the family. And because we didn't carry that on, instead we have the language and so I
8 always say we 'inherited our diploma' [were given our diploma at birth].
```

Mrs B's knowledge of German, handed down mainly from her monolingual Viennese grandmother, is not only a birthright, it is also her 'craft'. It has become the basis of her profession and it is a form of 'compensation', because due to their gender she and her sister were not able to carry on the family tradition of (manual) craftsmanship. This elaboration makes her professional choice look very straightforward, but the reference to gender also makes it appear almost like a duty, or a mission, where she did not actually have a choice.

However, beneath the surface of the seemingly natural language choice there is also a realization that she did not have the natural bilingualism of previous generations, which became apparent when she faced the choice of how to bring up her own children (see Extract 2b).

2b Mrs B from Sopron: bilingual dilemmas

```
1 und jetzt wo ich SELber . eine Familie . HAbe . jetzt hat mein MANN darauf eh
2 bestanden also dass dass ich mit den Kindern zuhause Deutsch sprechen soll/ aber bei
3 mir war das nicht mehr so naTUERlich weil eh . weil doch die zwei Sprachen
4 vorHANden sind aber Ungarisch . domiNIERT/ und dann . haben es die Kinder
5 eigentlich meinem MANN zu verdanken dass sie Deutsch koennen weil dann hab ich
6 beim DRITten Kind hab ich gesagt gut . dann muss ich das ueberWINden und . bei der
7 ersten Windel anfangen
```

1 And now that I have my own family, now my husband insisted that I speak German to
2 the children at home. But it wasn't so natural for me anymore, because both
3 languages [German and Hungarian] are there but Hungarian is dominant. And then the
4 children owe it to my husband that they can speak German because when I had my
5 third child I said 'well I just have to get over this and start [speaking German] with the
6 first nappy'.

Entering this new life phase, Mrs B was confronted with the dilemma of whether or not to pass on her linguistic 'inheritance'. Her own first encounter with German had been in the private, domestic domain but her use of German had subsequently been confined to the public, occupational domain of the classroom. Her monolingual, Hungarian-speaking husband clearly identified knowledge of German as an asset, one that only she could offer their children, but her recounting of this phase of her life is in terms of an emotional struggle that she only overcame with the birth of their third child. However, while she first speaks in the role of 'animator' (in the sense of Goffman 1981), articulating family language policy designed by her husband, she then reasserts her own agency as both 'author' and 'principal'. In lines 1–2, she uses reported speech to represent her husband's action, but through her self-quotation in direct speech (lines 5–6) she intensifies the affective force of her own decision and retrospectively constructs a 'moral stance' (Relaño-Pastor and De Fina 2005: 46) as a 'good mother'.

Extract 2b introduces language loss as a theme, but the actual loss, the loss of the traditional dialect, is only made explicit in extract 2c, where Mrs B reflects on what makes a language 'genuine'.

2c Mrs B from Sopron: genuine family language

1 in der [...]-Familie . dort . das weiss das hoer ich von meinem Sohn . dort wird nur
2 Deutsch gesprochen / also das ist eine echt- also das ist das will ich nicht sagen . also .
3 ECHT . aber bei UNS hat ECHT wahrscheinlich aufgehoert mit . mit meinen ELTern
4 also mit dieser Generation/ o- obwohl ich auch sagen muss so lange war das- war die
5 Sprache in der Familie lebendig . solange die Grossmutter gelebt hat/ solange die Oma
6 gelebt hat/ und eh . ja . und danach hat dann Ungarisch dominiert nur wir waren dann
7 schon . ehm . irgendwie mit Deutsch als – auf der- .hh es war schon die BAHN die-/ .../
8 und . ich hab zum Beispiel den Dialekt auch nicht gelernt / [...]da hat mich der Herr
9 Professor [...]und der hat mich immer so gegeisselt und hat gesagt ,ja wenn die [...] den
10 Dialekt vom Vater gelernt haette'/

1 In that family, I know that from my son, they only speak German. That's a genuine,
2 well, that's, I wouldn't say, well, genuine, but in our case 'genuine' stopped with my
3 parents, with their generation. Although I must say, until then the language was still
4 alive in the family, as long as grandmother was alive, as long as grandma was alive.
5 After that, Hungarian became dominant, only we were then somehow with German –
6 that was the way ... And for example I didn't learn the dialect. ... The 'Herr
7 Professor', he always chastised me, he said 'well, if she had only learned the dialect
8 from her father'.

Triggered by the comparison with the family of a friend of her son's, where all the members of the family speak only German at home, she reflects on when German ceased to be the 'genuine' language in her family, and it emerges that it was only kept 'alive' by her Viennese grandmother, and only during her parents' generation was it still used naturally. And she only then also 'admits' that she did not learn the local dialect – the distinction between dialect and standard German had not been made before this point in the interview – which she seemingly came to identify as a deficit only when she was faced with the criticism of her university professor, whose authoritative voice she cites in lines 7–8. His criticism draws further attention to the loss of the 'natural' language she became aware of when she had her children, and it adds another dimension to it by highlighting the loss of the local tradition through the dialect, which had been concealed until then – until this moment in the interview, but perhaps also until that moment in her life – by the seemingly natural presence of 'German'.

Mrs C from Pécs also presents a troubled relationship with the German language, but in a different way. Even though German has always played an important part in her life – like Mrs B, she is a trained teacher of German and although she is not now working in this profession, she has always used her German language skills professionally – she has always struggled with it and does not want to be reduced to her Germanness.

3 Mrs C from Pécs/HU; 45 years old: finding your own way

```
 1  aber ich muss sagen dass eh – eh die deutsche Sprache und die deutsche Kultur
 2  nicht eh . ganz also . eh – wie soll ich das sagen?<lacht> - also ich ich finde ich habe
 3  sehr viel Mueh- viel Muehe eh . damit gehabt . aber . ich eh kann mich damit nicht eh .
 4  eh . eh . ganz identifizieren und deshalb habe ich andere Wege gesucht/ [...] man hat eh
 5  eigene Gedanken man- eh . eh wie man im Leben weiter ((Schritt hat)) sucht immer
 6  was- wofuer ich da bin und was eh fuer Ziele ich eh haben muss . und .hh was ich hier
 7  SCHAFfen muss in diesem Leben und eh und ich bin zwar eh so in eine deutsche
 8  Familie geboren aber eh . ich eh – ich bin ueberzeugt dass ich nicht da mein LEBen
 9  finden muss aber also .hh ich kann das nicht- schwer erklaeren/ also nicht die Sprache
10  und und nicht die Eltern sondern man findet andere WERte und man geht man
11  danach- [...]
```

```
 1  I have to say that, well the German language and the German culture is not so, how
 2  shall I say this? <laughs> well I find I struggled with it a lot but I really can't identify
 3  with it and therefore I have looked for other ways. [...] You have your own ideas, about
 4  how you carry on in life, you always look for – what I'm here for and what kind of
 5  aims I must have, and what I have to achieve in this life, and, well, I was born into a
 6  German family, it's true, but I'm convinced that I don't have to find my life there, I
 7  can't, it's hard to explain. I mean not the language and not the parents, but you find
 8  other values and you live according to them – [...]
```

In extract 3, Mrs C recounts how she struggles to define her own subjectivity, what her values and goals in life are, and how she has sought to make her own way. As in the previous extracts, narrative strategies are used here to weave together the warp of her personal story with the weft of a wider social narrative (Lefkowitz 2004: 23): shifts in tense and subject pronouns are part of a strategy of 'referential defocusing' (Barth 2004), through which the narrator constructs a stance at once individual and conventional. Her personal struggle in relation to 'the German language and culture' stems from the fact that she '*was born* into a German family' but '*can't* identify' with this linguistic and cultural heritage and therefore '[*has*] *looked* for' other sources of identificational potential (emphases added). Embedded within the narrator-I's individual journey through time, however, is a general assertion of moral autonomy articulated through a shift to the present tense and to the generic personal pronoun 'you' and an equivalent non-specific 'I' (lines 3–5, 7–8).

Mrs C's brother, Mr D, shares many of her experiences but evaluates them in an entirely different way. In contrast to his sister, Mr D has a very clear sense of who he is, what he wants to achieve in life, and he is very categorical in his descriptions of his life-choices (see extract 4a).

4a Mr D from Pécs, 42 years old, Mrs C's brother: using the mother tongue

1 also- also bei mir . eh . war es eigentlich so . also meine Muttersprache ist Deutsch
2 denn meine Mutter hat mit mir bis zum . Kindergartenalter nur Deutsch gesprochen/
3 also ich habe erst im Kindergarten Ungarisch gelernt/ aber weil im- . also ich bin im
4 Moment 42 Jahre alt das heisst . im . in den 60er Jahren . ((oder)) im- . ja da war's- da
5 gab's hier noch kein guter Deutschunterricht/ da war ja . noch Kommunismus und das
6 heisst in den- in der SCHULzeit hab ich . eh . nur Ungarisch gelernt/ also . ich hatte
7 Deutschstunden besucht aber die waren nicht so praegend/ also . eh ich konnte
8 praktisch nicht . eh so viel Deutsch sprechen/ ich sprach DAMALs eine . eine
9 OERTliche Mundart/ - eine . eine SCHWAEbische . eine schwaebische Mundart/ … eh
10 dann kam langsam die WENDE und dann hat man hier DRINGend Deutschlehrer
11 gebraucht/ und bei MIR ist das dann gut zusammengefallen denn . eh ich konnte mich
12 in DREI MONaten soVIEL vorbereiten dass ich auf die Uni aufgenommen WURDe/
13 und da hab ich . e-e-eh Deutschlehrer.ausbildung gemacht/ also . eh . in drei Jahren
14 wurde ich dann Deutschlehrer/ also . hatte ich ein GROSses Glueck dass ich Deutsch
15 konnte/ und eh schon VORHer . war das immer ein WUNSCH von mir so WIRKlich
16 gut Deutsch zu sprechen wenn ich schon deutscher Abstammung bin/

1 Well in my case, my mother tongue is German because until I went to kindergarten my
2 mother only spoke German with me. So I only learnt Hungarian in kindergarten. But
3 because during- I am 42 years old, that means in the 1960s, well there were no good
4 German classes here. This was still during Communism and so in school I only learnt
5 Hungarian. Well I had some German lessons but they didn't have much effect. So I
6 couldn't really speak a lot of German, I spoke a local dialect in those days, a
7 *schwäbisch* dialect. […] And then the *Wende* came along and they urgently needed
8 German language teachers. And that worked out well for me because within three
9 months I was able to prepare so well that I was offered a place at university where I

10 studied to be a German language teacher. [...] It was very lucky for me that I spoke
11 German, and even before it had always been my wish to be able to speak German
12 really well, as I'm of German origin, after all.

In this first episode in his linguistic autobiography, Mr D structures his account in relation to changes in external social and political conditions, which tie his personal story both to the wider 'national' story of postwar Hungary and to other personal narratives. The transformative impact on his life of the political turning point (*Wende*) in 1989–90 is represented here as an opportunity to convert what had been a disadvantage during the Communist period into a privilege: his 'good fortune' in being 'of German origin' and a German speaker enables him to move from a passive to an active stance. His self-categorization as German at the end of this episode echoes the declaration of having German as a mother tongue at the beginning: these two assertions frame the account and construct a sense of the restoration of stability and normality.

The shift to a more active narrative stance is taken further in extract 4b, where he relates linguistic choices made in connection with his family life.

4b Mr D from Pécs: family language

1 und . <lacht> mir war's auch SEHR . WICHtig wenn es auch so komisch klingen mag
2 dass eh meine FRAU Deutsch spricht/ also ich habe eine Frau die genauso gut Deutsch
3 spricht wie ich/ ... und . eh jetzt habe ich deswegen das Glueck dass meine GANZE
4 FAMILIE das heisst meine Schwiegereltern AUCH ALLE Deutsch sprechen/ und SO
5 sind wir eine AUSNAHme und zwar weil wir auch mit unseren EIGenen KINdern ich
6 habe drei Kinder wir sprechen auch mit unseren eigenen Kindern nur Deutsch {I hm}/
7 das heisst WIEder eine oertliche Mundart also kein- zuhause spricht man nicht die
8 Hochsprache

1 And <laughs> it was very important for me, however funny it may sound, that my
2 wife should speak German. So I have a wife who speaks German just as well as me.
3 And so now I have the good fortune that my whole family, I mean my parents-in-law,
4 all speak German, and so we're an exception, because we also speak only German
5 with our own children, we have three children, that's to say a local dialect again, at
6 home we don't speak standard German.

Again, this is a very categorical account of his choices, which not only concern his own linguistic practices but also extend to the choice of his wife from a German background so that the language could be handed down to the next generation. The story is thus carefully assembled from selected moments in his past life and follows his progression from assimilated Hungarian speaker to exemplary *Ungarndeutscher* and thus the realization of his personal aspiration.[3]

Although it displays many similarities with Mr D's account, such as the positive identification with their respective ethnic Germanness, and the awareness of the impact of political systems on their lives, Mr E is much more reflective, especially as far as the different life stages that he constructs in his narrative are concerned, where the German language – or the absence of it – is accorded an important role.

5a Mr E from Pécs, 37: mother tongue and public language

1 bis zu meinem vierten Lebensjahr da kam ich in den Kindergarten war ich einsprachig/
2 ich hab die Mundart gesprochen/ . ich konnte es mir auch kaum vorstellen- oder oder in
3 meinem . eh . WELTbild gab's das nicht dass jemand Deutsch nicht spricht/ / <lacht>
4 also das MiliEU das ich noch bis- also in dieser fruehen Kindheit erlebt habe . eh . das
5 war deutsch/ . . . - na und dann . im KINdergarten- <lacht>ich kann mich . an diese . eh .
6 KonfrontaTION so LEICHT erinnern/ also es war eh erSTAUNlich fuer mich es war
7 auch so eine . eh GRENZsituation die ich erlebt habe weil . .hh dort hat man Ungarisch
8 gesprochen also die . eh Kindergaertnerinnen und die Angestellten und und auch die
9 MEHRzahl der Kinder/ aber in dem Alter passt man sich halt schnell an/ und man
10 PASST sich nicht nur an sondern man will auch zur Mehrheit geHOEren glaube ich

1 Until I was four when I went to kindergarten I was monolingual. I spoke the dialect.
2 I also couldn't imagine, or it didn't exist in my image of the world that somebody
3 couldn't speak German. <laughs> So the environment in my early childhood was
4 German. [...] Well, and then in kindergarten <laughs> I can easily remember the
5 confrontation. Well for me it was amazing and it was also a borderline situation that I
6 experienced there because they spoke Hungarian there, the teachers and the staff and
7 most of the children. But at that age you just adapt quickly. And you don't just adapt,
8 you want to belong to the majority, I think.

Like Mr D, Mr E perceives the transition from home to kindergarten as a transition from a monolingual, German-speaking, private space to a monolingual, Hungarian-speaking, public one. But whereas Mr D represented the transition in a rather unemotional way, Mr E reconstructs this experience as an existential crisis, which he describes as a 'confrontation' (line 5) and also a 'borderline' experience that seems to have turned his image of the world upside-down. He concludes this short narrative episode by shifting from the narrator-I perspective to the generic 'you', which provides a rationalization for his compliant linguistic behaviour, a point that will become important later in his narrative.

In extract 5b, Mr E goes on to talk about how he 'lost' the German language, and how he 'found' it again. But, again unlike Mr D, he talks about the process of becoming aware of the loss, and what he did to revive German in his family.

5b Mr E from Pécs, 37: family language, past and present

1 und dann eh hat das dazu B gefuehrt dass die deutsche Sprache . die Mundart . begann .
2 in . den . Hintergrund . zu gelangen/ . ehm . dann ist meine GROSSmutter gestorben .
3 eh . die so ein . starker Traeger der Identitaet und der Sprache geWEsen ist in der
4 Familie/ . und . eh . dann . war ich so . 15 16 Jahre alt als es mir beWUSst wurde eh
5 dass die Sprache bei uns in der Familie ausgestorben ist quasi/ aber dann . begann ich
6 es . eh . zu verbalisieren und eh anzustreben dass die Mundart gebraucht wird in der
7 Familie/ verLERNT haben wir sie ja nicht nur nicht gebraucht/ und seitdem . ist es so
8 ein . SprachengeMISCH/ also Deutsch . also jetzt die Litera- HOCHdeutsch Mundart
9 und Ungarisch/ also . die Mundart ist ja so ein.e KonSERve die in der Entwicklung
10 stehengeblieben ist irgendwann und natuerlich . vieles nicht . AUSgedrueckt werden
11 kann so richtig/ und dann muss man halt . eh Begriffe aus dem . HEUTigen Deutsch
12 oder . aus dem Ungarischen holen und <lacht; beide lachen> so exisTIERT aber die
13 Sprache bei uns/ und . ich hab auch eine Ungarndeutsche als Frau/ - so klappt's . auch
14 in meiner . heutigen Familie – mit der deutschen Sprache/

1 And then the German language, the dialect, began to move into the background, then
2 my grandmother died, she had maintained the identity so strongly in the family, and
3 the language. And then, I was 15, 16 years old when I became aware of the fact that
4 the language had sort of died out in our family. But then I began to verbalise it and to
5 try to get the dialect used in the family. We didn't forget it, we just didn't use it. And
6 since then it's a kind of mixture of languages, I mean German, well now standard
7 German, dialect and Hungarian. I mean, the dialect is sort of preserved in aspic, its
8 development stopped at some point and of course lots of things can't be expressed
9 properly, and so you have to take concepts from today's German [aus dem heutigen
10 Deutsch] or from Hungarian. <laughs> But that's how language is here, and I have an
11 *ungarndeutsch* wife, and so it works in my present family [in meiner heutigen
12 Familie], with the German language.

In this extract, Mr E moves from a local perspective relating to his family in the past through a generalized discussion of language development and use to a particular focus on his family in the present. He presents his adolescence as the time when he realized that he and his family had lost the German language as a family language and when he actively tried to reverse the situation. The 'recovery', however, did not happen through a full-scale reversal of linguistic practices from Hungarian to German, but by adopting a mix of languages, of the *ungarndeutsch* dialect, standard German and Hungarian. Within this constellation he explicitly signifies both the dialect and standard German as indexical of time: in his view, the dialect is a relic, a 'preserve' from the past, which is linked to tradition but cannot express modern life, whereas standard German is called 'today's German', which has a strong place also in his present family. This correspondence between linguistic form and life stage is marked lexically by his choice of the same epithet (heutig, today's/present) in relation to both ('das *heutige* Deutsch' and 'meine *heutige* Familie'; 'today's German' and 'my present family').

Having established the central plotline of his story, Mr E then goes on to elaborate on the details of his journey, articulating his increasing sense of alienation from the majority culture and how he sets himself apart from the monolingual Hungarian mainstream.

5c Mr E from Pécs, 37: journey back to the mother tongue

1   ja wie gesagt in meiner fruehen Kindheit war das normal/ dann eh haben die MEISten
2   meines Jahrgangs im Dorf nicht zurueckgefunden zur deutschen Sprache oder zum
3   Dialekt/ bis heute wenn ich sie spreche sagen sie ,naja so Reste klingen noch im Ohr'
4   aber sie sprechen die Sprache nicht mehr und eh – bemaengeln sie meistens auch nicht/

1   Well, as I said, in my early childhood it was normal [to be bilingual]. Later most of
2   the people of my age in the village didn't find their way back to speaking German or
3   dialect. Even today when I speak to them they say 'well tiny bits are still in my head'
4   but they don't speak the language anymore and for the most part they don't find
5   anything wrong with that either.

In Extract 5c, he recapitulates his contemporaries' migration from the bilingual space of their childhood to a monolingual Hungarian one, a journey few of them have since made in reverse. According to him they have accepted this situation, but he sets himself apart by placing himself outside the majority, as separate from 'most of the people of my age'. However, it is only in the next excerpt that he speaks about his sense of alienation proper, and its extent (see extract 5d).

5d Mr E from Pécs, 37: living on the margins

1   da MUSS man dazugehoeren/ also wenn man- wenn man . eh . BISSchen am Rande ist
2   wird man rausgest- ausgestossen/ man muss sehr am Rand sein damit man eine eigene-
3   einen eigenen Standpunkt aufbauen kann wo dann die UmGEbung das . akzepTIERT/
4   naja ich sag das vorsichtig ich weiss nicht ob die Umgebung das akzeptiert aber a-aber
5   wo es einen nicht mehr intereSSIERT ob's die Umgebung akzeptiert/ das <lacht> ehm .
6   DAS hat bei mir AUCH gedauert/ sicherlich . haben mich dara- darin auch die Jahre im
7   Ausland gestaerkt/ wie- als ich zurueckgekommen bin war das ein voellig fremdes
8   Land fuer mich/ DAS ist es bis HEUte/ also ich- ich eh . ich koennte nicht ande- ich
9   koennte SEHR SCHWER anderswo leben/ ich koennte anderswo leben aber SEHR
10   SCHWER/ aber HIER . hier bin weitgehend nicht zuhause/ also . es ist ein FREMdes
11   Land so wie ich dem Land auch fremd bin/

1   You have to fit in. If you're a bit on the margins you get rejected. You have to be right
2   on the margins in order to develop your own position, so that your environment
3   accepts it. Well OK, I'll put that more cautiously, I don't know whether the
4   environment accepts it, but where you don't care any more whether the environment
5   accepts it.... When I came back [from abroad] it was a completely foreign country to
6   me....I couldn't live anywhere else, I'd find it very hard to live anywhere else, but
7   here I'm pretty much not at home. I mean, it's a foreign country to me just as I'm
8   foreign to the country.

Here, like Mrs C above, Mr E uses the double voice of a rhetorical imper-
sonal 'you' and a personal 'I', in this case apparently to rationalize
his ambivalence towards his home. Adopting the defiant stance of an
active bilingual risks marginalization but it is only on the margins of
the mainstream society that he is able to find a place that accommo-
dates his conflicting feelings. As later passages in his interview show,
both his alienation and his defiance seem to have been strengthened
by his dislocation and subsequent relocation occasioned by his periods
spent abroad (in the GDR and in Austria), from which he brought back
a reinforced attachment to the German language.

Mr F, from Liberec (Czech Republic), shares Mr E's resistance to hegemonic cultural norms but has very different experiences in that he is a
member of the older generation, who has first-hand experiences of the
Second World War and the following expulsion and marginalization of
Germans in the former Czechoslovakia. These experiences form the core
of the first extract from his narrative (see Extract 6a).

*6a Mr F from Liberec/CZ and his daughter; 75 and 45 years old: The
German language after the Second World War*

1   die ErFAHRUNg mit der deutschen Sprache nach dem Krieg war ja die dass man sie
2   nicht sprechen durfte/ also . insofern ist die Erfahrung natuerlich . fuer ALLE
3   Deutschen in der damaligen Zeit katastrophal gewesen sofern sie nicht die
4   Staatssprache beherrschten/ und das das war das Problem MEINER Mutter und das war
5   das Problem ihrer <zeigt auf seine Tochter> Grossmutter muetterlicherseits/ und da
6   gab's natuerlich furchtbare Szenen und und da . hat man sich natuerlich aergern
7   muessen . und man wurde auch pro- provoziert und und ich hab mir ja auch NIE was
8   gefallen lassen/ das war vielleicht mein NACHteil/ ich hatte insofern also mit mit mit
9   der SPRAche MEIner- MEIner Mutter oder meiner Schwiegermutter gegenueber dann
10 immer Schwierigkeiten [I hm] weil ich- weil ich dann ((sein-)) ganz einfach mich
11 beRUFEn fuehlte sich fuer diese alten Herrschaften einzutreten ja?

1   The experience with the German language after the war was that you weren't allowed
2   to speak it. So to that extent of course the experience for all Germans at that time was
3   catastrophic, if they couldn't speak the state language. And that was my mother's
4   problem, and that was the problem of her <points to his daughter > maternal
5   grandmother, and of course there were terrible scenes, and of course you had to feel
6   angry, and you were provoked, and I never put up with any of that. That was probably
7   my disadvantage. So I always had difficulties over language with my mother and my
8   mother-in-law, because I just felt I had to stand up for the old folks, you know?

Mr F, a particularly striking example of what Rosenwald and Ochberg
(1992: 6) call a 'self-historicizing subject', paints here a picture of discrimination and reprisals, and the general condition of the German
community at that time has become very much engrained in his own
experiences from which he constructs his sense of self. Although his

narrative as a whole moves from a point in the past immediately after the war and concludes with reference to the present, the organization of individual narrative episodes is thematically rather than temporally driven. In extract 6a, the development is a movement not through historical time but from the construction of a 'problem' to its resolution through the narrator speaking not only as 'author' of the story but also as 'principal' and 'figure' in the storyworld (see again Goffman 1981). The episode is populated by a variety of figures – generic 'you', 'all Germans', 'the old folks', 'my mother', 'my mother-in-law' – who are subject to 'catastrophic experiences' and 'terrible scenes', while the narrator-protagonist alone is active in confronting the situation. Extract 6b then gives a more specific characterization of the defiant individual confronting the monolithic state apparatus.

6b Mr F from Liberec/CZ: defying the Party

```
1  ich hab auch die Staatspruefung in Deutsch nach((getan)) dann noch gemacht ... und eh
2  ich hab's anundfuersich nie gebraucht aber eh eh ich hab's also ((xxx)) bloss aus Trotz
3  gemacht weil ehhh bei diesen KADER.eh.ueberpruefungen da musste man ja eh eh eh
4  aufSCHREIben welche FREMDsprachen sprichst du/ bei mir war ja immer
5  problematisch was ist fuer mich FREMDsprache/ fuer mich ist Fremdsprache
6  Tschechisch/ das war aber fuer die KEINE Fremdsprache/ fuer die war das richtige
7  STAATSsprache sozusagen/ also hab ich dann immer Fremdsprache ‚Deutsch'
8  geschrieben/ da hat der- wir hatten so einen Trottel als als ((xxx)) der sagte ‚naja aber
9  Staatspruefung hat er keine'/ <lacht laut> das hat mich dann- ich dachte- ich dachte so
10 ein Arschloch/ er kann kaum Tschechisch selber ja? und da hab ich dann gesagt ‚so
11 jetzt mach ich sie'/ und da habe ich sie gemacht/ war fuer mich kein Problem
12 natuerlich/
```

```
1  I did the state exam in German later ... and I never really used it, but I just did it out
2  of defiance, because in those official checks the Party ran you had to write down
3  which foreign languages you spoke. For me it was always problematic: what is a
4  foreign language for me? For me Czech is a foreign language, but for them it wasn't,
5  for them it was the proper language of the state, so to speak. So then I always wrote
6  'foreign language: German'. We had this idiot, he said 'well, but he hasn't got a state
7  exam' <laughs out loud> so I thought, what an arsehole, he can hardly speak Czech
8  himself, so then I said, OK I'll do it then, and so I did it, it was no problem for me of
9  course.
```

The reference point of the story – the act of taking a state exam in German – opens and closes the episode, but the narrative function of the story – constructing the narrator as 'bold resister' and problematizing conceptions of language within a particular ideological regime – is developed within this frame. The 'tellability' (Labov and Waletzky 1967) of his story depends on there being a reason for his selecting this aspect of his formal education as salient in his life story. The initial discounting of an instrumental motivation for taking the exam opens up a narrative gap (why tell us about the qualification if he didn't use it?) and his declaration of a political motivation moves the story towards its justification.

From the habitual gesture of tactical compliance (writing 'foreign language: German' on official forms) the narrative progresses to a specific conflictual event reconstructed and foregrounded through the dialogic interaction between narrator-as-figure and the state official. In chronological terms, the temporal specification of the event (taking the exam) is not important; it is significant only as the moment of resolution, the moment at which the narrator-as-figure exerted control by choosing to take a particular action. Both his apparent compliance in declaring German 'his' foreign language and the act of defiance in obtaining the required qualification under his own terms – calling the state's bluff, as it were – are constructed as a challenge to the hegemonic order and enable him, more emphatically than Mrs A or Mr E, to 'claim a moral space' (Relaño-Pastor and De Fina 2005: 55–6).

Justification for Mr F's construction of himself as a defender of his community and active resister of the communist state's linguistic regime emerges towards the end of his interview when he talks of his grandson, who is brought up bilingually Czech-German in the family – by Mr F and his daughter, who herself is bilingual Czech-German – as well as through his place in a kindergarten across the border in Germany, which has a great impact on the boy's fluency in German.

6c Mr F from Liberec/CZ and his daughter: speaking without an accent

1 [Tochter] ja und das letzte dann . <raeuspert sich> ich hab natuerlich versucht mit den
2 Kindern Deutsch zu reden ... und jetzt . das fuenfte . da hab ich's irgendwie .
3 durchgesetzt . obwohl es mich viel Nerven kostet manchmal/ ... und jetzt haben wir
4 einen . Platz im- in Zittau im Kindergarten bekommen [...] er hat herVORRagende
5 Erfolge dort . weil . er auch wirklich Deutsch redet Deutsch antwortet/ [...]
6 [Herr F.] naja aber der der Junge- ich hab ja- ich hab- mhhh . [..]s Mann der war SEHR
7 interessiert dass der Junge eben Deutsch lernt/ und hat auch MIR immer ans Herz
8 gelegt ,spreche nur mit ihm Deutsch'/ das hab ich auch gemacht/ und er hat . er hat
9 immer alles verstanden aber hat nie geantwortet/ aber seit er in den Kindergarten geht
10 spricht der Deutsch/ ... UND was mir natuerlich auffaellt er SPRICHT ja das Deutsch
11 OHNE AKZENT / er spricht ein EINWANDFREIES DEUTSCH/ ... aber was mich
12 natuerlich beGEISTert ist dass- dass kein tschechischer Akzent dabei ist/

1 (His daughter) Well, the last one then, of course I tried to speak German with the
2 children ... and now with the fifth one I've managed it somehow, although it causes
3 me a lot of stress sometimes. And now we've got a place at the kindergarten in Zittau.
4 He's doing outstandingly well there, because he's really speaking German, answers in
5 German. [...]
6 (Mr F again) Well yes, her husband was always very keen that the boy should learn
7 German, and he always really went on at me: 'Only speak German with him'. And I
8 did that, and he always understood everything but never answered, but since he's been

9 going to the kindergarten he's been speaking German. And of course what really
10 strikes me is that he speaks German without an accent, he speaks perfect German...
11 what I'm really delighted about is that there's no Czech accent in there.

It becomes clear that Mr F and his daughter perceive the boy's success in German as a great accomplishment that rewards the efforts that
the family has put into his upbringing. The gratification appears to be
derived not only from the economic advantage the boy will gain from
this asset, but also because the 'investment' of Mr F's resistance against
assimilation seems to have paid off. This is possible because the political transformations in Central Europe have abolished the borders that
would previously have made this sort of education impossible (see also
Černá, this volume): ironically, the kindergarten (albeit in the neighbouring state Germany) is now the location for developing rather than
abandoning German, lending institutional support to the family policy that has regained legitimacy in the broader transnational context
of the region. Furthermore, by quoting his son-in-law's plea to 'only
speak German with him [his grandson]', Mr F concedes authorship of
the policy to another, indirectly validating the objectives of his own
longer-term actions.

Mr F, however, seems to gain additional gratification from this as he
notes that the boy speaks German 'without an accent'. This statement
is reiterated twice, but each time it is qualified by a different, stronger
epithet. In line 10, Mr F says the boy speaks 'perfect German', which
is enhanced in line 11 when he says that there is 'no Czech accent'
in the boy's speech. This is a significant statement, as it sets the boy
apart from his Czech compatriots, who would not have achieved this
degree of fluency, but it also resonates with Mr F's own resilience and
his self-categorization as German. His obvious pleasure at this family
success story is then ultimately a vindication of his choice to frame his
experiences not through the concept of *loss* but of *resistance* and his
achievement in retaining his attachment to his first language.

Conclusions

In this chapter, we have tried to show how concepts of time and loss
together function in different ways to shape and organize the narrative
structure of individual life stories. The stories to which we have referred
here share a common theme – the experience of challenges posed to
individual and collective linguistic practices under broadly similar social
and historical conditions – but the conceptualization of this experience

and the way it is used to represent or articulate the relationship between past and present in the narrators' lives show marked differences. In some cases, the past is recalled in terms of discrete, decisive events, while in others it is reconstructed as a more diffuse process; and while all identify language loss as a motif in their biographies, they represent it and compensate for it in different ways. For some it is inevitable and irretrievable, but for others it is temporary, negotiable, contestable and contingent on changing circumstances. This in turn raises questions of agency: there may have been no perceived alternative to accommodation and adaptation, but where defiance and resistance appeared to be available options they may in retrospect be constructed as an emotional investment that has ultimately paid off. Finally, we have seen how loss is not only experienced as occurring *in* time, but also structures people's experience *of* time and provides them with an important narrative resource.

Transcription conventions

In the transcripts of the original German passages, we have used the following conventions:

CAPITALS	indicates relative loudness
/	the end of a tone group or chunk of talk
.	short pause
-	incomplete word or utterance
((xx))	inaudible or indistinct words
((raeuspert sich))	vocal effects such as clearing throat

For ease of reading, we have used normal orthography in the English translations.

Notes

1. The interviews referred to here were conducted as part of a research programme funded by the UK Arts and Humanities Research Council (The German Language and the Future of Europe; see www.glipp.soton.ac.uk).
2. Line references to the transcripts are to the English translations.
3. His account of family language use contains several ambiguities and contradictions, especially in the concept of 'German' itself, but there is no space to discuss these here (see Stevenson and Carl forthcoming).

References

Atkinson, P. and Delamont, S. (eds) (2006) *Narrative Methods*. Volume II, *Narrative Applications* (London: Sage).

Barth, D. (2004) 'Referential defocusing: dangerous topics and language use in language biographies of East Germans', in Franceschini and Miecznikowski (2004), 75–96.

Baynham, M. (2006) 'Narratives in space and time: beyond "backdrop" accounts of narrative orientation', in Atkinson and Delamont (2006), 177–90.

Baynham, M. and de Fina, A. (eds) (2005) *Dislocations/Relocations. Narratives of Displacement* (Manchester: St Jerome).

Blommaert, J. (2005) *Discourse: A Critical Introduction* (Cambridge: Cambridge University Press).

Braudel, F. (1958/1969) 'Histoire et sciences socials: la longue durée', in *Ecrits sur l'Histoire* (Paris: Flammarion), 41–83.

Brockmeier, J. (2000) 'Autobiographical time', *Narrative Inquiry* 10, 51–73.

Brockmeier, J. (2001) 'From the end to the beginning: retrospective teleology in autobiography', in Brockmeier and Carbaugh (2001), 247–80.

Brockmeier, J. and Carbaugh, D. (eds) (2001) *Narrative and Identity: Studies in Autobiography, Self and Culture* (Amsterdam: Benjamins).

Carl, J. and Stevenson, P. (2007) 'Being a German-speaker in Central Europe: language policies and the negotiation of identities', in Fandrych and Salverda (2007), 99–112.

De Fina, A., Schiffrin, D. and Bamberg, M. (eds) (2006) *Discourse and Identity* (Cambridge: Cambridge University Press).

Dickinson, H. and Erben, M. (2006) 'Nostalgia and autobiography: the past in the present', *Auto/Biography* 14, 223–44.

Fandrych, C. and Salverda, R. (eds) (2007) *Standard, Variation und Sprachwandel in germanischen Sprachen* (Tübingen: Narr).

Franceschini, R. and Miecznikowski, J. (eds) (2004) *Leben mit mehreren Sprachen/Vivre avec plusieurs langues: Sprachbiographien/biographies langagières* (Bern: Peter Lang).

Gal, S. (2006) 'Migration, minorities and multilingualism: language ideologies in Europe', in Mar-Molinero and Stevenson (2006), 13–27.

Gal, S. and Woolard, K. (eds) (2001a) *Languages and Publics: The Making of Authority* (Manchester: St Jerome).

Gal, S. and Woolard, K. (2001b) 'Constructing languages and publics: authority and representation', in Gal and Woolard (2001a), 1–12.

Goffman, E. (1981) *Forms of Talk* (Philadelphia: University of Pennsylvania Press).

Helm, J. (ed.) (1967) *Essays on the Verbal and Visual Arts* (Seattle: University of Washington Press).

Labov, W. and Waletzky, J. (1967) 'Narrative analysis: oral versions of personal experience', in Helm (1967), 12–44.

Lefkowitz, D. (2004) *Words and Stones: The Politics of Language and Identity in Israel* (Oxford: Oxford University Press).

Mar-Molinero, C. and Stevenson, P. (eds) (2006) *Language Ideologies, Policies and Practices: Language and the Future of Europe* (Basingstoke: Palgrave Macmillan).

Mishler, E. (2006) 'Narrative and identity: the double arrow of time', in De Fina et al. (2006), 30–47.

Relaño-Pastor, A. and De Fina, A. (2005) 'Contesting social place: narratives of language conflict', in Baynham and De Fina (2005), 36–60.

Rosenwald, G. and Ochberg, R. (1992a) *Storied Lives: The Cultural Politics of Self-Understanding* (New Haven, CT and London: Yale University Press).

Rosenwald, G. and Ochberg, R. (1992b) 'Introduction: life stories, cultural politics, and self-understanding', in Rosenwald and Ochberg (1992a), 1–18.

Schulze, M., John, D. G., Liebscher, G., Siebel-Achenbach, S. and Skidmore, J. M. (eds) (2008) *German Diasporic Experiences: Identity, Migration, and Loss* (Waterloo, Ontario: Wilfrid Laurier University Press).

Schutz, A. and Luckmann, T. (1974) *The Structures of the Lifeworld* (London: Heinemann).

Shaw, C. and Chase, M. (eds) (1989a) *The Imagined Past* (Manchester: Manchester University Press).

Shaw, C. and Chase, M. (1989b) 'The dimensions of nostalgia', in Shaw and Chase (1989a), 2–3.

Stevenson, P. and Carl, J. (2008) 'Language and the negotiation of identities among German-speaking diasporic communities in Central Europe', in Schulze et al. (2008).

Stevenson, P. and Carl, J. (forthcoming) *Language and Social Change in Central Europe: Discourses on Policy, Identity and the German Language* (Edinburgh: Edinburgh University Press).

9
Dialect Use and Discursive Identities of Migrants from the West in Eastern Germany

Jennifer Dailey-O'Cain and Grit Liebscher

This chapter[1] investigates the connection between dialect use, identity and migration in the German context. In particular, we are concerned with the ways in which individuals from western Germany[2] who moved to the eastern German region of Saxony after the fall of the Berlin Wall in 1989 use the Saxon dialect – which they hear on a daily basis in their everyday surroundings – to make various aspects of their selves and others relevant in the interaction. The process of doing this is also one of relating their individual identities to social categories that are present in their environment. In our analysis, we look specifically at the ways in which these people use the local dialect of their new surroundings – often with other linguistic material – in order to draw attention to the relationship between existing social categories and identities. In contrast with many of the other chapters in this volume, this approach can be characterized as a focus on the 'lower-case d discourse' analysis of the German language in interaction, rather than an analysis of the 'capital D discourses' which are concerned with the social and political processes that shape the production of German texts (Gee [1999] 2005; see also Černá, Carl and Stevenson, Horner, this volume).

It is important to note that the social backdrop against which this chapter is cast is a complex one. After the collapse of the GDR in 1989 and the subsequent unification of Germany in 1990, a well-known and large-scale migration took place in which people from eastern Germany moved west in search of work and a new way of life. Less visible, however, was a separate and smaller group of migrants who travelled from west to east, who made the move for personal reasons, such as to take on positions that had not existed in the GDR (in banks or in business), to fill positions left vacant by ousted socialists (in academia or the legal system) or to buy properties unaffordable or unavailable in the west. The social situation in which these people found themselves was fraught with the tension of the attempt to bring together two very different cultural groups, and the sociolinguistic situation reflected these differences. Saxon German in particular bore the brunt of negative language attitudes and became associated for many westerners with negative stereotypes about the east (Dailey-O'Cain 2000). The use of the Saxon dialect by westerners can then suggest a disregard for these negative connotations and index a closeness and appreciation of the local language and its people.

The use of the Saxon dialect by people who have moved to Saxony from the west is therefore not a trivial matter, but one that raises complex questions of identity which involve the social categories of *Wessi* ('western German') and *Ossi* ('eastern German'), as well as possible in-between identities. It is one of these 'more widely known classifications of personhood linked to speech' (Agha 2007: 136) based on a link between language use and identity. Since the Saxon dialect plays such a central role in the construction of eastern and western German identities, it is an important aspect of the migrants' identity negotiation. These identities are viewed not as a matter of who counts as a 'real German' (cf. Schneider, this volume), but as different ways of being German. By looking at issues of identity and dialect use within a still volatile political climate like post-unification Germany, we hope to shed light on the role that dialect use can play in identity construction in situations of migration in central Europe.

The terms 'migrant' and 'migration' are used primarily in the fields of sociology and geography, where they refer to the movement of people both within (Stillwell and Congdon 1991) and across political borders (Toro-Morn und Alicea 2004). They are also common in the sociolinguistic research about post-unification Germany (for example, Grosskopf et al. 1996), where this ambiguity seems to be both intentional and desirable, since eastern and western identities were once linked to different national identities and are even today still tied to socio-culturally distinct regions. Generally, however, one can speak of migration as occurring when people move from one place to another, and it is in this respect that we situate our work within the current research on migration and national identity in central Europe (for example, Triandafyllidou 2006; Krzyżanowski and Wodak 2008) despite the fact that it is not different languages our migrants encounter but different varieties of the same language. Our contribution to these migration studies is to examine belonging and identity using both discourse-analytic and sociolinguistic approaches to the study of migration (cf. Wodak 2006). In line with Krzyżanowski and Wodak (2008: 96), we examine 'relevant aspects of migrant identities by analysing them from the point of view of their construction in/through discourse, that is, the main locus of reformulations and negotiations of migrant identifications'. For Krzyżanowski and Wodak and in this chapter, the focus is on migration as the emic perspective of a person or family as it is contained within migration as a larger socio-political phenomenon.

Theory and methodology

We conceive of identity here as having two separate aspects. The first is personal identity (Ricker 2000: 9), which is built on the life history of each individual. This form of identity consists of biographical facts about people, such as where they have lived, who their family and friends are and their exposure to different linguistic environments. This is relevant in this chapter in the sense that these western German migrants' move to eastern Germany necessarily has an impact on their personal identity, and this includes a confrontation with a new and particularly stigmatized dialect. Another more important aspect of our analysis, however, is discursive identity, which for us is tied to the question of what the migrants do with the Saxon dialect as a new linguistic resource. We analyse this kind of identity as it is constructed in interaction rather than as a series of fixed categories (see Antaki and Widdicombe 1998; Pavlenko and Blackledge 2004; Meinhof and Galasiński 2005; Černá, this volume). While we do observe the relationship between the Saxon dialect and identity, it is clear that there is no one-to-one relationship between those linguistic resources and different identities (Meinhof and Galasiński 2005: 16). Instead, we refer to the process by which interactants make identities relevant as *positioning* (Harré and van Langenhove 1991; van Langenhove and Harré 1993; Wolf 1999), which we define as the ways in which interactants index their own and others' relationships to roles and social categories by means of interactive resources known as *contextualization cues* (Gumperz 1982: 31). We see positioning as 'a dynamic alternative to the more static concept of role' (Harré and van Langenhove 1991: 393), because these category memberships are not permanent, but highly context-dependent, and can even change from one moment to the next for a single individual. Agha refers to such uses of linguistic resources in interaction as 'denotational footing, [which] is merely a special case of the more general phenomenon of interactional role alignment' (2007: 134).

It is through positioning, then, that social categories are evoked and distinctions between different category memberships are made.[3]

While positioning is a natural and unavoidable process in any conversation, it is perhaps particularly important to view identity in this way in situations of migration, since linguistic signs are renegotiated through the presence of heterogeneity of language and culture in this 'third space' (Kramsch 1999: 46–8, following Bhabha 1994). This also means that these migrants may see themselves as fitting into different social categories depending on aspects of the interactional situation. While social categories may be pre-existing in these individuals' cultural contexts, these categories alone do not constitute identities in and of themselves, as the individuals must first make the categories relevant in the interaction (cf. McKinlay and Dunnett 1998), and they do this in our case through the use of the Saxon dialect and other contextualization cues. The Saxon dialect plays such an important role in this identity construction because it is strongly associated not only with the local community of Saxony, but also with East Germany as a whole,[4] which is especially pertinent when it comes to speakers who can draw on multiple linguistic resources for identity construction, including a variety of standard German, the dialect of their origin, and Saxon as the dialect of the place to which they migrated. In that sense, linguistic forms produced in the Saxon dialect in the present evoke a relationship to the East German past, similar to the way Carl and Stevenson (this volume) connect time, language and place in the narratives of ethnic Germans in Eastern Europe.

This chapter draws on data from a larger project which included 16 families and individuals, including both adults and children, whom we worked with from 2000 to 2003. All the participants had moved from western Germany to the eastern German region of Saxony after the fall of the Berlin Wall, and the data consists of casual, video- or audiotaped conversations between these families or individuals and the two fieldworkers (the authors of this chapter), usually over a meal. We seek to answer three questions: *To what extent* do migrants from western Germany to Saxony use Saxon German? *How and why* do they do this? *What impact* does this have on their identity? Because we view identity as discursively constructed, the primary way in which we investigate these questions is through a systematic qualitative discourse analysis of the ways in which participants use the Saxon dialect as a resource in positioning themselves and others. The two types of positioning we identify in this chapter consist of *narrative* positioning, that is, formulating one's identity as 'I am X' and stating explicitly how one sees oneself and hopes to be seen by others, and *formulaic* positioning, by which conversation participants formulate their identities through the use of contextualization cues. Additionally, it is also relevant to take into account whether the speaker is the *author* or the *animator* of the words uttered (Goffman 1974), by which we mean a distinction between whether the speaker is giving voice to her own ideas, or 'animating' the ideas of others (see also Carl and Stevenson, this volume). If we link this distinction to our understanding of identity construction, it seems that expressing something as the author positions the speaker with a stronger authority[5] than speaking through the voice of another. The voice of the author thus goes along with a stronger claim or stance to the particular identity category indexed by the contextualization cues. In contrast, formulating something as the animator shows a display of knowledge but no claim to the identity category associated with that knowledge.

These constructivist, discourse analytical methods of analysis are necessary to answer our *how* and *why* research questions, but additional, more quantitative methods are needed in order to answer the *to what extent* questions. While there has traditionally been a divide in sociolinguistics between those methods that are constructivist in orientation and those that are positivist or post-positivist in orientation, we reject this and instead turn to the mixed methodologies that have been emerging within other social sciences such as psychology and educational research (for example, Newman et al. 1998; Tashakkori and Teddlie 1998; Todd et al. 2004). These mixed methods are *pragmatist* in orientation, regarding the research question as paramount, and choose from available analytical techniques based solely on what the researcher seeks to discover. By making use of mixed methods, we can draw on the strengths of both qualitative and quantitative analytical techniques, not only combining depth with breadth, but also allowing the results of each analysis to inform the other so as to provide a combination of detail and generalizability (cf. Nekvapil and Sherman, this volume).

The quantitative methodology that we draw on falls within the tradition of variationist sociolinguistics (for example, Milroy and Gordon 2003). In the variationist tradition, identity is seen as a pattern of choice among variants (Eckert 2000; Kiesling 2005), and a social group which predominantly uses one particular variant or set of variants is often interpreted as adopting the identity associated with that variant or set of variants. In order to avoid the fixed interpretation of identity that can result from such a one-to-one correspondence between identity and linguistic variables, however, we instead view each occurrence of each variable as a formulaic positioning, and only one of several potential ways in which the participant can position himself. Shifting between positionings becomes possible because speakers have access to other linguistic resources beyond the Saxon dialect with which to position themselves, such as standard German and their own dialect of origin, among other linguistic material. We view variation in these positionings not as multiple warring identities among which the most frequent one eventually prevails, but as the participant exploiting variation to construct the identity that is relevant in each particular circumstance. Our method of analysis therefore has four steps: first, examining our corpus of data with a view to identifying what positioning is occurring in the talk whenever the Saxon dialect is used; second, identifying typical examples of the different things that can happen and doing an in-depth analysis of the ways in which Saxon dialect and other contextualization cues are used to accomplish this positioning within these examples; third, coding occurrences of a set of linguistic variables in conversational data taken from the same participants found in the examples we used for our qualitative analysis; and fourth, calculating the percentage of Saxon and standard variants used for each variable in that second data set, in order to learn how frequently these individuals use Saxon German dialect in general. We refer to such a methodology as a *sequential mixed model* (cf. Tashakkori and Teddlie 1998) since the results of the qualitative analysis directly inform the quantitative analysis.

Usefully for the sociolinguist, the Saxon dialect is 'easily described (and recognized) by a small number of phonological features' (Auer et al. 1998: 170), and the variables we analyse in steps three and four are taken from the nine vocalic and three consonantal variables, also used in previous work done by Auer et al. (1998) and Barden and Grosskopf (1998) on native Saxon migrants to western Germany. However, two of the variables have been deleted from our analysis (/CH/ and /P,T,K/) because the Saxon variants also exist in dialects that some of our participants speak as their native dialects. Table 9.1 shows the set of variables we have used.

We coded every occurrence of each variable as to whether the variety spoken was Saxon, standard or the participant's native dialect, although there were no occurrences which fell into the third category, thus reducing this to a binary variable. We also coded each occurrence for whether

Table 9.1   Phonological variables

/A:/	/E:/	/Ü:/	/Ü/	/O:/	/U:/	/OI/	/AI/	/AU/	/G/
'wahr'	'leben'	'üben'	'Hütte'	'bloss'	'absolut'	'Freund'	'kein'	'auch'	'Wagen'

the speaker was acting as *author* or as *animator* (Goffman 1981). Though this distinction is by no means unproblematic (since ambiguities may arise and speakers can be assigned to these categories by other conversationalists), we find that this distinction alerts us to the fact that not all uses of Saxon position the speaker *as* a Saxon, since the use as animator clearly does not. This is relevant because it has an impact on the speaker's identity construction. If a speaker is acting as animator, for example if a use of the Saxon dialect is an imitation of native Saxons, the speaker does not lay claim to a self-identification as a Saxon. If, however, a speaker is acting as author, that is, 'owning' her or his dialect use, the speaker *is* laying that claim. We coded those cases as animator which suggest that the speaker clearly indicated quoting or acting out somebody, either through verbal or non-verbal cues. Other occurrences were then quantified in order to determine whether the occurrence in the example reflected the overall use of Saxon as author or animator by the same speaker. Whenever possible, at least 30 variants of each variable were coded for each individual participant, for a total of 1,183 occurrences of all variables.

Analysis

The analysis section is structured such that the qualitative analysis of each example is immediately contrasted with quantitative results with regards to the language use of speakers in the example. This allows us to juxtapose contextualized, possibly one-time claims to identity in the form of positioning with repeated language behaviour as expressions of identity observed through quantitative analysis. Example 1 contains a fairly straightforward case of what we have termed narrative positioning. The situation is one of the migrant Walter[6] sitting down with the two fieldworkers for cake and coffee. The conversation is about the various types of cake available.

Example 1 Saxon egg cake[7]

1 W: also des scheint irgendwie
         so that seems somehow
2 JD: [das is
         [*that's*
         [
3 W: [das ist- und das is
         [*that's- and that's*

4 eierschecke (.) das erkenne selbst ich als zugereister
   Saxon egg cake (.) even I as a migrant[8] recognize that
5 JD/GL: {laughter}

In line 4, Walter uses a narrative positioning, formulated as *das erkenne selbst ich als Zugereister* ('even I as a migrant recognize that'), to show how he sees himself, as well as how he wants to be seen by the fieldworkers, JD and GL. This is a deliberate self-positioning as a migrant that carves out for Walter a sort of third space between the two constructed categories of western German and eastern German. In line 5, then, the resulting laughter from the fieldworkers is a comment on this identification.

This example tells us that Walter readily associates a specific kind of cake (*Eierschecke* or Saxon egg cake) with the place where he lives now, though it is unclear whether the specific reference is the town in Saxony, Saxony itself or eastern Germany in general. For Walter, the vocabulary thus carries the 'sense' (in Vygotskian terms (1997)) of the local community. Walter uses this specifically local vocabulary in a way that positions him as sufficiently knowledgeable about the local culture to use its vocabulary, but at the same time he formulates himself as a 'Zugereister'. This means that he claims to be a special kind of local and prides himself in acquiring local knowledge. This takes him further away from constructing his identity as non-local or in terms of his origins, and instead he constructs his identity in terms of a third space that is neither an eastern nor a western German in this example. In supplementing this qualitative analysis with a quantitative variationist analysis, we can now analyse whether this kind of third space positioning is typical for Walter in terms of his overall dialect use, including the extent to which he uses Saxon German in general. In order to investigate this, we took a total of 309 tokens of all the potentially Saxon German variables, and calculated the percentage of the time that he used standard German and the percentage of the time he used Saxon German. In distinguishing which of the tokens were of him as animator and which were of him as author, it turned out that all of the tokens were used from the perspective of the author. The results in terms of his dialect use were equally simple: he used standard German 100 per cent of the time. This finding corresponds with his positioning in example 1, in that the use of standard German is neither a claim to a Saxon identity nor an identity indicative of a speaker of a western German variety, but rather indexes again a third space in which he constructs a pan-German identity for himself.

Example 2 contains both narrative and formulaic positioning. In this interaction between the fieldworkers JD and GL and participants Bernd and Silke, JD asks an explicit question about their self-identification.

Example 2 Dresden

1 JD: und wenn ihr in (.) ZÜRICH seid (.) und- und jemand fragt wo
       and when you're in (.) ZURICH (.) and- and somebody asks where
2   kommt ihr HER (.) was sagt ihr dann
       you're FROM (.) what do you say then
3 B: DRESden (standard)
       DRESden
4 S: DRÄZSCHden (dialect)
       DRESden
5 JD: {laughter}

The question posed in lines 1–2 is a deliberate request for a narrative positioning – that is, a request for the participants to tell the fieldworkers how they perceive themselves and wish to be perceived by others. In fact, with no hesitation in line 3, the migrant Bernd uses narrative positioning to identify himself as being from Dresden, the Saxon city where he now lives. In line 4, his wife Silke repeats his narrative positioning, but at the same time also displays a formulaic positioning by using a version of the local dialect as a contextualization cue. In doing this, she personalizes the answer to the question about where they are from by using the dialect to show a personal stance in terms of her closeness to the place. While it may look like she is simply mimicking the locals (as animator)[9] and therefore positioning herself as sufficiently knowledgeable about but separate from them, she may instead have meant to position herself as the author, that is, as somebody who can be fully credited with using the local dialect. The laughter in line 5, however, seems to indicate that this is not how she is being understood or positioned. Instead, the laughter shows that her use of the dialect is being acknowledged and appreciated by the fieldworker JD as a creative and (for Silke) unusual form of language use worth commenting on. JD positions Silke as a non-local who nevertheless is able to play with and display her knowledge of the local dialect.

Though JD can position Silke as the non-local (that is, the animator) or the local (the author), the question is still open as to how Silke's use of the dialect corresponds to her overall use of Saxon as author or as animator. It is possible, then, for a variationist analysis to accomplish two things with respect to Bernd and Silke: first, it can tell us

Table 9.2 Bernd and Silke's usage of Saxon and standard German

Bernd		Silke	
Saxon	Standard	Saxon	standard
6.6% (n = 20)	93.4% (n = 282)	9.3% (n = 27)	90.7% (n = 264)

to what extent their positionings in this example are consistent with their overall dialect use; and second, it can help us to contextualize JD's interpretation of Silke's utterance as animator as an exception or as something Silke does regularly.

Table 9.2 shows the overall use of both Saxon and standard German by Bernd and Silke. In a total of 302 tokens, Bernd used Saxon German 6.6 per cent of the time and standard German 93.4 per cent of the time, and only once was he clearly the animator in the use of a Saxon variant. Similarly, in a total of 291 tokens, Silke used Saxon German 9.3 per cent of the time and standard German 90.7 per cent of the time. In the stretch of talk analysed for Silke's use of these variables, no instance of animator use could be detected. With respect to the variable /E:/ in particular, she only used the Saxon variant once, indicating that that particular usage is quite rare for her. This tilts the interpretation of her linguistic behaviour in line 4 as being the animator of the Saxon pronunciation of 'Dresden' rather than as the author. However, it is clear from the fact that both Bernd and Silke display some use of the Saxon dialect that they construct their identity, in part, as Saxon, whether this use is intentional or not. This corresponds, in a way, to how they present themselves through their respective narrative positionings in example 2.

Example 3 is far more complex. The situation is one in which the nine-year-old migrant Marie is discussing her school classes with the two fieldworkers, in the presence of her father, Werner.

Example 3 Extra Practice

1 M: mathe, deutsch, sport, kunst, englisch (...) äh {laughter}
      maths, German, sports, art, English (...) uh {laughter}
2   fördern {Saxon}
      extra practice
3 GL: was war das?
      what was that?
4 M: fördern {Saxon}
      extra practice

5 GL: [hm (X)
     [
6 W: [jetzt, sag, erklär das mal
      [*now, explain what that is*
7 JD: füttern {standard}
      feeding
8 W: [nein nein·
     [*no no*
     [
9 M: [FöRDERN {standard}
     [*EXTRA PRACTICE*
10 W: erklär ma was das is
      explain what that is
11 M: also wenn man (.) wenn man noch was nachholn muss oder so (.)
      when you (.) when you have to catch up on something or something
12   dann muss man in fördern {standard} gehn (.) oder wenn man zu
      (.) then you have to go to extra practice (.) or when you're bad
13   schlecht is dann kann ma alles dort noch lern
      then you can still learn everything there
14 JD:ach so
      oh
15 GL: mhm
16 W: is ein förderkurs {standard}
      it's a practice course
17 M: hm
18 W: die Sachsn die schluckn das immer mit, fördern {Saxon} ja
      Saxons always swallow it, extra practice yeah
19   {laughter}
20 W: fördern {Saxon} (.) s kann mer leicht verwechsln mit füttern
      extra practice (.) it's easy to confuse that with feeding
21   {laughter}
22 W: da könn mer heute (X) keine scherze über sachsn machn, s sitzt
      we can't make any (X) jokes about Saxons today, there's one
23   nämich eine am tisch
      sitting at the table
24   {laughter}
25 JD: und was bist du? bist du SACHSE? (.) oder bist du (.) schwabe
      and what are you? are you a Saxon? (.) or are you (.) a Swabian
26 M: sachse
      a Saxon

In line 2, when Marie says the word *fördern* ('practice'), she uses the Saxon pronunciation, which can be interpreted as a formulaic positioning that ascribes to her a Saxon identity. In line 3, when the fieldworker GL asks for clarification of the term, Marie does not switch to standard German, but repeats the term using the Saxon pronunciation, reinforcing the original formulaic positioning and thereby also positioning GL as someone who is able to understand the Saxon dialect. In line 10, Marie's father asks her to explain what the course is about, and the fieldworker JD says what word she had heard, *füttern* ('feeding'). In response, Marie repeats the term again, this time not only more loudly, but also with a standard pronunciation. Through this new formulaic positioning, she demonstrates her ability to code-switch, as well as her ability to take up different identities through her positioning herself as a non-Saxon this time. Marie also reinforces this new positioning in line 12 by repeating the standard pronunciation as part of her explanation of what the course is, and in line 16, her father gives a further explanation, using a standard pronunciation for *fördern* and positioning himself as a non-Saxon as well.

In line 18, Werner explains the Saxon pronunciation of the word *fördern* by saying that the Saxons 'swallow' the word. But through the formulaic positioning of referring to the local group as *die Sachsen, die* ('the Saxons, they'), he not only excludes himself from that group, but includes his daughter Marie, as she is the one who used the 'swallowing' pronunciation only moments earlier. This use of the demonstrative pronoun *die* is therefore a formulaic positioning not only of himself, but also simultaneously of Marie. In lines 18 and 20, Werner then goes on to use the Saxon pronunciation of the term, but only as animator, that is, only in imitation of Saxons. This formulaic positioning is therefore not of himself *as* a Saxon, but one of acting the part of a Saxon in order to make a point. This positioning is reinforced through the laughter by the group in lines 19 and 21; while no one laughed when Marie used that pronunciation, Werner's use of it does provoke laughter.

In line 22, Werner goes on to state that they can't make any jokes about Saxons today, which suggests that they usually can. An explanation for the unusual circumstances that change their ordinary joke-making abilities is then given: there's one sitting at the table. Since this can only be a Saxon who isn't normally at the table, it's clear that he can only mean the fieldworker GL, who grew up in Saxony. Through this formulaic positioning, Werner positions GL as a Saxon, but also positions himself and his daughter Marie as non-Saxon. This marks a shift in identity for Marie, who was positioned by her father as Saxon only a few lines earlier. Finally, the fieldworker JD explicitly asks Marie whether she considers herself a Saxon or a Swabian, which is the region of western Germany where she was born. Like the question asked in example 2, this is a question that explicitly asks the participant to formulate her response as a narrative positioning, and Marie complies, positioning herself as a Saxon. Marie does not see the Saxon part of her identity as a loss of some prior Swabianness (cf. Carl and Stevenson, this volume), but instead embraces it wholeheartedly. It is relevant to note here, though, that it was JD who presented only two categorical options, and we do not know how Marie might have positioned herself if there had also been a third option similar to Walter's 'third space' in example 1.

As with Walter, Bernd and Silke in examples 1 and 2, though, a variationist analysis can serve to show to what extent the self- and other-positionings found in this example are consistent with their overall language use. Table 9.3 shows the overall use of both Saxon and standard German by Werner and by Marie.

In a total of 343 tokens (one as animator), Werner uses Saxon German 15.5 per cent of the time, and standard German 84.5 per cent of the time. This is a higher percentage of Saxon forms than not only Walter, who did not use Saxon German at all, but also than Bernd and Silke, and is also consistent with Werner's positioning of himself in example 3 as a not-quite-Saxon who is nonetheless very integrated into his Saxon environment and knowledgeable about the Saxon dialect. Marie, on the other hand, uses more Saxon German overall than any of the other speakers, including her father, using Saxon variants 35.6 per cent of the time and standard variants 64.4 per cent of the time in a total of 247 tokens. While we do not have Saxon-born participants of Marie's age for comparison, it seems likely that this usage is similar to locals of her own age, and is therefore consistent with Marie's frequent positioning of herself as a 'real' Saxon throughout example 3.

Table 9.3   Werner and Marie's usage of Saxon and standard German

Werner		Marie	
Saxon	Standard	Saxon	standard
15.5% (n = 53)	84.5% (n = 290)	35.6% (n = 88)	64.4% (n = 159)

Conclusions

In this chapter, we have identified parallels between the findings of the qualitative analysis and the findings of the quantitative analysis. In example 1, for instance, we have Walter, who positions himself not as an eastern or as a western German, but in terms of a third space. This is, in turn, reflected in his overall dialect use as well, since he exclusively uses standard German variants of the series of variables we examined for potential use of Saxon German. This complete absence of Saxon German phonology marks him as a non-Saxon, but not necessarily as a western German, which is completely consistent with the third space positioning. With Bernd and Silke (example 2), then, we have a similar sort of resonance between qualitative and quantitative data. Both identify themselves through narrative positioning as now coming 'from Dresden', something that is also reflected in both participants' occasional use of the Saxon dialect variants as investigated by the quantitative analysis. However, we have also suggested, based on the quantitative analysis, that Silke's use of some form of Saxon German in her pronunciation of the word 'Dresden' is that of the animator, rather than the author, which would mean that she positions herself outside of the group of Saxons, displaying her knowledge of Saxon dialect only by mimicking them.

Finally, we have Werner and his daughter Marie, whose positionings in example 3 often shift from one moment to the next, suggesting that their identities are complex and quite context-dependent. Werner positions himself as knowledgeable enough about Saxon German to use it, but always as something other than an actual Saxon. Marie, on the other hand, is positioned by her father alternately as a Saxon and as a non-Saxon, but she consistently positions herself as a Saxon, except when she steps briefly out of that mode to use the standard pronunciation of a word for clarification for one of her interlocutors. The quantitative analysis reflects these differences as well: although Werner uses more Saxon German than both Bernd and Silke, he still uses less than his daughter Marie, who is more comparable to Saxon-born children in her use of dialect and standard variants. While it seems important to mention that one cannot always expect such resonance between the use of dialect as positioning in individual stretches of talk and the overall use of dialect by particular speakers, it is striking that it seems to be present here. The use of a quantitative analysis as a supplement to a qualitative analysis seems to have borne fruit.

We also find that both kinds of positioning – narrative and formulaic – serve to construct complex identities in interaction. In examples 1 and 2, the three participants construct their identities through the use of narrative positioning, that is, by stating outright how they see themselves and wish to be seen. In example 2, however, there is an additional layer of a formulaic positioning in which Silke serves as the animator of a Saxon voice. Example 3 is a complex mosaic of narrative and formulaic positionings in which the Saxon dialect is used alternately by Marie to position herself as a Saxon and as a non-Saxon, and by Werner as animator to position himself as someone who is not quite Saxon but still knowledgeable enough to use the dialect. We also find, especially in example 3, that participants are responsive to each other's formulaic positionings and use them to position themselves and others.

Overall, the findings about language use based on qualitative discursive analysis was largely confirmed through and informed by quantitative analysis. For example, when we learn from a quantitative analysis that Silke's use of the Saxon variant of the /E:/ variable is quite infrequent, it helps us interpret her use of Saxon German in example 2 as positioning her as animator rather than speaking with her own Saxon voice. Similarly, the qualitative analysis can inform the quantitative analysis if we take a constructivist perspective on the quantitative analysis as well, and see variability not as a conflict between two incompatible identities, but as different positionings that are, on the one hand, highly mutable and context-dependent, and, on the other hand, still generalizable to present an overall picture of dialect use in each individual speaker. Using this kind of mixed methodology has provided us with a tool to uncover the complexities of identity, dialect use, and migration among western Germans migrating to Saxony in eastern Germany.

This combination of discourse-analytic and sociolinguistic approaches to the study of migration has provided us with insights into the intricacies of negotiating belonging and identification. Dialect, as we have argued, is used as a resource to position self and others along the lines of group boundaries determined by dialect boundaries that are associated with groups and nations. Different levels of identification are achieved through different kinds of narrative and formulaic positioning. The importance of paying attention to these micro-discursive processes became especially evident when analysing the use of the dialect as an author or an animator. Our analysis has shown that the new variety, Saxon, has become part of the migrants' lives and of their personal identities in the sense that they must all deal with it in some way.

On the one hand, the use of Saxon can be considered something which these migrants have gained in that they have more linguistic resources than they had prior to their migration. On the other hand, it may also be seen as a burden, in that the use (or non-use) of Saxon necessarily positions the speakers within their new environment. We conclude with the observation that language and, in particular, dialect use is an important tool in the construction of identities not only in this German context but potentially in situations of migration in general.

Notes

1. This chapter forms part of a larger project entitled '(Inter)acting identities in dialect and discourse: migrant western Germans in eastern Germany', carried out by the authors and funded in 2003 by the Social Sciences and Humanities Research Council of Canada (File number: 410-2003-0378). We are also grateful for funding from the University of Alberta and the University of Waterloo.
2. In this chapter, the terms 'East Germany' and 'West Germany' refer to the two separate countries prior to 3 October 1990, the date of unification. The term German Democratic Republic (GDR) refers to East Germany as a political unit until 1989. The terms 'eastern Germany' and 'western Germany' refer to the same geographic territory subsequent to unification. 'Eastern German' and 'western German' are analytic categories for anything associated with one or the other territory. These terms are also used in reference to people who position themselves as eastern or western German.
3. While this chapter explores the way this is accomplished through the use of dialect, this is something which is also commonly accomplished by means of deixis (cf. Liebscher and Dailey-O'Cain 2007; Černá, this volume).
4. It is often believed by people unfamiliar with the eastern German dialects that Saxon German was spoken throughout East Germany (cf. Dailey-O'Cain 1997).
5. 'Authority' is meant here in the sense that Heritage and Raymond (2005) use it, that is to say in terms of the expressed distance of the speaker to claims of authorship of knowledge or, in our case, of categories of identity.
6. Names and certain other identifying details have been changed to protect participants' identities.
7. Transcription conventions are as follows: German utterances are in normal type and English translations follow in italics. The transcript differs from usual orthographic spelling; for example, capitalization in the transcript is used to mark loudness. Conversational overlap is indicated with square brackets. Pauses lasting a beat (.) or two (..) are indicated as shown; longer pauses are indicated in seconds. Laughter and parts deleted to save space are written in ((double brackets)), and = equals signs = are used to indicate a continuation between previous and following lines of talk.
8. A literal translation of *Zugereister* is 'a person who moved to a new place'. We use the translation of 'migrant' here in order to keep the translation to a single English word, as well as to allude to the internal migration within Germany.
9. In that sense, it could be seen as an instance of Rampton's (2005) crossing.

References

Agha, A. (2007) *Language and Social Relations* (Cambridge: Cambridge University Press).

Antaki, C. and Widdicombe, S. (eds) (1998) *Identities in Talk* (London: Sage).

Auer, P. (ed.) (2007) *Style and Social Identities: Alternative Approaches to Linguistic Heterogeneity* (Amsterdam and New York: de Gruyter).

Auer, P., Barden, B. and Grosskopf, B. (1998) 'Subjective and objective parameters determining "salience" in long-term dialect accommodation', *Journal of Sociolinguistics* 2(2), 163–87.

Barden, B. and Grosskopf, B. (1998) *Sprachliche Akkommodation und soziale Integration: sächsische Übersiedler und Übersiedlerinnen im rhein-/moselfränkischen und alemannischen Sprachraum* (Tübingen: Niemeyer).

Bhabha, H. K. (1994) *The Location of Culture* (London: Routledge).

Caldas-Coulthard, C. R. and Iedema, R. (eds) (2008) *Identity Trouble. Critical Discourse and Contested Identities* (Basingstoke: Palgrave Macmillan).

Coupland, N. J., Nussbaum, F. and Grossman, A. (eds) (1993) *Discourse and Lifespan Identity* (London: Sage).

Dailey-O'Cain, J. (1997) 'Geographic and Socio-Political Influences on Language Ideology and Attitudes Toward Language Variation in Post-Unification Germany', unpublished PhD dissertation, University of Michigan.

Dailey-O'Cain, J. (2000) 'Competing language ideologies in post-unification Germany: when east meets west', in Stevenson and Theobald (2000), 248–66.

Delanty, G. and Kumar, K. (eds) (2006) *The Sage Handbook of Nations and Nationalism* (London: Sage).

Eckert, P. (2000) *Linguistic Variation as Social Practice* (Oxford: Blackwell).

Gee, J.P. [1999] (2005) *An Introduction to Discourse Analysis: Theory and Method* (London: Routledge).

Goffman, E. (1974) *Frame analysis* (New York: Harper & Row).

Goffman, E. (1981) *Forms of Talk* (Philadelphia: University of Pennsylvania Press).

Grosskopf, B., Barden, B. and Auer, P. (1996) 'Sprachliche Anpassung und soziale Haltung: zur verstehenden Soziolinguistik der innerdeutschen Migration', *Folia Linguistica* 30(3–4), 359–84.

Gumperz, J. J. (1982) *Discourse Strategies (Studies in Interactional Sociolinguistics 1)* (Cambridge: Cambridge University Press).

Harré, R. and van Langenhove, L. (1991) 'Varieties of positioning', *Journal for the Theory of Social Behaviour* 21, 393–407.

Heritage, J. and Raymond, G. (2005) 'The terms of agreement: indexing epistemic authority and subordination in talk-in-interaction', *Social Psychology Quarterly* 68 (1), 15–38.

Kiesling, S. (2005) 'Variation, stance, and style: word-final -er, high rising tone, and ethnicity in Australian English', in *English World Wide* 26, 1–44.

Kramsch, C. (1999) 'Thirdness: the intercultural stance', in Verstergaards (1999), 41–58.

Krzyżanowski, M. and Wodak, R. (2008) 'Multiple identities, migration and belonging: "voices of migrants"', in Caldas-Coulthard and Iedema (2008), 95–119.

Liebscher, G. and Dailey-O'Cain, J. (2007) 'Variability, identity and positioning in interactive knowledge displays', in Auer (2007), 247–78.

McKinlay, A. and Dunnett, A. (1998) 'How gun-owners accomplish being deadly average', in Antaki and Widdicombe (1998), 34–51.

Meinhof, U. and Galasiński, D. (eds) (2005) *The Language of Belonging* (Basingstoke: Palgrave Macmillan).

Milroy, L. and Gordon, M. (2003) *Sociolinguistics: Method and Interpretation* (Oxford: Blackwell).

Newman, I., Benz, C. R. and Ridenour, C. (1998) *Qualitative-Quantitative Research Methodology: Exploring the Interactive Continuum* (Carbondale, IL: Southern Illinois University Press).

Pavlenko, A. and Blackledge, A. (eds) (2004) *Negotiation of Identities in Multilingual Contexts* (Clevedon: Multilingual Matters).

Rampton, B. (2005) *Crossing: Language and Ethnicity among Adolescents* (Manchester: St Jerome).

Ricker, K. (2000) *Migration, Sprache, und Identität: Eine biographieanalytische Studie zu Migrationsprozessen von Französinnen in Deutschland* (Bremen: Donat Verlag).

Stevenson, P. and Theobald, J. (eds) (2000) *Relocating Germanness: Discursive Disunity in Unified Germany* (Basingstoke and New York: Macmillan and St. Martin's Press).

Stillwell, J. and Congdon, P. (eds) (1991) *Migration Models: Macro and Micro Approaches* (London and New York: Belhaven).

Tashakkori, A. and Teddlie, C. (1998) *Mixed Methodology: Combining Qualitative and Quantitative Approaches* (London: Sage).

Todd, Z. B. N., McKeown, S. and Clarke, D. D. (2004) *Mixing Methods in Psychology: The Integration of Qualitative and Quantitative Methods in Theory and Practice* (Hove and New York: Psychology Press).

Toro-Morn, M. I. and Alicea, M. (eds) (2004) *Migration and Immigration: A Global View* (Westport, CT: Greenwood).

Triandafyllidou, A. (2006) 'Nations, migrants and transnational identifications: an interactive approach to nationalism', in Delanty and Kumar (2006), 285–94.

van Langenhove, L. and Harré, R. (1993) 'Positioning and autobiography: Telling your life', in Coupland, Nussbaum and Grossman (1993), 81–99.

Verstergaards, T. (ed.) (1999) *Language, Culture and Identity* (Aalborg: Aalborg University Press).

Vygotsky, L. (1997) *Thought and Language*, trans. and ed. J. Preston (Cambridge and New York: Cambridge University Press).

Wodak, R. (2006) 'Discourse-analytic and socio-linguistic approaches to the study of nation(alism)', in Delanty and Kumar (2006), 104–17.

Wolf, R (1999) 'Soziale Positionierung im Gespräch', *Deutsche Sprache* 1, 69–94.

10
¿Hablemos el mismo idioma?[1] Salsa, Multilingualism and National Monolingual Ideology

Britta Schneider

Introduction

Nationalist language epistemology that conceives of the relationship of culture, space and language in a one-dimensional way has a reasonably long and stable tradition in Western societies (Wimmer and Schiller 2002); thus it comes as no surprise that in Central Europe public discourses on language and the integration of migrants are deeply influenced by nationalist frameworks. However, in Germany and elsewhere, cultural phenomena have arisen that are difficult to capture within such national frameworks of thought. This is not only true for national literature canons, as Cooper (this volume) shows, there are also many types of music culture, most of which are popular in Germany, that form traditions that have never been especially associated with particular nation-states. Hip-hop, house music and Salsa belong to the better-known of these transnational music traditions. The notion of transnationalism not only tries to describe phenomena that cross national borders but refers to cultural practices that transcend territories and at the same time question epistemological frameworks that see the nation, its culture, its territory and its borders as a given point of departure for social research (see Pietrobruno 2006: chapter 1; also Hannerz 1996; Glick Schiller et al. 1997; Pries 2001; Pennycook 2007: chapter 3).

In this chapter, linguistic identities and language ideologies of a transnational 'community of practice' (CofP) in Germany are related to contemporary German discourses on language and integration. Eckert and McConnell-Ginet (1998: 490) have defined a CofP as

an aggregate of people who come together around mutual engage-
ments in some common endeavour. Ways of doing things, ways of
talking, beliefs, values, power relations – in short, practices – emerge
in the course of their joint activity around that endeavour.

In studying language in transnational settings, the concept of the community of practice is useful in order to overcome essentialist concepts
such as ethnic or national groups, as membership in a community of
this order is defined by cultural practice and not by descent (for an
introduction to the concept see, for example, Holmes and Meyerhoff
1999). The community taken as an example here is based on Salsa, a
transnational cultural phenomenon based on music and dance found
worldwide as well as in most German cities. How do language practices and patterns of linguistic identification within a German, but at
the same time transnational, context contrast with national mainstream
language ideologies? And what can we learn from that with regards to
the role of German as a national language and the development of new
patterns of exclusion in an age of multilingualism and globalization?

Approaches to multilingualism in public discourses of Germany

German discourses concerning migration, integration and language are
characterized by comparatively strong monolingual tendencies. The
causes of this have to be seen in the historical development of Germany.
The concept of an ethnic *Volk* nation was the ideological basis for the
formation of the state, thus the political ideology of the *jus sanguinis* pre-
vailed until 2000 (Koopmans 2001). Here, where *Volk* is understood as
a 'biologically' related group of people, the role of language has always
been salient. Language, in the historical context of Germany, served as
the prime symbol and affirmation of the proclaimed organic entity (see
Blommaert and Verschueren 1998: 195; Barbour and Carmichael 2000).
Thus, monolingual, nationalist tendencies are easy to find at both the
policy level and the level of public discourse (see also Stevenson 2006).

As one rather obvious example of a monocultural and monolingual
ideology, the 'German-only' policy of many schools and kindergartens
should be noted, where it is forbidden to use any language other than
German (Spiegel Online, 23 January 2006). There is also a plethora
of examples from newspaper articles that regard multilingualism on
school playgrounds as hindering educational success (see also Stevenson

and Schanze in press). A report about a conference on language policy in Germany (Leitner and Schütte 2006), which criticizes the fact that Germany lacks a proper language policy that understands (migrant) multilingualism as an asset rather than as a threat, characterizes the situation; the report also comments negatively on the 'monolingual habitus' in Germany and in European nation-states in general.

The emphasis on German language skills by the German government is also evidenced by the compulsory language classes for foreigners wanting to be naturalized, which were introduced in 2005. These classes comprise 600 hours of language teaching plus 30 hours of cultural orientation (Bundesamt für Migration und Flüchtlinge (BAMF) 2005; Stevenson and Schanze in press). Although the classes are of obvious practical advantage, it is notable that a rather advanced knowledge of German is considered to be crucial in order to obtain German citizenship. Against the historical background of Germany, where, for a long time, guestworkers and their children had little chance of becoming citizens, language and cultural orientation classes as a prerequisite to becoming German may be interpreted as having a rather nationalist flavour. Additionally, it is interesting to note that these compulsory language classes were introduced at roughly the same time as a new law concerning citizenship, whereby children who are born in Germany now have the right to be naturalized. Concomitant with this, it seems the importance of becoming 'ideologically' German on a linguistic and cultural level is reinforced.

Nevertheless, it should be acknowledged that the assimilationist, monocultural habitus of German state policies has exceptions. Bilingual schooling exists, but mainly for prestige languages like French and English and not for the languages spoken by most ethnic minorities in Germany: Turkish, Italian, Arabic or languages from the former Yugoslavia. 'Instrumental bilingualism' (Hoffmann 1991) with prestige languages, as found in German high schools, is seen as an asset on global markets and is not considered to touch on questions of identity (see also Hessisches Kultusministerium 2004).

One may suggest that in Germany officially abandoned ethnic nationalism is tacitly maintained in the guise of a monolingual, assimilationist ideology. This confirms Stevenson's observation that representations in German language policy 're-assert an idea of the integrity of the nation still based on a stable monolingual norm that is increasingly contradicted by dynamic multilingual realities' (Stevenson 2006: 160-1). Indeed, looking closely at multilingual realities in German cities, the picture becomes more complex and we have to ask what the actual 'target' of the monolingual ideology is and what its effects and functions are in an era of cultural globalization and transnational cultural development.

Transnational Salsa communities

Transnational, multi-ethnic communities of practice (Wenger 1998) based on Salsa dancing are interesting examples of the multilingual practices of local German environments. Salsa subcultures have been chosen as a unit of analysis here in order to prevent the circular reproduction of essentialist categories such as citizenship, country of origin or mother tongue and also to allow for contemporary theories of cultural practice (Holmes and Meyerhoff 1999; Barton and Tusting 2005).

Salsa is a transnational cultural phenomenon, comparable in its transnationality to hip hop (Pennycook 2007) or house music. Developed by Latin American musicians in the 1970s in New York (Aparicio 1998), this style has entered the music scene and nightlife in many parts of the world, ranging from the US through Europe to Japan (Hosokawa 1997). Aside from music, of which the lyrics are, irrespective of their origin, almost always in Spanish, dance is the central feature of this cultural practice. The particular relocation (see Robertson 1998) – or local performance – of global Salsa culture differs between countries, and even cities. In Germany, communities are found in all large cities. Members of these CofPs have various ethnic backgrounds, ranging from Latin American to German, and also to other, often non-European ethnicities (various African ethnic/national groups, as well as Turkish, Arabic, Greek, etc.). Interestingly, Latin Americans very often become Salsa aficionados or 'Latinos', as they are often called in the German context, only when they are abroad (Papadopulos 2003); in many Latin American countries, Salsa tends to be classified as music of the lower milieux.[2]

German Salsa aficionados – or better: Salsa aficionados in Germany – not only meet to dance in Salsa venues, but very often also perform a particular type of identity and lifestyle. This includes the attendance of dance classes, a certain style of dress, a particular way of moving – there are even classes for women to show them how to move like a 'real' Latina – preference for certain types of drinks (for example, Cuba Libre), regular attendance of Salsa concerts, workshops and parties. If affordable, trips to Latin American countries are made, especially Cuba, and interestingly, for many, speaking Spanish also belongs to an authentic performance of this type of identity. Within these communities of practice we thus find different groups of people who are native or non-native speakers of Spanish. The use of Spanish here cannot be understood as having an instrumental function in the sense that it would, for example, be helpful in getting a job; it is, rather, a crucial tool in the production and performance of a particular type of identity (for the theoretical background of poststructuralist understandings of identity and performativity, see Butler [1993] 2000; Hall 2000; Wirth 2002a). It is important to note that these identities are not merely based on ethnic or national aspirations. These specific identities have to be understood as the products of interwoven German, Hispanic *and* transnational discourses. The acquisition of Spanish in this context seems to enhance the status of those performing Salsa identities. This relates to Wilkinson's observation (this volume) that Bourdieu's notion of 'linguistic capital' (Bourdieu [1980] 2005) can be applied not only in one-language or diglossic communities, but it is also vital for language identification in transnational contexts that cross borders of formerly unrelated languages and cultures.

The following account of language identity and ideology in a German Salsa community of practice is based on an ethnographic research project that was carried out in Frankfurt am Main in 2006. Qualitative interviews (Witzel 1996) were part of the ethnographic research design employed in this study. Next to participant observation, they are the main source for analysing this transnationally oriented community. The interest of this study is not so much in the actual usage of language but in the investigation of discourses that accompany the usage, maintenance and/or acquisition of Spanish. In this sense, the study is concerned with language ideology (Woolard 1998; Blommaert 1999; Irvine and Gal 2000; Kroskrity 2000a) and belongs to the area of sociolinguistic enquiry that 'investigates the discourses in which processes of attribution of value to linguistic forms and practices are inscribed, along with the processes of construction of social difference and social inequality with which they are associated' (Heller 2007a: 15).

The following section portrays the internal complexity of the different linguistic identities and language ideologies of Salsa scenes. Here, the 'attribution of value to linguistic forms and practice' sometimes differs significantly from that in official and public discourses.

Frankfurt's Salseras and Salseros – language ideologies and identities in transnational contexts

Despite the aim of this research to overcome essentialist notions of identity – for example, nationality, ethnicity or mother tongue – these categories nevertheless appear in empirical research. In order to be able to analyse the data found and to make the material more accessible, the categories of nationality and (native) language competence are used as a basis for analytical categories. It has to be kept in mind, however, that these categories are understood as being constructed performatively in discourse (see Tabouret-Keller 1997).

First, it has to be noted that far from all Salsa aficionados speak Spanish. Many members of the CofP are monolingual German speakers or bilingual with German and other languages than Spanish, especially English – it has already been mentioned that the community is constituted via dance practice and not on grounds of language. These members can be described as belonging to the mainstream of German society.[3] Discourses on linguistic integration, language maintenance or shift, and so on are not directed at these individuals; they seem to conform to the ostensible monolingual ideology of German language policy and discourse. Monolingual native Spanish speakers who do not speak German at all are those to whom the monolingual discourse is directed. However, next to the fact that no informant has been met who could be said to belong to this category, the following examination of bilinguals shows that it is not language competence and nationality alone that are crucial factors in becoming a 'target' of monolingual language policy and societal monolingual discourse. It turns out that class is as much an important feature as ethnicity or nationality in the rating of language usage and competence.

It is then striking to note that many members of the CofP have to be considered elite bilinguals, like German or Latin American students or professionals who speak Spanish and German fluently. In public discourses, their bilingual competence is both welcomed and desired; this type of bilingualism is, for example, considered helpful in getting a job (see above). From the point of view of mainstream public discourse, where instrumental bilingualism is seen as a valuable asset, ethnic identity does not seem to be questioned by this type of bilingual competence.

However, the ethnic identity of native Germans is to a certain extent questioned by the interviewees themselves. They describe their acquisition of Spanish not in terms of instrumentality, but as a way to 'become someone else'. The forms of language crossing that are found in this context index this construction of the self as 'other'. Language crossing has been defined as the 'use of a language or variety that, in one way or another, feels anomalously "other" ' (Rampton 2000: 55) – the use of a language that is not related to the speaker's 'original' ethnic heritage. Studying the functions of cross-ethnic language usage promises to be revealing in transnational cultures as language crossing may be related to the emergence of new, non-essential forms of linguistic identity and post-national language ideologies. While so far the phenomenon has been studied mainly in urban youth culture contexts (see particularly Rampton 1995), crossing, as it occurs in the Salsa sphere, is rather connected to discourses of travel, leisure, fun and a privileged position that allows interest in the language and culture of others. German women especially say that speaking Spanish makes them feel very joyful and also that doing so involves the construction of an 'other' identity, which is not 'the frosty central European':

> ... ich hab schon das Gefühl, das macht mich immer fröhlich, wenn ich Spanisch sprechen kann, *total*, das find ich total *klásse*... ich weiss auch nich, ja, es is schwer zu sagen, was es eigentlich is... doch so'n bisschen...ja wirklich, dieses aus der eigenen Rolle...der unterkühlten Mitteleuropäerin bisschen aus...zu...dingsen

> (... I do have the feeling, it always makes me happy, when I can speak Spanish, *absolutely*, I find it *really* amazing...I don't know, yeah, it is difficult to say, what it actually is...but a little bit...yeah, really, this breaking out of this out-of-your-own-role...of the frosty central European, a little bit)

> (A 1: 206–10)[4]

The expression of emotions and also communication about emotions seem to be tied to the usage of Spanish:

> Also wenn ich Spanisch spreche, das macht mich immer *unheimlich* glücklich, das macht mich unheimlich frei, ja, viele Sachen sind viel einfacher, vor allem über Gefühle zu reden, ja, und ich komm auch immer in so 'ne...relativ schnell in so 'ne aufgedrehte glückliche Stimmung.

> (Well, when I speak Spanish, it always makes me *incredibly* happy, it makes me incredibly free, yeah, many things are a lot easier, especially to speak about emotions, yeah, and I always get into an energetic, happy mood.)

> (I, 1: 33–9)

In this sense, Spanish seems to function as a type of Shangri La;[5] Spanish seems to have utopian functions in that it serves for Germans as a tool to perform an 'other' identity. Additionally, language crossing to Spanish is a way of constructing a certain degree of authenticity in the context, although people are aware that they are probably not able to truly 'cross' ethnic boundaries:

> Ich würd's echt gerne perfektionieren, ja und es ist wahrscheinlich auch der Wunsch von jedem (1,5) ähm, der irgendwie so Spanisch lernt ... dass man's halt irgendwann möglichst akzentfrei spricht und von den, von den Latinos ... na ja gut, als ihresgleichen aufgenommen wird man wahrscheinlich nicht (lacht)

> (I'd really love to perfect it, yeah, and it's probably also the desire of everybody who learns Spanish ... that one day you'll speak it without an accent and be ... well OK, you probably won't be accepted by the Latinos, as one of them (laughs))

> (A 1: 230–3)

This general desire of becoming an 'other' is also described as an unspecified 'longing' (*Sehnsucht*):

> Ja, warum ist diese Kultur so beliebt? Ich glaube, es ist einfach diese ... Sehnsucht ... irgendwie ... diese Sehnsucht. ... Das drückt es eigentlich ganz gut aus.

> (So why is this culture so popular? I think it is just, this ... longing ... somehow ... this longing. ... That expresses it pretty well.)

> (M, 0: 75–6)

It is also interesting to note that Spanish in this context may come to symbolize a challenge to English as a global language. While English is considered to be a technical instrument, Spanish is described as bearing emotions and a certain degree of warm-heartedness:

> Englisch, das lernt man eben, muss man ja, schon in der Schule. Spanisch ist eben viel mehr so Gefühl als Englisch.

> (English, you just learn it. You have to, don't you, at school. Spanish is much more emotion than English.)

> (A, 0: 34–5)

Considering the strong anti-US discourse within Latin America, Spanish can also be interpreted here as bearing connotations of political resistance and anti-(US) Americanism. This is also expressed by many visual images within the Salsa scene, where red stars, pictures of Che

Guevara and flags of the Cuban nation are omnipresent. Trips to Cuba and a positive attitude towards Cuba's regime are very common among German Salsa lovers, while capitalism and the US, together with English, are often described as the cold and technical opposite (personal observation and communication). There are also many lyrics within Salsa songs that express this attitude, see for example the very famous *Plástico* by Willie Colón and Rubén Blades (1977; see http://www.fania.com/disco_detalle.php?id = 981&coleccion = 221. Accessed 23 September 2008).

The whole enterprise of becoming an 'other' and the description of 'longing' also have to be understood in relation to heterosexual and nostalgic aspirations. When entering a Salsa venue for the first time, the degree of heteronormativity[6] can be astonishing. The performance of masculine and feminine identity in 'traditional' ways is quite drastic, starting from what people wear to the norms of behaviour, where women are supposed to perform the passive role – they usually have to wait until asked to dance and are led when dancing – and men take the active part – they are supposed to ask and to lead the dance. The persistence of extremely traditional gender categories is compelling and may have to do with the relative fluidity of ethnic categories. Where ethnic categories dissolve, where it is no longer possible to sort people according to their ethnic background, it may become necessary to gain ground on other levels, as in, for example, the fixity of gender categories in order to make behaviour meaningful and understandable. This phenomenon has also been interpreted as a 'return to a past imagined as more ordered' as 'engaging in this dance marks a return to prefeminist gendered relations' (Pietrobruno 2006: 19). According to Robertson (1992: 162), it is the highly fluid nature of global change that nourishes the nostalgic tendency for more certain and stable forms of 'world order' (see also Pietrobruno 2006: 20).

Heteronormativity is also found in the production of identity of native Latin Americans, who often prefer to speak Spanish in this environment. Ethnic authenticity is of value, created via language and other means. Some non-Latin interviewees thus express the feeling that Latin people do not truly mingle with the others as they feel superior to 'non-authentic' Salseras:

Zu den Latinos passt man sowieso nicht, die ja sowieso irgendwie ihre mehr oder minder ... Enklave da noch bilden und da auch die Leute eigentlich gar nicht so wirklich reinlassen, beziehungsweise, wir sind hier die Latinos und ihr seid hier halt schon so die Deutschen, die halt hier so tanzen und wenn ihr das gut macht, dann ist das schon cool, aber naja …

(You don't fit in with the Latinos anyway, who more or less form their own … enclave and who don't really let other people in, or, we're the Latinos here and you're just, like, the Germans, who just like dance around here and when you're good at it, then it's pretty cool, but, well…)

(A1: 5–10)

'Authentic' ethnicity functions as symbolic capital in this context. Dancing in a particular style seems to lead to increased status, but 'real' Latin American ethnicity still functions as a boundary-marker. It is symptomatic of this value of authenticity that there is one venue in Frankfurt (a club called Living) that gives free entrance to people with Latin American passports on Salsa nights. Having real 'Latinos' at a Salsa party increases the authentic value of the event and selling the image of the 'real Latin Lover' is part of the club's marketing strategy (see www.livingxxl.de, summer 2007). And indeed, especially male Latin Americans often perform a stereotypical 'Latin lover' identity. Interestingly, they often use Spanish even if their German is very good and the Spanish of their (female) counterparts mediocre. This is an interesting observation with regard to gender and language acquisition. As far as can be said from participant observation, more (German) women, in fact, learn Spanish as a second language than (German) men, whereas Latin American men seem to adhere to their native language. When asked about these language acquisition practices and the potential reasons for that, all interviewees state that women learn languages more easily because of their 'natural' talent to do so:

… ich geh tendenziell davon aus, dass Frauen Sprachen leichter lernen als Männer, ich weiss nich, ob das 'n Vorurteil is, aber irgendwie geh ich schon davon aus. Aufgrund der höheren Emotionalität von Frauen, ich weiss nich, ob man das irgendwie so sagen kann, aber irgendwie… (2,5) denk ich dass Frauen Sprachen leichter lernen.

(I tend to assume that women learn languages more easily than men, I don't know if that's a prejudice, but somehow I assume that. Because women are more emotional than men, I don't know if you can say that but somehow … (2,5) I do think that women learn languages more easily.)

(A 1: 251–4)

Next to the female tendency to be 'emotional', women are mentioned as being more predisposed to wanting to 'adjust' to their partners:

> Ich glaub sowieso dass Frauen eher sprachbegabt sind, deswegen denk ich natürlich schon, dass es eher viele Frauen sind und dann glaub ich auch, also wenn's so Pärchen sind, denk ich immer, dass die Frauen dann Spanisch lernen und wenn's andersrum is, dann lernen die Frauen eher deutsch, ja. Die Frauen lernen eben die Sprache ihrer Männer. ... [weil die Frauen] sich eher an den Mann anpassen, heute noch wahrscheinlich.

> (I believe anyway that women are more talented at learning languages, and therefore, of course, I think that it's more women and then I also believe that, if it's couples, I always think that the women learn Spanish and if it's the other way around, women rather learn German, yeah. Women just learn the language of their men...[because women] are more likely to adjust to their men, probably even today.)

> (I 1: 94–105)

Language ideologies concerning language learning and gender in their relation to the production of a particular gendered identity (see also Pavlenko et al. 2001) – women as empathic, understanding partners for their men – become very obvious here. Next to that, language functions as an important means in the construction of ethnic authenticity, which in this context is highly valued – in contrast to the images that are created in German discourses on migrants, integration and the role of the German language.

When asked about code-switching practices, there is an interesting feature in nearly all interviews: most interviewees describe code-switching as an everyday practice that is regarded very positively. Interviewees react almost enthusiastically when asked about language-mixing and switching (the difference between the two concepts is not analysed in this chapter; for details, see Myers-Scotton 2005: chapter 9). Code-switching – not the act of speaking Spanish – is described as something that is enabling 'on all levels', 'opens a whole new world' and, interestingly here, evokes the metaphor of tentacles:

> [Code-switching] zeigt halt einfach, dass man in allen Ebenen irgendwie da so, also es kommt halt einfach, es kommt mir so vor wie so Tentakel, dass man überall sein Dingens drin hat, sozusagen und

dass man sich einfach irgendwo dazwischen bewegt und das eröffnet einem so eine ganz neue Welt.

([Code-switching] just shows that on all levels you're somehow, well, it just, it feels to me like tentacles, that you have your thingies everywhere, so to speak, and that you move somewhere in between and that just opens up a whole new world.)

(A, 2: 347–51)

Or as in this short, but highly compelling quote:

Es como 'Pimp my language'.[7]

(It is just like 'Pimp my language'.)

(J, 2: 122)

The interviewee here refers to a television programme on MTV ('Pimp my Ride') in which cars get a makeover. Speech can be 'restyled' or 'upgraded' if bits and pieces from several languages are used. With an eye on newer developments within sociolinguistic theory (Rampton 1995; Errington 2001; Heller 2007a; Makoni and Pennycook 2007a), this may be interpreted as a form of deconstruction of national language categories. Both German and Spanish are described as if they were part of *one* language competence. This language competence can be related to the emergence of transnational and multilingual forms of identity. Thus, speaking Spanish and German (and potentially any other language that carries symbolic capital) in a mixed fashion for these individuals is a way to create a multilingual, cosmopolitan identity, where cosmopolitanism is understood as 'an intellectual and aesthetic stance of openness towards divergent cultural experiences, a search for contrast rather than uniformity' (Hannerz 1990: 239). Obviously, this type of multilingualism, which is often found in the Frankfurt Salsa scene, is not 'meant' by German language policy and monolingual discourse. Furthermore, the comments made by the group pose questions about our understanding of 'languages' as given structural entities in general.

A second sub-group of the Salsa community can be described as 'minority bilinguals'. In some cases, the labelling of 'minority' is not made on the basis of the nationality alone but is, as above, made on grounds of nationality and class alike. In the Salsa context, poor German is rated negatively, but only in the case of Spanish native speakers do interviewees differentiate individuals on the basis of language background *and* class. Economically precarious situations count here as a reason for not succeeding in learning the language:

Gente Latino que no aprende alemán, si hay ... pero eso depende de la clase. Si uno no tiene educación y vive aquí feliz, no es grave. Y también tienen que trabajar tanto que no tienen tiempo para aprender el lenguaje.

(Latin people who don't learn German ... but this depends on class. If somebody has no education and lives here happily, it doesn't matter. And also, these people have to work so much, they don't have time to learn the language.)

(J, 3: 425–8)

This differentiation is not made for all other language backgrounds, however, where the language background alone seems to be sufficient for perceiving individuals as having a minority status that is rated as negative. As has been observed by Collins and Slembrouck (2008: 5, 12), it seems to be common not only in popular but also in academic and policy discourse to discuss deficit multilingualism in isolation from the effects of socioeconomic background. Thus, the exception that is made here for people with a Spanish language background may be interpreted as sympathy for those who are perceived as in-group members and who may be known personally to interviewees through contact in the Salsa scene.

Concerning more monolithic, undifferentiated perceptions of linguistic 'otherness', it is striking to note that during the interviews, when it comes to the context of language acquisition and integration, all interviewees mention the Turkish minority in Germany and claim that 'the Turks' – 'die Türken' – are those who 'do not want to learn German' and who are in this sense seen as problematic, as in the following passage:

Ja natürlich gibt es da schon auch Probleme hier in Deutschland, mit den Leuten, die sich nicht integrieren wollen, wie ja zum Beispiel die Türken, die kein Deutsch lernen. Das ist natürlich total respektlos.

(Well yes, of course, there are problems, here in Germany, with those who don't want to integrate, like, for example, the Turks who don't learn German. That is of course very disrespectful.)

(I, 4: 230–2)

This is particularly interesting because in none of the interviews did the interviewer mention this ethnic group at all. The ethnic group of

Turks is perceived as unwilling to acquire German and seems to be symbolic of the general undesired 'other', while people with a Latin background who do not learn German are usually excused because of their difficult economic situation, as in the quote above. Within the Salsa CofP in Frankfurt, however, there is a group with a Latin American background that is sometimes differentiated from transnational elites: Colombians with a refugee background who spend their free time in Salsa venues. It is *their* allegedly poor German that is considered a problem. Within the Salsa scene, there exists the prejudice that Colombian women generally work in red light districts (personal communication; see also Papadopulos 2003: 93) or have married German men in order to get a residence permit. It is conceived that their bilingual ability is not acquired on the basis of a voluntary decision; it is therefore never mentioned as valuable linguistic capital. Although their bilingual competence may be quite high, the ability to speak in Spanish and German is not valued in the same way as if they had acquired it in a more formal setting. It may be assumed that the language competence of economically marginal speakers does not adhere to standardized norms, whether in German or Spanish. Thus, German speakers sometimes describe Colombians as non-German speakers:

> Frankfurt hat ja natürlich auch eine spezielle Szene, die auch leider sehr viel mit Kolumbianern zu tun hat. Und diese Szene speziell, oder diese Kolumbianer, die reden, also die können auch kein deutsch sprechen, ja, leben eigentlich nur unter sich selber ...

> (Frankfurt has, of course, a special scene, which unfortunately has a lot to do with Colombians. And this scene especially, or these Colombians, they speak, well, they can't speak German, actually only live among themselves ...)

> (M, see Papadopulos 2003: 93)

Accusing non-Germans of being unwilling to 'integrate' into German society – a common accusation in German public discourse – is directed here against particular groups of economically marginal non-Europeans. However, Spanish speakers are lucky in that their native language is relatively prestigious in its global ranking, which is why it is still considered 'better' to speak Spanish and German than, for example, Turkish and German (see above). This leads to a third subgroup identified during the research, again based on the empirical validity of essentialist terms, especially that of nationhood and ethnicity. This group runs counter to the traditional view on language and ethnic identity: 'other' minorities of Germany, for example Turks, Arabs, Sub-Saharan Africans or southern Europeans, are also vital members of the community. Here, it is especially males who seem to attempt to acquire an ethnic identity that is of higher cultural value than their own ethnic identity: Latinos or Salseros as 'better' foreigners. Not only is it easy to find these men in Salsa venues, where their phenotype is not marked as 'other' negatively, but there are also some who have acquired Spanish and who thus perform a male identity that is of higher cultural capital than their 'original' ethnicity (participant observation). The identification with Spanish in the case of one individual goes as far as adopting a Spanish name in an attempt to abandon his ethnic Afghan identity (see Papadopulos 2003). This special type of mimicry (Bhabha 1994) has to be understood within the German context, with its particular history of *Gastarbeiter* migration (Terkessidis 2000), where Spanish speakers and speakers of other languages of today's EU (Italian, Portuguese) have never been as marginalized as speakers of non-European languages. On a global level, where some countries and their citizens are perceived as wealthier or as underdeveloped respectively, class plays a key role in the desire for ethnic and language crossing. And again, as it is mostly men from these ethnic backgrounds who perform Salsero identities, gender also turns out to be a crucial factor in the motivation for language acquisition and the linguistic construction of identity.

The implications of a monolingual ideology in transnational contexts

It has become clear that German discourses and ideologies concerning language and integration have repercussions that go beyond language competence alone. In the example of Salsa CofPs, the imposition (Pavlenko and Blackledge 2004a) of a 'deficient' linguistic identity is made on grounds of language competence *and* nationality *and* class *and* (to a certain extent) gender. Thus, the ostensible aim of the German monolingual discourse seems at first sight to be one-dimensional and anachronistic. The hidden, underlying arguments of this discourse, however, show that the instrument 'language', as a symbol, functions fairly well in the exclusion of undesired 'others', although not in the traditional logic of nationalism.

While certain types of bilingualism are supported and desired in terms of the global marketplace and for constructing cosmopolitan, elite

identities, others are suppressed. The suppression of certain types of language usage and identification, however, is not, as officially claimed,
based solely on the ideal of monolingual language competence and a
monolingual society but on the marginalization of those who are considered foreign, uneducated *and* poor. A large group of ethnically 'others'
is not excluded, as it is now possible to acquire a cosmopolitan, multilingual identity and thus be seen as a legitimate part of the contemporary
culture of Germany. The whole Salsa movement can be understood
accordingly. Here, the dynamics of globalization cross national ideology.
Local cultures are pervaded by globalized cultures (see also the notion
of glocalization in Robertson 1998) and the monocultural aim of public
discourses is oriented towards a marginalized minority.

Contemporary nationalist ideology can only be understood within its
global context where autonomous nationalism no longer exists – now it
is impossible to see a single nation as an isolated vessel. Policies and discourses that may originally have been intended to carry meaning on a
national level only, gain new and other meanings in globalized, transnational cultures and discourses, which are now a vital part of everyday
life, in Germany and elsewhere. The 'myth of a stable monolingual
norm' (Stevenson 2006: 148) in German national language policies may
rather be a sign of the 'growing instability' (ibid.) of a national ideology in globalized cultures. In this global context, the conception of a
national ideology has to be deconstructed as a class discourse. This also
relates to Pujolar's observation of new multilingual, but nevertheless
nationalist, strategies, where

> [m]ultilingual policies may be devised in ways that ensure the privi-
> leged position of dominant groups who foster knowledge of powerful
> 'foreign' languages in their standard forms but delegitimize or ignore
> other languages and other forms of multilingual competence and
> performance (for example code-switching, heterogeneous skills).
>
> (Pujolar 2007: 78)

Conclusion

Linguistic identity, as this example shows, is not only connected to ethnic or national identity; this was never the case. However, research in
transnational communities shows that speaking 'a language' is, as with
speaking 'a dialect', clearly also connected to class, gender and lifestyle.
Again, this relates to Wilkinson's (this volume) observation that today

the logic of linguistic capital can function across cultural and linguistic boundaries. Rather than expressing ethnic or national identity, certain forms of multilingual language competence are constitutive of a lifestyle that connects to the language ideology of a transnational, multilingual, educated class. The role of the German language in this context is that of one among several sources of identification and not an exclusive one, contrary to claims of social inclusion made by German mainstream public discourse.

As the construct of 'a language' is dialectically interwoven with the construction of the nation-state (Gogolin 1998; Pennycook 2004; Heller 2007a), quotes like the 'Pimp my language' comment show that it is the modernist concept of language that also has to be questioned. With the changing role of the nation-state, the concept of the 'national language' changes simultaneously. The complexity and interrelation of constructions of language, nation and class are invisible in many national language policies. Their often one-dimensional approaches can be understood as symptomatic of language problems in the contemporary world (Makoni and Pennycook 2007a), where one may suspect

> [t]hat the 'problem' may not be language at all, but that language instead may be serving as a terrain for the construction of boundaries and relations of power in ways that are legitimate within dominant discursive regimes.... That operating with the idea of language as bounded in the first place may be primarily a matter of reproducing specific discursive regimes.
>
> (Heller 2007b: 345)

Studying the role of language in the reproduction of national and global regimes of power and the way in which individuals appropriate languages within such regimes – as national or ethnic markers, as indicators of cosmopolitan, hybrid identities or as commodities on a global market – is vital for studying social change in a globalized society.

Notes

1. Quote from the song 'Hablemos el mismo idioma' by Gloria Estefan (1993).
2. The history of the cultural meaning of Salsa is, of course, far more complex. For a thorough introduction see Aparicio (1998).
3. Those who speak German *and* Spanish as a second language and have other native languages are referred to below.
4. In referring to interviewees, anonymized abbreviations in the form of capital letters are used.

5. Shangri La is the Tibetan utopia in James Hilton's novel *Lost Horizon* (1933). The term is also used to describe imagined ideal spaces, especially if they are retreats from the pressures of civilization (see, for example, Bishop 1989).
6. The term 'heteronormativity' is a critique of symbolic orders and practices that understand heterosexuality as the norm and naturalize bipolar, mutually exclusive gender categories, where all other forms of gendered identity or sexuality are constructed as deviant from a presumed natural norm (Wagenknecht 2007: 17).
7. English in the original quote; the interview was conducted in Spanish.

References

Aparicio, F. R. (1998) *Listening to Salsa: Gender, Latin Popular Music, and Puerto Rican Cultures* (Hanover, NH: Wesleyan University Press).
Barbour, S. and Carmichael, C. (eds) (2000) *Language and Nationalism in Europe* (Oxford: Oxford University Press).
Barton, D. and Tusting, K. (eds) (2005) *Beyond Communities of Practice: Language, Power, and Social Context* (Cambridge: Cambridge University Press).
Beck, U. (ed.) (1998) *Perspektiven der Weltgesellschaft* (Frankfurt am Main: Suhrkamp).
Bergmann, S. and Römhild, R. (eds) (2003) *Global Heimat* (Frankfurt am Main: Notizen).
Bhabha, H. K. (1994) *The Location of Culture* (London: Routledge).
Bishop, P. (1989) *The Myth of Shangri-La. Tibet, Travel Writing, and the Western Creation of Sacred Landscape* (Berkeley, CA: University of California Press).
Blommaert, J. (ed) (1999) *Language Ideological Debates* (Berlin: de Gruyter).
Blommaert, J. and Verschueren, J. (1998) 'The role of language in European nationalist ideologies', in Schieffelin et al. (1998), 189–210.
Bourdieu, P. [1980] (2005) *Was heißt sprechen? Die Ökonomie des sprachlichen Tausches* (Wien: Braumüller).
Bundesamt für Migration und Flüchtlinge (BAMF) (2005) *Konzept für einen bundesweiten Integrationskurs* (Nürnberg: BAMF).
Butler, J. [1993] (2000) 'Critically queer', in du Gay et al. (2000), 108–18.
Coates, J. (ed.) (1998) *Language and Gender: A Reader* (Oxford: Blackwell).
Collins, J. and Slembrouck, S. (2008) 'Is class relevant in constructing a multilingual Europe?', in *Working Papers in Urban Language & Literacies*, 52, http://www.kcl.ac.uk/content/1/c6/01/42/29/WP52CollinsSlembrouckonclass multilingualism.pdf
Colón, W. and Blades, R. (1977) 'Plástico', album sleeve, *Siembra* (New York: Fania Records).
Coulmas, F. (ed.) (1997) *The Handbook of Sociolinguistics* (Oxford: Blackwell).
Eckert, P. and McConnell-Ginet, S. (1998) 'Communities of practice: where language, gender, and power all live', in Coates (1998), 484–94.
Errington, J. (2001) 'Colonial linguistics', *Annual Review of Anthropology* 30, 19–39.
Estefan, G. (1993) 'Hablemos el mismo idioma', album sleeve, *Mi Tierra* (Sony BMG).

Extra, G., van Avermaet, P. and Spotti, M. (in press) *Testing Regimes: Cross-national Perspectives on Language, Migration and Citizenship* (London: Continuum).

Gay, P. du et al. (eds) (2000) *Identity: A Reader* (London: Sage).

Glick Schiller, N., Basch, N. and Szanton Blanc, C. (1997) 'From immigrant to transmigrant: theorizing transnational migration', in Pries (1997), 121–40.

Gogolin, I. (1998) 'Sprachen rein halten – eine Obsession', in Gogolin et al. (1998), 71–96.

Gogolin, I. et al. (1998) *Erziehungsziel Zweisprachigkeit. Konturen eines sprachpädagogischen Konzepts für die multikulturelle Schule* (Hamburg: Bergmann+Helbig).

Hall, S. (2000) 'Who needs 'identity'?', in du Gay et al. (2000), 15–30.

Hannerz, U. (1990) 'Cosmopolitans and locals in world culture', *Theory, Culture & Society* 7, 237–51.

Hannerz, U. (1996) *Transnational Connections. Culture, People, Places* (London: Routledge).

Hartmann, J. et al. (2007) *Heteronormativität. Empirische Studien zu Geschlecht, Sexualität und Macht* (Wiesbaden: VS Verlag).

Heller, M. (2007a) 'Bilingualism as ideology and practice', in Heller (2007c), 1–22.

Heller, M. (2007b) 'The future of bilingualism', in Heller (2007c), 340–5.

Heller, M. (ed.) (2007c) *Bilingualism: A Social Approach* (Basingstoke: Palgrave Macmillan).

Hessisches Kultusministerium (2004) Integration durch Bildung – Was Hessens Schulen leisten, www.kultusministerium.hessen.de. Accessed 28 February 2004.

Hoffmann, C. (1991) *An Introduction to Bilingualism* (London: Longman).

Holmes, J. and Meyerhoff, M. (1999) 'The community of practice: theories and methodologies in language and gender research', *Language in Society* 28, 173–83.

Hosokawa, S. (1997) ' "Salsa no tiene frontera": Orquesta de la luz or the globalization and Japanization of Afro-Caribbean music', *Revista Transcultural de Música – Transcultural Music Review*, 3, http://www.sibetrans.com/trans/trans3/hosokawa.htm. Accessed 9 March 2007.

Irvine, J. T. and Gal, S. (2000) 'Language ideology and linguistic differentiation', in Kroskrity (2000b), 35–83.

Koopmans, R. (2001) 'Deutschland und seine Einwanderer: Ein gespaltenes Verhältnis', in *Blätter für deutsche und internationale Politik* 2, 1–28.

Kroskrity, P. V. (2000a) 'Regimenting languages. Language ideological perspectives', in Kroskrity (2000b), 1–34.

Kroskrity, P. V. (ed.) (2000b) *Regimes of Language. Ideologies, Polities and Identities* (Santa Fe, NM: School of American Research Press).

Leitner, G and Schütte, G. (2006) *Braucht Deutschland eine bewusstere, kohäsive Sprachpolitik?* http://avh.de/de/netzwerk/veranstalt/expert_2006_index.htm

Makoni, S. and Pennycook, A. (2007a) 'Disinventing and reconstituting languages', in Makoni and Pennycook (2007b), 1–41.

Makoni, S. and Pennycook, A. (eds) (2007b) *Disinventing and Reconstituting Languages* (Clevedon: Multilingual Matters).

Myers-Scotton, C. (2005) *Multiple Voices: An Introduction to Bilingualism* (Oxford: Blackwell).

Papadopulos, M. (2003) 'Salsa no tiene Frontera. Eine Szene ohne Grenzen?' in Bergmann and Römhild (2003), 75–104.

Pavlenko, A. and Blackledge, A. (2004a) 'Introduction: new theoretical approaches to the study of negotiation of identities in multilingual contexts', in Pavlenko and Blackledge (2004b), 1–33.

Pavlenko, A. and Blackledge, A. (eds) (2004b) *Negotiation of Identities in Multilingual Contexts* (Clevedon: Multilingual Matters).

Pavlenko, A. et al. (eds) (2001) *Multilingualism, Second Language Learning, and Gender* (Berlin: de Gruyter).

Pennycook, A. (2004) 'Performativity and language studies', *Critical Inquiry in Language Studies* 1, 1–19.

Pennycook, A. (2007) *Global Englishes and Transcultural Flows* (London: Routledge).

Pietrobruno, S. (2006) *Salsa and its Transnational Moves* (Lanham, MD: Lexington Books).

Pries, L. (1997) *Transnationale Migration* (Baden Baden: Nomos).

Pries, L. (2001) 'Internationale Migration' (Bielefeld: transcript).

Pujolar, J. (2007) 'Bilingualism and the nation-state in the post-national era', in Heller (2007c), 71–95.

Rampton, B. (1995) *Crossing: Language and Ethnicity among Adolescents* (London: Longman).

Rampton, B. (2000) 'Crossing', *Journal of Linguistic Anthropology*, 9, 54–6.

Robertson, R. (1992) *Globalization: Social Theory and Global Culture* (London: Sage).

Robertson, R. (1998) 'Glokalisierung: Homogenität und Heterogenität in Raum und Zeit', in Beck (1998), 192–220.

Schieffelin, B. B. et al. (eds) (1998) *Language Ideologies. Practice and Theory* (Oxford: Oxford University Press).

Spiegel Online (23 January 2006) 'Schüler begrüßen Deutsch-Pflicht', *Spiegel Online*, http://www.spiegel.de/schulspiegel/0,1518,396842,00.html

Stevenson, P. (2006) ' "National" languages in transnational contexts: language, migration and citizenship in Europe', in Stevenson and Mar-Molinero (2006), 147–61.

Stevenson, P. and Mar-Molinero, C. (eds) (2006) *Language Ideologies, Policies and Practices: Language and the Future of Europe* (Basingstoke: Palgrave Macmillan).

Stevenson, P. and Schanze, L. (in press) 'Language, migration and citizenship in Germany', in Extra et al. (in press).

Strobl, R. and Böttger, A. (eds) (1996) *Wahre Geschichten? Zur Theorie und Praxis qualitativer Interviews* (Baden-Baden: Nomos).

Tabouret-Keller, A. (1997) 'Language and Identity', in Coulmas (1997), 315–26.

Terkessidis, M. (2000) *Migranten* (Hamburg: Rotbuch Verlag).

Wagenknecht, P. (2007) 'Was ist Heteronormativität? Zu Geschichte und Gehalt des Begriffs' in Hartmann et al. (2007), 17–34.

Wenger, E. (1998) *Communities of Practice. Learning, Meaning and Identity* (Cambridge: Cambridge University Press).

Wimmer, A. and Schiller, N. G. (2002) 'Methodological nationalism and beyond: nation-State building, migration and the social sciences', *Global Networks* 2, 301–34.

Wirth, U. (2002a) 'Der Performanzbegriff im Spannungsfeld von Illokution, Iteration und Indexikalität', in Wirth (2002b), 9–60.

Wirth, U. (ed.) (2002b) *Performanz. Zwischen Sprachphilosophie und Kulturwissenschaften* (Frankfurt am Main: Suhrkamp).

Witzel, A. (1996) 'Auswertung problemzentrierter Interviews: Grundlagen und Erfahrungen', in Strobl and Böttger (1996), 49–76.

Woolard, K. A. (1998) 'Introduction. Language ideology as field of inquiry', in Schieffelin et al. (1998), 3–47.

11
Towards a Multinational Concept of Culture: Romanian German Literature in Romanian and Hungarian Literature

Thomas Cooper

Introduction

If one were to raise questions concerning the future of German in Romania (as the country which has been home to one of the larger German-speaking minorities of Central Europe since the end of the First World War) it might be worthwhile to consider the current place of the German language literature of the country, not merely as an addendum to questions ostensibly more immediate, such as German as a language of education, administration or commerce, but rather as an investigation of the substance of German as a local cultural influence. While the use of German in governmental and commercial bodies is arguably driven primarily by the political and economic influence of Germany itself, the presence of German language literature native to Romania – specifically the regions of Transylvania and Banat – and distinct from the literature of Germany suggests that German itself continues to figure not merely as a medium of exchange, the prestige of which derives from exterior factors, but as an internally generative cultural force. This chapter proposes to demonstrate the continuing presence of Romanian German literature by examining its influence on the Romanian and Hungarian language literature of Transylvania and Banat. After a brief discussion of distinctive features of postwar Romanian German literature, in comparison with the postwar literature of Germany, I consider the presence of this literature in the two largest national literatures of Romania – Hungarian and Romanian – through figures of allusion and translation and the incorporation on the institutional level of the German language culture of Romania into the Romanian cultural canon.

Context

With the fall of the Soviet Union and the collapse of communist regimes in Central Europe has come a reappraisal of visions and representations of nationhood. One often speaks today of large-scale globalization and various scales of regionalization, both processes that transgress the borders of the linguistic nation and the nation-state. In this context considerable attention has been accorded to the formation of collective identities, especially ethnic identities that have proved to be of long duration within socio-political frameworks of nation-building. As home to several linguistic groups, Romania has been a favourite ground for such surveys, and there has been keen interest in the country's ethnic diversity and the ways in which the entangled histories of different cultural/linguistic groups have interacted and affected state formation and geopolitical processes. However, the critical revision of hegemonic cultural and historical canons through dialogue and effective renegotiation of the main identity discourses of the cultures is an issue that remains to be tackled. Previous attempts have failed largely because they made little attempt to address instances of cross-cultural influence that disrupt the national paradigm, instead accumulating components of competing narratives and accentuating their proliferation and alleged incompatibility (Gáll, 1994; Bocşan et al. 1995; Mureşanu, 1996; Zub, 1996). As *International Postmodernism: Theory and Practice* (part of the series *Comparative History of Literatures in European Languages* sponsored by the International Comparative Literature Association) makes clear, in scholarship in the humanities on Central Europe the national continues to prevail as a discrete category, even in discussions centred on a topic as allegedly international as postmodernism. The various chapters on Central Europe are divided along strictly national lines and there is little discussion within individual chapters of the other national literatures of the region except in broad references to certain aspects of shared history. While the construction of identities in Romania has unquestionably been affected by parochialism and mutual distrust amply reflected in the historiography, these identities are nonetheless overlapping, sharing the same territory and much of the same politico-cultural heritage. What is needed in lieu of an approach that charts the perceived incongruity of 'Hungarian', 'Romanian' and 'ethnic German' is an attempt to trace these overlaps by addressing moments of convergence in the cultural artefacts through which these identities gain their substance.

Yet the continued pervasiveness of polemical national mythologies in the historiography on cultures in Romania notwithstanding, there has been some effort among scholars in the humanities to draw attention to the ways in which works of art from the region, including music, the visual arts and literature, both partake of and affirm what can be thought of as the shared cultural legacy of the different linguistic (i.e. national) groups. In the late 1990s scholars from Central and Western Europe began putting together plans for a comparative literary history of the region that would compensate for the narratives of internally homogeneous national cultures offered by national literary histories by examining junctures where these traditions intersect. These efforts came to fruition with the publication of the first three of four volumes of the *History of the Literary Cultures of East-Central Europe* edited by John Neubauer and Marcel Cornis-Pope, and published by John Benjamins as part of the same series in which *International Postmodernism* was published. Unlike traditional national literary histories, the *Comparative History* conceptualizes linguistic difference not only as a boundary but also as a site of exchange. In addition, recent comparative work of several scholars from Central Europe on cross-cultural influence in the national literatures of the region challenges the chauvinism of national collective identity by exploring interstices and intersections, rather than articulating – and thereby reifying – borders (Babeți and Ungureanu, 1997; Culic et al. 1998; Ungureanu, 2004).

Regarding the German language literature of Romania today, a quick survey of the contemporary literary landscape may leave one with the initial impression that, with the virtual disappearance of German-speaking communities from Transylvania and Banat, this literature subsists, at most, either as a curiosity or as a relic of now vanished communities. Whereas the German-speaking population of western Romania, including the Banat Swabians and the Saxons of the neighbouring region of Transylvania, had numbered some 53,000 in 1941 and 330,000 in 1948, by 2002 this number had dropped to below 50,000 (Kocsis, 2007: 182). Considering these figures one might be tempted to concur with the Banat author Helmut Britz, who, as part of a conference held in Timişoara in 1990, gave a presentation entitled 'A romániai német irodalomnak vége. Éljen a német irodalom Romániában!' ('Romanian German literature has come to an end. Long live German literature in Romania!') or with the Transylvanian Saxon poet Franz Hodjak who contended as part of a roundtable talk held the same year in Munich, 'A romániai német irodalom a vasfüggöny terméke, eltávolításával törvényszerűen megszűnik' ('Romanian-German literature was a product of the Iron Curtain. With the disappearance of the Iron Curtain it will cease to exist') (cited in Hungarian translation in

Végh, 1993: 1). Yet however accurate these contentions may be from the practical perspective of the German-language author living in Romania, they are tenable for the study of the literature of the region only if one subscribes to a conservative, essentialist notion of culture. Indeed, the separation of literature from the immediate context implicit in Britz's title (the emphasis on German language literature in Romania instead of Romanian German literature) constitutes a (possibly ironic) return to the Romantic concept of the nation as an organic whole united by its language (e.g. Herder's contention that '[providence] wonderfully separated nationalities not only by woods and mountains, seas and deserts, rivers and climates, but more particularly by languages', cited in Butler 1968: 26). Adherence to such a notion of culture would represent not only a validation of concepts of identity rooted in divisiveness, but also a denial of the transnational nature of the German-language literature of Romania and the place this literature has come to occupy in the literatures of the other languages of Transylvania and Banat, namely Romanian and Hungarian. Moreover, it would represent a failure to consider the ways in which this literature, itself on the margins of several national literatures, reframes the national paradigm and foregrounds the processes of exclusion on which it relies in the construction of allegedly discrete unities. Ultimately, to consider the German-language literature of Romania as German literature that happens to be in Romania is to neglect one of the most significant features of this literature: its participation in the construction of a transnational cultural ethos in a multilingual region.

It is in this spirit that this chapter attempts to retrieve the multinational character of the German literature of Romania by considering the ways in which this literature has figured in the Romanian and Hungarian literature of Transylvania. By contextualizing this literature in the literatures of other national groups, I intend to advance an understanding of the cultures of the region as products of interaction between different linguistic groups. I offer this in part as a challenge to the persistent study of the cultures of this region of Europe as national or nationalist, an approach that abets nationalist claims concerning organic unity. Far from affirming national borders, numerous cultural artefacts from Central Europe transgress these borders and subject myths of national identity to questioning, recasting cultural identity as the fluid subject of continuous negotiation. I suggest three provisional approaches to the study of the place of the German language literature of Romania in Romanian and Hungarian literature: an examination of a few writings by Transylvanian German authors as outside of rather than peripheral to the canon of German literature in Germany following the Second World War and consideration of the affinities these works have with works in Romanian and Hungarian; consideration of instances of the integration of German language literature of Transylvania into Romanian literary histories; and an examination of the ways in which this literature figures in specific works of literature in Romanian and Hungarian, through translation, allusion or citation. My intention in each instance is by no means to offer an exhaustive account, but rather to suggest directions for further inquiry.

German literature and Romanian German literature

Without tending to overstatement, one may hazard the contention that in the first two decades following the Second World War German literature in Germany seemed to confirm Adorno's assertion that, 'To write poetry after Auschwitz is barbaric' (Adorno 1981: 34). The tendency towards social engagement and a confrontation with the events of the war in the works of Heinrich Böll, Hans Magnus Enzensberger and Günter Grass were of far more immediate concern and attracted a wider readership than the antiquated formalism of the lyric. Against this backdrop, the poetry of the Transylvanian Saxon authors Wolf von Aichelburg, Hans Wolfram Hockl and Georg Scherg, to name just three, may seem out of context or even anachronistic. Consider the following lines from Aichelburg's poem 'Rückblick' written in the 1960s:

> Die Mutter hat mich seltsam gestaltet,
> und als sie's erkannte, erschrak sie zutiefst.
> Sie bannte nicht mehr, was über mir waltet...
> Wer gab dir die Seele, als du noch schliefst?
> . . .
> Und muß der Zug zur Schrift sich biegen,
> und schreib ich meines Lebens Sinn,
> bleibt stummer Schmerzen Überwiegen,
> daß ich aus fremdem Holze bin
> (von Aichelburg, 1969: 106).

> (My mother formed me somewhat strange,
> And when she realized took deep fright.
> Spellbound no more by what reigned over me,
> Who gave you your soul as you slept?

...
And must my bent incline to writing,
And I write the meaning of my life
An overbalance of mute pain remains,
That I am of a foreign timber.)[1]

One cannot help but be struck by the echo of the opening lines of the poem 'Bénédiction' (Benediction) by Charles Baudelaire, cited here in the original and the translation by Edna St. Vincent Millay:

Lorsque, par un décret des puissances suprêmes,
Le Poète apparaît en ce monde ennuyé,
Sa mère épouvantée et pleine de blasphèmes
Crispe ses poings vers Dieu, qui la prend en pitié:
'Ah! que n'ai-je mis bas tout un noeud de vipers[.]'

(When, on a certain day, into this harassed world
The Poet, by decree of the high powers, was born,
His mother, overwhelmed by shame and fury, hurled
These blasphemies at God, clenching her fists in scorn:
'Would I had whelped a knot of vipers[.]')

This image of the poet as an outsider, a prominent theme of a great deal of nineteenth-century European literature, is in stark contrast to, for instance, the social engagement of the poetry of Germany of the 1960s (one might think, for instance, of Enzensberger's 1957 volume *Verteidigung der Wölfe* [In Defence of the Wolves]). Indeed, much of Aichelburg's poetry shows strong affinities with the works of prominent poets of Romanticism, such as Joseph von Eichendorff, Percy Bysshe Shelley or Charles Baudelaire. Almost all the poems in his largest collection, *Herbergen im Wind* (Hostelries in the Wind), are lyrics in which an object in nature figures as the occasion for the construction of an allegorical reflection on the human condition. Poems such as 'Zypresse' (The Cypress), 'Der Oliven Baum' (The Olive Tree), 'Die Eulen' (The Owls), 'Die Wellen' (The Waves) or 'Das Vogelei' (The Bird's Egg) offer representations of nature that are inherently figurative. Except that they were written in the latter half of the twentieth century these poems could be cited as exemplary of the characteristics of nineteenth-century Romanticism identified by the scholar of comparative literature René Wellek (1965), in that they turn to nature for their view of the world and to symbol and myth for poetic style. Aichelburg's poetry is no less distinct in its content than the postwar literature of West Germany. The poem 'Spätes Liebeslied' contains references to his homeland that would have radically different connotations were they to figure in the work of an author from West Germany:

> Heimat, einzige, die mir verblieben:
> lieben, immer dich lieben,
> hoffnungsarm, ergeben,
> dir, frühes Leben! (p. 132)

> (Homeland, only thing left to me:
> to love, always to love you,
> beggared of hopes, devoted,
> to you, early life!)

In the Romanian-German context the appeal to homeland bears a different meaning from what it might have in West Germany or even English translation, and it is significant that the facing page Romanian translation in *Herbergen im Wind* renders *Heimat* as *leagăn* or cradle, thus invoking less nationalistic connotations and skirting entirely the heavily value-laden implications of a reference to 'homeland' by a member of a German minority community.

While such poems could only be assimilated with considerable violence to the canon of postwar German literature in Germany, they show strong thematic and formal similarities to poems written in the same period by Transylvanian Romanians. In his poem 'The Poet's Profession', Dan Dănilă, for instance, expresses a similar concept of the poet as outsider:

> Oare meseria poetului e tristeţea
> de a fi neînţeles în propria limbă,
> sau tocmai înţelegerea tuturor
> l-ar ucide?

> (Is it the profession of the poet to grieve that
> He is not understood in his own language,
> Or would being understood by all
> Mean his perishing?)

This image of the poet as misunderstood is again a prominent theme of much of the literature of the nineteenth century. Its invocation in these poems by members of different national groupings suggests that the cultural ties of the region straddle the borders of language (it is worth noting that Dănilă's poem was translated into German by the Transylvanian German poet Hans Bergel). In the words of the Transylvanian Romanian poet Ovidiu Pecian, 'literatura transilvană există. Ea a produs opere valoroase în toate limbile Ardealului' ('Transylvanian literature exists. It has produced valuable works in all the languages of Transylvania') (Pecian 2000).

Romanian German literature in Romanian literary histories

The concept of the literary canon is in itself highly problematic and relies for its coherence on the principles of exclusion. Despite strivings to arrive at methodologies that release culture from its centripetal force, the notion of the national literary canon continues to exert a tremendous sway on the study of literature, whether on the level of institutional divisions into departments based on language or the writing of new national literary histories. It is therefore all the more remarkable that two of the most recent literary histories to be published in Romania, *Istoria literaturii române* (History of Romanian Literature) and *Istoria literaturii române de azi pe mâine* (History of Romanian Literature from Today to Tomorrow), devote sections to the German language literature of the country, mentioning specific authors, translators and literary journals. The shorter of the two, edited by Alexandru Piru (published one year after his death in 1993), admittedly gives only token acknowledgement to these works with no analysis, but the more extensive history by Marian Popa published in 2001 devotes an entire chapter to the literatures of linguistic minorities. Particularly illuminating for the contemporary reception and place of the German literature of Romania in Romanian literature is the remarkable contrast between Popa's treatment of this literature and his treatment of the Hungarian literature of Romania. The subsection on Hungarian literature, after pages devoted to little more than a rehearsal of condemnations made by Romanian authors of the irredentism allegedly implicit in the writings of Transylvanian Hungarians, concludes that:

> A considera literatură maghiară din România altfel decât o literatură străină nu mai pare exagerat. Desigur, sunt scriitori români şi unguri care pot avea relaţii personale amicable, fără a se simţi obligaţi să se considere edificatorii unei literaturi unice.
>
> (Popa, 2001: 190)

(It does not seem exaggerated to consider the Hungarian literature of Romania nothing other than a foreign literature. Certainly there are Romanian and Hungarian writers who have friendly personal relationships, but without feeling obliged to consider themselves representatives of a single literature.)

By contrast, in the section devoted to the German literature of Romania, Popa contends that German authors, if perhaps isolating themselves from Romanian writers, 'în cadrul socialist de ultimă oră ei reflectă relativ realităţi române' ('within the framework of socialism reflect, up until the last hour, the realities of Romania') (2001: 191).

However problematic the individual sections on the minority language literatures of Romania in Popa's history may be, the mere fact that both he and Piru felt it appropriate to include this literature within the context of a national literary history constitutes a departure from common practice in both Romania and Central Europe. While it is true that in his literary history written in 1865 the Hungarian author Ferenc Toldy (born to a German-speaking family named Schedel, which he officially changed in 1847) considered as Hungarian any work of literature written within the territory of the medieval kingdom of Hungary, this regional approach to cultural history was quickly submerged beneath the rising tide of national sentiment and by the end of the nineteenth century such a conception of literature was scarcely viable. One can consider the canonical history of Romanian literature, *Istoria literaturii române de la origini până în present* (History of Romanian Literature from its Origins to the Present), by the prominent Romanian literary historian George Calinescu, first published in 1941 and republished numerous times, paradigmatic. The section of his highly influential history on so-called foreign authors defines these authors not as writers in other languages living in Romania, but as writers of Romanian origins who left the country and wrote in other languages abroad. Indeed, Calinescu even includes Anne de Noailles, who was born in Paris and wrote in French. The fundamentally nationalist nature of this approach is epitomized in Calinescu's remark concerning authors who chose to write in a language other than Romanian that 'Gestul nu se recomandă, dar este explicabil' ('the gesture is not recommended, but it is understandable') (Calinescu, 1982: 969).

Piru's and Popa's inclusion within a national literary history of writers in other languages suggests the (re)beginnings of an approach to the study of culture in the region that considers language not an impermeable border, but rather a vehicle of exchange. This approach is by no means unique to their works, but rather can be seen in other institutional forms. In 2002, for instance, the Collegium Hungaricum Berlin hosted the Hungarian Transylvanian poet Géza Szőcs, the German native of Banat novelist Herta Müller, and the Romanian Transylvanian poet Simona Popescu. The same writers were hosted again that year by the Romanian Cultural Institute Titu Maiorescu. The inclusion of three artists writing in different languages by cultural organizations of two countries is an indication that the regional approach to culture is gaining ground on the institutional level. It would be unfortunate, given the admittedly provisional nature of this approach, to return to an understanding of culture based on division.

Romanian German literature in Hungarian and Romanian literature: allusion, citation, translation

In considering the place of the German language literature of Transylvania and Banat in Romanian and Hungarian literature its most immediate presence is through translation. Numerous novels, collections of shorter prose works and volumes of poetry have been published in Hungarian and Romanian translation. Of particular interest is the anthology of poems edited by Peter Motzan entitled *Vânt potrivit pâna la tare* (A Moderate to Strong Wind), which included the works of ten Romanian German authors translated into Romanian. In an article written in 1990, the Transylvanian Romanian poet Simona Popescu, herself a native of Brasov, once home to the second largest Saxon community in Transylvania, comments:

> aceasta poesie spune mai mult şi intr-o formă plină de forţa si artisticitate...decât o face poezia românească...o poeticitate care cuprînde mai multe elemente şi nuanţe: de la tranşantă la delicatete, de la emotiv la obiectiv...Poesia aceasta e o sinteză a mentalitaţii, expresivitaţii, sensibilitaţii individuale şi comunitare in acelaşi timp.
>
> (cited in Mihaiu)

(This poetry said more and in a form full of force and artistry...than Romanian poetry...A poetry that embraced more elements and nuances; from trenchant to delicate, emotional to objective...this poetry was a synthesis of the mentality, expressivity, and sensibility, individual and communal, of that time.)

Popescu continues, 'Poesia celor din *Vânt potrivit până la tare* este profund actuală, profund românească si necesară' ('The poetry of the volume was profoundly current, profoundly Romanian, and vital'). The Romanian literary scholar Virgil Mihaiu, writing in 1997 on the same volume, concurs:

> din acel moment, reprezentaţii iconoclastei noastre 'generaţii optzeciste' devin constienţi de existenţă, în acelaşi perimetru statal, a unor confraţi ce devansaseră gustul liric al timpului.

> (at the moment [of its publication] the representatives of our iconoclastic writers of the 1980s became aware of the existence, in this peripheral state, of their brothers, who had pushed forward the lyrical style of the time.)

If translation constitutes one of the forms in which Romanian German literature assumes its presence in Romanian and Hungarian literature, stylistic affinities also suggest inter-lingual influences. In the poetry of Hungarian authors from Transylvania such as Géza Paksándi, László Kolozsvári Papp and Sándor Kányádi one finds descriptions of nature that, like those of Aichelburg, are inherently figurative and invested with allegorical meanings. Indeed, Kányádi is a translator of the poetry of Transylvanian Saxons such as Wolf von Aichelburg and Joachim Wittstock, whose poems have also been translated into Romanian by Dan Dănilă. Worthy of mention is Kányádi's translation of the poem 'Dorfturm' (Village Tower) by Aichelburg, in which the tower of an abandoned village church, which has an iconic status in Transylvania as a symbol of the Saxon cultural presence, becomes a metonym for the communities that have, over the past two decades, almost completely vanished. It is also worth mentioning that Kányádi translates the title of the poem as 'Falusi torony Erdélyben' ('Village Tower in Transylvania'), thereby emphasizing the importance of a geographical context that is not bound to a specific language or national literature. The poem acquires poignancy in Hungarian, as many Transylvanian Hungarian speakers, correctly or incorrectly, perceive that the landmarks of their culture are slowly becoming gravestones of their communities. Here the act of translation transplants a narrative of loss and the symbols through which that poetic narrative is anchored to a territory into the language of a culture that perceives itself as in an analogous position, thereby inviting the culture of the target language to populate the narrative with its own symbols.

If Kányádi's work as a translator has contributed to the creation of a place for the German language literature of Romania in Hungarian literature, his poetry itself is no less deserving of attention. In the poem 'Hallotak napja Bécsben' (All Souls' Day in Vienna), which has been translated into several languages, including English (by Paul Sohar), Kányádi actually cites a line from a Saxon folk poem which he himself translated into Hungarian, but in this poem he cites it in German, and follows this with a Hungarian translation of the next line of the Saxon song:

> Befonnak egyszer téged is
> valami pompás koszorúba
> idegen lesz majd és hideg
> minden akár e bécsi utca
> wie die glocken ihren schall verloren
> felejted hamar minden örömöd

Sohar's translation preserves this feature of the original Hungarian:

> (They will braid you too some day
> in a wreath with pomp replete
> but the world will feel as cold
> and strange as this Vienna street
> wie die glocken ihren schall verloren
> forget your joy you will so soon.)

The last two lines are taken from a Saxon song 'Wie kam der Tod?' (How Did Death Come?), an excerpt of which is offered here in Transylvanian Saxon, German translation by Hermann Roth, and my English translation:

> Wae kâum dier Duit? Hie brâch mech nider,
> hîe zebrâch mir alle mene Glider;
> wae kâum dier Duit ond haûf mech of?

> Sai draugn mech aus Vuoters Haus,
> wuor verschuorn sei mech? – an de kail Jert;
> do lauch der Laif schnêwêis ond giel –
> Wän dai Klôken îren Schaul verluoren,
> esu vergôß ech men Fraud mäd allem Flaiß.

Wie kam der Tod? Er brach mich nieder,
er zerbrach mir alle meine Glieder;
wie kam der Tod und hob mich auf?

Sie trugen mich fort aus Vaters Haus,
Wohin verscharrten sie mich? In die kühle Erd,
da lag der Leib schneeweiß und gelb.

Wie die Glocken ihren Schall verloren,
so vergaß ich meine Freud mit allem Fleiß

(How did death come? He laid me low,
And shattered all my limbs;
How did death come, and lift me up?

They carried me forth from father's house,
Where did they bury me? In the cool earth,
There lay my body snow-white and yellow.
Like the bells their clang lost,
So hastily I forgot my joy.)

In his collection of essays, poems, diary entries and other writings entitled *So Nah, so Fremd: Heimatlegenden* (So Near, So Strange: Legends of
Homeland) the Transylvanian poet Dieter Schlesak mentions this song
as part of familiar everyday cultural life of his childhood in Schäßburg
(Sighişoara in Romanian, Segesvár in Hungarian), the Transylvanian city
of his birth. What was once part of the folklore of a now vanished community has become part of the contemporary poetry of a still thriving
minority literature.

Conclusion

This discussion of the ways in which the German language literature
of Romania has assumed a place in Romanian and Hungarian literature
should demonstrate that the concept of discrete, self-sufficient national
culture can no more be applied to the literatures of this region of Central
Europe than can the literatures of Central Europe be used to demonstrate the self-sufficiency of national cultures. Indeed as Schneider (this
volume) cogently demonstrates, this is true not only of the literature but
also of the musical culture of the region. Far from reifying national identities, much of the cultural life of Central Europe makes these groupings
appear illusory. It is a curious irony that literature in particular, which
it has been argued (notably by Anderson 1983) was the most influential

medium in the creation of national identity, now functions in part as a forum for its deconstruction. Readings of the national literatures of the region that are attentive to the echoes intermingling in these literatures can further a revision of concepts of culture based on the exclusionary practices involved in the construction of national canons.

Acknowledgement

I would like to extend my sincerest thanks to the Institute for Comparative Literature and Society at Columbia University for its generous support of the research on which this chapter is based.

Note

1. All translations are mine unless otherwise indicated.

References

Adorno, T. (1981) *Prisms*, trans. S. and S. Weber (Cambridge, MA: MIT Press).
Anderson, B. (1983) *Imagined Communities: Reflections on the Origin and Spread of Nationalism* (London and New York: Verso).
Babeți, A. and Ungureanu, C. (eds) (1997) *Europa Centrală: Nevroze, dileme, utopii* (Iași: Polirom).
Bocșan, N., Förster, H. and Teicu, D. (1995) *Kulturraum mittlere und untere Donau: Traditionen und Perspektiven des Zusammenlebens* (Reșita: Museum für Geschichte des Kreises Karasch-Sewerin).
Butler, R. d'O. (1968) *The Roots of National Socialism: 1783–1933*, 2nd edition (New York: E. P. Dutton).
Calinescu, G. (1982) *Istoria literaturii române de la origini până în present* (Bucharest: Minerva).
Culic, I., Horváth, I., Magyari, N. and Lazăr, M. (1998) *Bazinul Carpatic: Români și maghiari în tranziție – Imagini mentale și relații interetnice în Transilvania* (Cluj: Research Center for Interethnic Relations).
Dănilă, D. (2006) *Poetry*, http://www.dan-danila.de/poezii.html. Accessed 21 December 2006.
Gáll, E. (1994) *A nacionalizmus színeváltozásai* (Oradea: Literátor).
Halsted, J. B. (ed.) (1965) *Romanticism: Problems of Definition, Explanation, and Evaluation* (Boston, MA: Heath).
Kányádi, S. (1976) *Hallotak napja Bécsben*, http://www.neumann-haz.hu/dia/diat/muvek/html/KANYADI/kanyadi00267/kanyadi00267.html. Accessed 3 December 2006.
Kányádi, S. (1976) *All Souls' Day*, trans. Paul Sohar, http://www.archipelago.org/vol3-4/kanyadi.htm. Accessed 3 December 2006.
Kocsis, K. (2007) 'Changing ethnic patterns in Transylvania since 1989', *Journal of Hungarian Studies* 21, 179–201.

Mihaiu, V. (1997) 'Scriitori germani din Romania: "Vânt potrivit până la tare"', *România Literară* 21. Available at http://www.memoria.ro/?location= view_article&id=966. Accessed 3 December 2006.

Motzan, P. (ed.) (1982) *Vânt potrivit pâna la tare. Anthologie neuerer rumänien-deutscher Lyrik in rumänischer Übersetzung*, translated into Romanian by Ioan Muslea (Bucharest: Kriterion).

Mureşanu, C. (1996) *Naţiune, naţionalism: Evoluţia naţionalităţilor* (Cluj: Fundaţia Culturală Română).

Pecian, O. (2000) *Aerul dimprejur*, http://www.provincia.ro/cikk_roman/ c000068.html. Accessed 29 January 2007.

Piru, A. (ed.) (1994) *Istoria literaturii române* (Bucharest: Grai şi suflet).

Popa, M. (ed.) (2001) *Istoria literaturii române de azi pe mâine* (Bucharest: Fundaţia Luceafărul).

Roth, H. (2007) *Wie kam der Tod*, translation of folk song *Wae kâum dier Duit?* http://ingeb.org/Lieder/wiekamde.html. Accessed 2 January 2007.

Schlesak, D. (1994) *So Nah, so Fremd: Heimatlegenden* (Ippesheim: Arbeitskreis für Geschichte und Kultur der deutschen Siedlungsgebiete).

Ungureanu, C. (2004) *Europa Centrală* (Bucharest: Curtea Veche).

Végh, B. (1993) 'Romániai német irodalom vagy német irodalom Romániában?', in *Regio – Kisebbség, politika, társadalom* 4.1 (Budapest: Teleki László Alapítvány and Teleki László Intézet Közép-Európai Tanulmányok Központja).

von Aichelburg, W. (1969) *Herbergen im Wind* (Bucharest: Literaturverl).

Wellek, R. (1965) 'The concept of "Romanticism" in literary history', *Halsted*, 45–52.

Zub, A. (1996) *Identitate şi alteritate în spaţiul cultural românesc* (Iaşi: Editura Universităţii Alexandru Ioan Cuza).

Part IV

Language and European Identities: Periphery and Centre

12
Revisiting History: The 2007 European Capital of Culture and the Integration of Fractal Europe

Kristine Horner

Introduction

Much has been written on the construction of a European identity, including debates as to whether it may be viewed as complementing or conflicting with national identities and, more fundamentally, whether such a concept is even conceivable (Delanty and Rumford 2005: 50–68). It has been argued that EU-sponsored attempts to foster a sense of European identity have recently shifted towards strategies seemingly devoid of cultural baggage, for example, emphasizing the practical benefits of EU membership (Stråth 2006; Caliendo 2007). While this sort of argument holds weight in certain contexts, attempts to construct a European identity framed explicitly in cultural terms have not been completely abandoned, as is illustrated by the annual European Capital of Culture (ECC). Based on an idea frequently credited to the former Greek Minister of Culture, Melina Mercouri, the first ECC was organized in Athens in 1985 and was subsequently hosted by individual cities in various EU member-states until 1999. In the year immediately preceding the introduction of the Euro, cities in nine European countries jointly hosted the 2000 ECC (Sassatelli 2002).[1] From 2001 to 2006, the ECC was held in either one or two cities in different EU member-states, with a European Cultural Month sometimes added as a satellite activity, often in a city in an EU candidate country.

This chapter takes the January 2007 accession of Romania and Bulgaria as new EU member-states and the related redrawing of European boundaries as a point of departure for exploring representations linked to the 2007 European Capital of Culture, which symbolically connected two opposite corners of the expanded European Union. On the one hand, marked by a strong sense of regionalism, Luxembourg and parts of Germany, France and Belgium are constructed as one territory – the 'Grande Région' – in promotional materials. On the other hand, Sibiu/Hermannstadt in the Transylvanian region of Romania is drawn into the discourse of European unification via moves to flag medieval settlements established by speakers of Germanic language varieties. This foregrounding of presupposed shared linguistic repertoires pre-dating the era of the nation-state serves to construct a continuity between historical patterns of migration and current transformations in Europe, as well as the unity or 'integration' of the space traversing the northwestern and southeastern stretches of an imagined European place.[2]

In the following sections, I explore the ways in which representations of linguistic and spatial boundaries in 2007 ECC materials resonate with attempts to construct a European identity, as well as the ways in which narratives of the nation-state and the legitimation of named languages of the state are being renegotiated in relation to global processes. A final question is how the discourse of unity in diversity is being drawn upon to resolve tensions bound up within the consolidation of EU infrastructures.

Inventing and disinventing the German language in an expanding Europe

During the twelfth century, speakers of Germanic language varieties from multiple points of origin in the (western) Holy Roman Empire, including the Moselle Valley, began to establish settlements in Transylvania, an area that extends from the geographic centre of present-day Romania towards the Maramures, Crisana and Banat regions framing its northwestern state borders. The settlers, who came to be known as the Transylvanian Saxons, initially arrived in response to incentives offered by King Géza II at the time when the region was part of the Kingdom of Hungary.[3] Transylvania was subsequently under the rule of the Habsburgs and, following the First World War, it was ceded to Romania in accordance with the Treaty of Trianon (1920), which resulted in the reallocation of a significant part of (then) Hungarian territory, a space that was home to many speakers of Hungarian and Germanic language varieties (Maitz and Sándor, this volume). While it can be said that fluctuations in the socio-political field from the late eighteenth century onwards led to the erosion of rights and privileges previously bestowed on speakers of Germanic language varieties in Transylvania, two historical moments in the twentieth century had a major impact as they significantly led to the numerical reduction of the Transylvanian Saxon population. First, events connected to the Second World War resulted in mass evacuations and expulsions of speakers of Germanic language varieties from Transylvania; and second, the fall of the Berlin Wall served as an impetus for additional, relatively large-scale migration to Germany during the early 1990s (Rein 1997: 1472–3). The irony of this 'return migration' lies in the fact that Transylvanian Saxons, who often considered themselves to be ethnically and linguistically German, have not always been regarded as such in Germany (cf. Weber-Newth 1995; Dietz 2000 on the migration of ethnic Germans from the former Soviet Union). Moreover, the Germanic language varieties spoken by Tranyslvanian Saxons have sometimes been stigmatized in this new environment, resulting in many speakers shifting to varieties that approximate standard, written German (Mummert 1995: 49–51). Because language varieties spoken by Transylvanian Saxons have often been devalorized and/or viewed as 'out of place' in Germany, it is somewhat paradoxical that they are depicted as a link between 'old' and 'new' EU member-states in 2007 ECC materials.

While spoken varieties that differ significantly from standard, written German are often regarded as 'bad' German in Germany (Davies and Langer 2006), the situation in contemporary Luxembourg is different. Due to myriad social-political developments, together with the endeavours of key social actors over the course of the twentieth century, the Moselle Franconian language varieties widely spoken in Luxembourg are not bound up with social stigmatization and, moreover, are commonly perceived as constituting a separate language, Luxembourgish, which is recognized as the 'national language' in the 1984 language law. Discourses circulating in the mainstream Luxembourgish press frequently construct the Moselle River as an impermeable linguistic boundary between Luxembourgish and German (Horner 2005). However, the boundary is blurred in 2007 ECC materials and references to the German language are sometimes interchanged with references to Moselle Franconian and Luxembourgish. While it is productive to unpack the processes of social construction – related to theorizations of the 'invention of tradition' (Hobsbawm and Ranger 1983) – that enable the categorization of abstractions such as languages, nations, and so on, this form of inquiry can be taken further by exploring how languages can be 'disinvented' (Makoni and Pennycook 2007b) by no longer being seen as bounded units. A close look at 2007 ECC materials reveals that the German language is to a certain extent strategically 'disinvented' in relation to goals of European unification informing the production of these materials, thus constituting the inverse of the widespread European practice of constructing languages with clear-cut boundaries.

The choice to foreground the German language for purposes of constructing shared 'Europeanness' may be viewed as a further paradox in the 2007 ECC representations, especially in light of associations of pan-Germanism with manifestations of ethnolinguistic or 'bad' nationalism (cf. May 2001). However, as Cooper (this volume) points out in his discussion of Romanian German literature, forms of cultural production sometimes mobilized by nationalist movements can also be drawn on to deconstruct essentialist concepts of culture. The 2007 ECC materials are not entirely dissimilar from the processes of cultural production described by Cooper in the sense that essentialist linkages underpinning nationalist ideologies conflating nation and state are challenged, while at the same time the Herderian ties between a common language and culture profoundly shape the 2007 ECC materials. Just as named languages and bound cultures are socially constructed, so too are named places, which brings us to the paradox about Europe as place, or in Liotta's (2005: 80) words: 'the irony of Europe is that its geographic identity has itself always been a bit of a fraud'. Liotta also discusses the perceived 'Otherness' of the Balkans and southeastern Europe, highlighting the question that preoccupies many present-day EU policy-makers: how can we integrate these spaces into Europe? With Germanic language varieties positioned as a key link, the 2007 ECC materials constitute an attempt to construct a sense of European place and, moreover, to incorporate parts of Europe that are often regarded as 'not quite European' from the perspective of the west.

Imagining a Europe unified in diversity

Although associated with Anderson's ([1983] 1991) concept of the imagined nation, the processes of imagining need not be limited to a national community as discourses can potentially be recast in relation to fluctuations in the socio-political field (cf. Sassatelli 2002). Pavlenko and Blackledge (2004b) underline the dynamics as well as the constraints of identity by asserting that it can potentially be assumed, imposed or negotiated; furthermore, they emphasize the role of imagining in relation to the processes of constructing and negotiating group boundaries. Central to imagining are discourses which are simultaneously creative and constrained, or as Johnstone (2002: 138) puts it: 'Repetition and variation – prior texts shaped to new contexts, old expectations drawn on in new situations – are at the heart of how discourse works.' Gee ([1999] 2005) encourages researchers to take into account different dimensions of discourse, which he refers to as small 'd' and big 'D' discourses (see also Dailey-O'Cain and Liebscher, this volume). The former entails close textual analysis as conducted by discourse and conversation analysts alike, for example, by exploring the ways in which boundaries are reproduced or challenged in stretches of language in use. Sometimes distinguishing work in discourse analysis from conversation analysis is the frequent engagement of the former with what Gee refers to as the big 'D' discourses, which pertain to the broader social, political and economic processes that shape textual production and uptake; the omnipresent European discourse of unity in diversity constitutes an example of a big 'D' discourse, which is particularly salient in materials produced under the auspices of the EU.

The 2007 ECC theme was marked by an innovative, two-pronged organizational strategy, seeking to promote a sense of pan-Europeanism more overtly than had been the case in previous years. Although Luxembourg was officially designated as the hosting EU member-state, 2007 ECC paraphernalia not only appeared in multiple sites across Luxembourg, but also in the adjacent regions of France, Belgium and Germany, which together were represented as one territory – the Grande Région – in promotional materials. 2007 ECC materials distributed in the Grande Région were produced in multiple sites, including Luxembourg city, Trier (Germany) and Metz (France). In these materials, which construct the Grande Région as a more salient unit than individual EU member-states, the image of the blue stag is portrayed as indexical of transcending boundaries, with the Grande Région depicted as the principal site for this process:[4]

(1) Weite Wälder prägen die Landschaft der gesamten Großregion – der Hirsch steht als Symbol für dieses verbindende Element. Als blauer Hirsch weist er den Weg über Grenzen hinweg, in die Welt der Träume, der Freiheit und des kreativen Schaffens ...
(Studio Martial Damblant 2007)

(Extensive forests mark the landscape of the entire Grande Région – the stag symbolizes this unifying element. The blue stag indicates the path [to follow] beyond the borders, into the world of dreams, liberty and creative production.)

Signalled by references to the natural world and the fantastic, together with the stag, excerpt (1) draws on romanticist traditions, which is of interest in light of recent suggestions that EU-related discourse is taking a more acultural or positivistic shape. The choice of the colour blue may similarly be linked to romantic imagery, though it is also the same shade of blue as on the Luxembourgish national flag (a red/white/light blue tricolour). Constituting the second prong of the 2007 ECC is the designation of Sibiu/Hermannstadt in the Transylvanian region of Romania as the 'second' or 'other' Capital of Culture. Also informed by romanticism, the link between Sibiu and the Grande Région is rooted in the Herderian equation of a shared language, ethnicity and homeland, which in this case foregrounds Germanic language varieties as a bridge spanning Europe; this representation strategy is enabled by medieval migration patterns from west to east as well as present-day cooperative undertakings.

As a springboard for further discussion of 2007 ECC discourses, it is productive to consider the ways in which the two prongs of the 2007 ECC are depicted in relation to each other in certain visual representations, as for example in Figure 12.1.

Two maps are shown in Figure 12.1, both of which represent Europe geographically without indicating state borders in a highly salient manner, due to the shading patterns. The centrally positioned map of the Grande Région includes the whole of Luxembourg as well as parts of Belgium, France and Germany. In the lower left-hand corner is a map of greater Europe with the Grande Région indicated as one territory, visually linked to the Romanian city of Sibiu by the use of white colouring of these places against a rich blue background. Although the link between Luxembourg and Sibiu is constructed in certain 2007 ECC materials by indexing the (allegedly) shared use of Moselle Franconian language varieties, the headings and captions on this map appear in the standard, written varieties of French, German and English. This seemingly paradoxical point will be discussed in the following sections in relation to the work of Irvine and Gal (2000) on linguistic differentiation. Just as there is 'no view from nowhere' with regard to the naming of languages, the same can be said for cartographical representations (cf. Shapiro 1999). In Figure 12.1 the gaze is from the west, with the 'rest of Europe' to the east positioned as secondary to the Grande Région, thus constituting an image that is not unrelated to Boia's ([2001] 2006: 8)

247

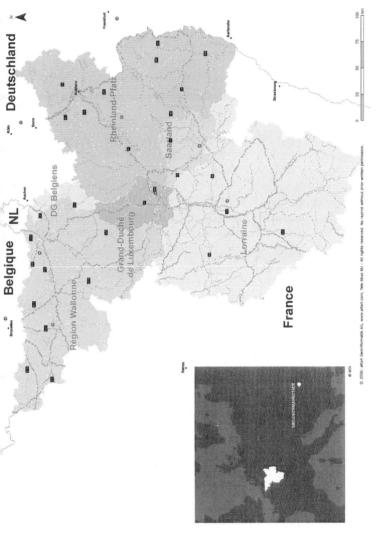

Figure 12.1 Crossing borders: Luxembourg and the 'Grande Région' alta4 Geoinformatik AG, Trier, © 2007

point concerning the ways in which Romania is sometimes regarded from the west:[5]

> Like any other country, Romania can be simplified and can be multiplied into all sorts of images and symbols. Seen from the west, its location alone is enough to make it seem an almost exotic land: somewhere 'out there', on the margins of Europe.

The 2007 European Capital of Culture: without borders?

The analysis of 2007 ECC materials focuses on representations of shifting European boundaries in relation to the consolidation of the EU and, in particular, the 2007 expansion phase entailing the entry of Bulgaria and Romania as new member-states. The first section deals with the negotiation of linguistic boundaries and draws on the work of Irvine and Gal (2000), who deal with the semiotic processes of (linguistic) differentiation. Informed by Gal's (2006) discussion of the 'fractal geography' of Europe, the second section concentrates on the negotiation of spatial boundaries. The final section analyses the ways in which places with varying degrees of perceived 'Europeanness' are brought together via an integrative as opposed to fractal geography of Europe, and shows how the concept of 'integrative geography' meshes with the discourse of unity in diversity informing 2007 ECC representations, which are bound up with the processes of imagining Europe.

Linguistic boundaries: legitimating stateless language varieties?

The nomination of Sibiu as the 'second' 2007 ECC stems in part from cooperative undertakings by the Luxembourgish and Romanian governments in recent years, with the restoration and reopening in 2004 of the Casa de Luxemburg on the Piata Mica in Sibiu, constituting the most high-profile initiative prior to the 2007 ECC. Fehlen (2007) takes a critical stance vis-à-vis these projects and, more specifically, aims to debunk mythical underpinnings drawn on to forge discursive links between Luxembourg and Sibiu. However exaggerated certain aspects of related historical narratives may be, I take a different tack by exploring the ways in which this pan-Germanic discourse – which Fehlen labels as 'nationalist' – has been disembedded or 'lifted out' from an existing discursive tradition bound up with the modernist ideal of nation-state congruence, and discuss how it has been recast in relation to the overarching 2007 ECC. The relationship between Luxembourg and Sibiu – and sometimes all of Transylvania – is frequently indexed by the supposed shared use of Moselle Franconian language varieties; representations of this nature pre-dating the 2007 ECC can be found, for example, in the Luxembourgish print media (excerpt (2)) and are pervasive in 2007 ECC materials (excerpt (3)):

(2) Es war König Geysa (Geza) II. von Ungarn, der im 12. Jahrhundert deutsche Siedler nach Siebenbürgen in die spätere "Hermannstädter Provinz" rief, um die Grenzen entlang der Karpaten zu verteidigen und zu befestigen und um das Land wirtschaftlich in Schwung zu bringen. Im 13. Jahrhundert errichtete der deutsche Ritterorden im Burzenland Burgen und Siedlungen. Man sprach in diesen Dörfern – und späteren Städten – jenes Moselfränkische, in dem die luxemburgische Sprache ihre Wurzeln hat und das bis heute in Siebenbürgen überlebt hat, wenn auch nur spärlich.

(Monique Hermes, *Luxemburger Wort*, 31 July 2002: 16)

(In order to defend and secure the borders along the Carpathians and to bring economic prosperity to the land, it was King Géza II of Hungary who invited German settlers to Transylvania to the future 'Province of Hermannstadt' in the twelfth century. In the thirteenth century the German Order of Knights established fortresses and settlements in Burzenland. People in these villages – and in future cities – spoke that Moselle Franconian in which the Luxembourgish language has its roots and which to this day has lived on in Transylvania, even if only in small numbers.)

(3) In order to achieve the goal they have set themselves, the two European Capitals of Culture 2007, Luxembourg and Greater Region [*sic*], as well as Sibiu in Romania meet many prerequisites: although geographically apart, the two regions have common roots and historical links which allotted them very similar cultures and traditions. The Saxons from Sibiu – descendants of the migrants who started building the city in the 12th century – still speak a language that is very close to the francique-mosellan [*sic*] which is spoken in the region enclosed by the Moselle and Rhine. Thus a relation between the two cultures seems very probable and the principal set of themes of the Capital of Culture 2007, migrations, is reinforced by this fact.

(LGRCEC 2007a)

In both excerpts, references to Moselle Franconian index a point of common origin between people in Luxembourg and Transylvania. However, in excerpt (3), taken from a 2007 ECC website under the heading 'Building bridges in an expanding Europe', the scope is broadened to include the Grande Région rather than just Luxembourg, but is narrowed to

Sibiu rather than all of Transylvania. This shift from Luxembourg to the entire Grande Région serves as an initial discursive move towards establishing shared 'Europeanness'. In addition, the text constitutes an attempt to foster a sense of European place across the continent by fore-grounding the causality between having 'common roots' and 'historical links' and therefore 'very similar cultures and traditions'. The repre-sentation of the linguistic link between the entire Grande Région and Sibiu in excerpt (3) stands in opposition to discourses regularly circu-lating in the Luxembourgish print media attempting to mark a clear boundary between what is spoken in Luxembourg and what is spo-ken directly on the 'other' side of the Moselle River, designating the state border between Luxembourg and Germany (Horner 2005). The strategy of evoking a shared history – discursively linked to essentialist biological or ecological metaphors such as 'roots' – is widely employed in nationalist discourses, but the goal in 2007 ECC materials is to uncouple the nation-state (cf. May 2001), and the ideal of bounded cultures is equated with regionalism rather than the model of the nation-state (cf. Blommaert and Verschueren 1992).

Given that Moselle Franconian is often referred to as a dialect rather than a language in other contexts (cf. extract (6) below), tensions con-cerning the naming of languages are erased or 'render[ed] invisible' (Irvine and Gal 2000: 38), as is the problematic nature of certain linguis-tic theories tracing this historical relationship (Hoffmann 1996: 171–4). Furthermore, the materials themselves are not written in Moselle Fran-conian but in standard German, French and English. In the 2007 ECC materials, the frequent indexing of Moselle Franconian is not bound up with an overarching shift towards the legitimation of non-officially rec-ognized European language varieties in addition to named languages of the state, nor does it suggest an abrupt shift in language ideologies and practices (cf. Wilkinson, this volume). Instead, the renegotiation of lin-guistic boundaries in this instance serves as a springboard to renegotiate spatial boundaries, which in turn allows for a sense of continuity from past to present, a discursive strategy facilitating the construction of a European sense of place.

Spatial boundaries: narrating beyond the nation-state?

The emphasis on regionalism in 2007 ECC materials resonates with related discursive attempts to shift the focus away from boundaries between EU member-states towards those between all that is and is not European (cf. Figure 12.1). In addition to narrating a common 'natural' history and indexing shared linguistic origins, as discussed in the previous section, the ways in which European space is represented constitute a further means of constructing European identity, as illustrated by excerpt (4) under the heading *Grenzenlos* ('Without Borders') from a 2007 ECC brochure:

(4) 4 Länder, 3 Sprachen, 5 Regionen im Herzen Europas – **Luxemburg Stadt** und **Land, Lothringen** (F), **Rheinland-Pfalz** (D), das **Saarland** (D), **Wallonien** (französische und deutschsprachige Gemeinschaft Belgiens): Die Kulturhauptstadt Europas 2007 geht über alle Grenzen hinweg! 2007 knüpft neue Netze für grenzüberschreitenden Austausch und schafft Raum für den Dialog zwischen lokalem Kunstschaffen und internationaler Kreation.

(Studio Martial Damblant 2007; original emphasis)

(4 countries, 3 languages and 5 regions in the heart of Europe – **Luxembourg city** and [the] **country, Lorraine, Rhineland-Palatinate, Saarland** and **Wallonia** (French and German speaking communities in Belgium): the 2007 European Capital of Culture transcends all borders! 2007 establishes new networks for border crossing exchange and creates a space for dialogue between local cultural endeavours and international creation.)

In excerpt (4), the Grande Région constitutes the focal point from which '4 countries', '3 languages' and '5 regions' derive, and the predominance of regional place is flagged by the choice of bold font to indicate the five (sub)regions subsumed by the Grande Région. Representations of Luxembourg as a region – or even part of the Grande Région – in 2007 ECC materials contradict discursive moves in multiple sources published over the course of the twentieth century to reinforce the status of Luxembourg as an independent state (Horner 2007). The narrative of excerpt (4) works intertextually with an image of a road sign indicating a blue stag as an appeal for the transcendence of state boundaries in the interest of furthering present-day cooperative endeavours. The representation of the Grande Région as the 'heart of Europe' positions it as the natural locus for the European project, perhaps even as a model which may be emulated.

Excerpt (5) is taken from the same 2007 ECC brochure under the heading 'Sibiu':

(5) Sibiu/Hermannstadt in Transsilvanien/Rumänien: Die zweite Kulturhauptstadt Europas des Jahres 2007. Gemeinsam mit **Luxemburg**

steht sie für grenzüberschreitende Projekte und Begegnungen, und ebenso für die Entwicklung und die Zukunft Europas. Die Kulturfabrik in **Esch/Alzette** (L) transformiert sich zu ihren Ehren ein ganzes Jahr lang in *little Sibiu – West meets East* mit einem bunt gemischten Programm und zahlreichen gemeinsamen Projekten von Künstlern aus der Großregion und Rumänien.

(Studio Martial Damblant 2007, original emphasis)

(Sibiu/Hermanndstadt in Transylvania/Romania: the second European Capital of Culture 2007. Together with **Luxembourg** it represents border crossing projects and encounters, as well as the development and future of Europe. For a whole year, the Kulturfabrik in **Esch/Alzette** (L) is transformed into *little Sibiu – West meets East* in its honour with a colourfully diverse programme and numerous joint projects [undertaken] by artists from the Grande Région and Romania.)

The reference to Sibiu as the 'second' 2007 ECC is indicative of the hierarchical relationship frequently posited between west and east. If the Grande Région is iconic or 'somehow depict[s] or display[s]' a sense of 'Europeanness' or the 'social group's inherent nature or essence' (Irvine and Gal 2000: 37), then Sibiu is positioned as almost but not quite European. Rooted in historical traditions forging binary oppositions between western and eastern Europe (cf. Delanty and Rumford 2005: 28–49), the 2007 ECC materials resonate with Gal's (2006: 25) discussion of the 'fractal geography' of Europe, which is indicative of moves to create further oppositions within Central and Eastern European countries (often in the former Soviet bloc) by indexing levels of 'Europeanness' or 'non-Europeanness', thus reproducing 'an infinitely splittable Europe, endlessly able to project stereotypical inclusion and exclusion according to perspective taken in interactional context'. Although the west/east divide is simultaneously reflected and constructed in 2007 ECC materials, discursive moves to 'build bridges' between the west and east are also made (cf. excerpt (3)), with the goal of shutting down the source of these fractal recursive processes described by Gal (2006: 25) so that 'the construction and future of Europe' may be undertaken, with as the ultimate goal the unification of Europe.

Unity in diversity: integrating fractal Europe?

Under the auspices of the 2007 ECC, attempts to position Romania as a viable EU member-state are also bound up with the organization of cultural events, including the series of exhibits and performances by Romanian artists that took place in the Kulturfabrik in the southern, Minette region of Luxembourg (cf. excerpt (5)). Musical performances on 8 and 16 June 2007 showcased bands from northwestern Transylvania (Taraf de Carei), Wallachia (Nadia and Napoleon), northern Moldavia (Taraf de Botosani) and northeastern Moldavia (Fanfare de Vorona). The choice of musicians from the major regions of Romania (cf. Boia [2001] 2006) casts it as a microcosm of Europe, embodying 'Europeanness' via its construction as a European place that is home to the ideal of unity in diversity; in this discourse any trace of intragroup conflict in Romania and the region of Transylvania is erased (cf. Baár and Ritivoi 2006; Brubaker et al. 2006). Representations of a harmonious Romania, 'unified in diversity', can be found in 2007 ECC materials, for example, in the official programme of events, which additionally highlights historical links between Sibiu and Luxembourg – together with the Grande Région – due to (allegedly) shared language:

(6) Sibiu/Hermannstadt in Romania is a city with a rich and chequered past that is characterized by a wide ethnic and cultural diversity. Romanians, Hungarians, Transylvanian Saxons, Roma ... different communities all contributing their particular ethnic influences to the intercultural flair of this city at the crossroads between East and West. ... The link between the inhabitants of Luxembourg and the Transylvanian Saxons was re-discovered in the 19th century through a comparison of the Luxembourgish and Saxon languages (a dialect related to Moselle Frankish [*sic*] as spoken in the Moselle/Rhine area)

(LGRCEC 2007b: 198).

Unlike the Grande Région, which is positioned in the 'heart of Europe', Sibiu is situated 'at the crossroads between East and West' (cf. Gal 2006). In this way, the outer frontier of Europe is shifted eastwards in line with the latest EU expansion. This discursive move serves to elevate the degree of 'Europeanness' of Sibiu – together with all of Romania – putting it more on a par with Luxembourg and the Grande Région. However, it is also the case that representations in 2007 ECC materials often suggest that further steps need to be taken for Romania to be properly 'integrated', and this process is to be facilitated by learning from the west, in particular from places

that are constructed as iconic of 'Europeanness' such as the Grande
Région:

> (7) In the context of globalisation and the process of European
> integration, cross-border cooperation between regions is increasingly
> important. Situated at the heart of the European Union and made up
> of Saarland, Lorraine, Luxembourg, Rhineland-Palatinate, Wallonia
> with the French- and the German-speaking communities of Belgium,
> our Greater Region is one of the most advanced models of inter-
> regional and cross-border cooperation. Various economic, social, and
> cultural elements – the product of the encounter of the Romanic
> and Germanic worlds – confer a specific character to the region. The
> interdependence of the entities comprising the Greater Region has
> a long history. Common cultural roots date back over a thousand
> years.... European Capital of Culture 2007 is a European project par
> excellence and it will enable the Greater Region to reach out well
> beyond its borders. In this respect, the participation of the city of
> Sibiu will be particularly important at a time when Romania will
> become a member state of the European Union.
>
> (LGRCEC 2007b: 2)

The representation of the Grande Région as 'the product of the
encounter of the Romanic and Germanic worlds' bears a striking resem-
blance to discourses of Luxembourgish nationalism, which position
Luxembourg as embodying the best of both worlds, simultaneously
making it distinct from and superior to its neighbouring states (Horner
2007). The employment of this discursive strategy in excerpt (7) is
unsurprising as it originates from a statement by the Luxembourgish
Prime Minister, Jean-Claude Juncker, in the context of EU-sponsored
materials. However, the additional, implicit reference to Charlemagne –
'[c]ommon cultural roots date back over a thousand years' – allows
it to be recast as post-nationalist, drawing on the tradition of 'stories
about Europe formed by a specific Christian or Antique heritage' (Stråth
2006: 437), which frequently underpins discourses of 'Europeanness'.
The discourse of integration, together with an integrative geography
of Europe, which is meant to contain the fractal geography of Europe,
combine in 2007 ECC materials to pave the way to reaching the future
goal of unity in diversity. The call for regional cooperation, which
may be understood as broader European cooperation, is constructed
as an essential survival strategy in relation to the forces of globalization. The narrative of a shared past in excerpt (7) projects a sense of

continuity and stability in relation to major social, political and economic fluctuations impacting on the lives of social actors in Europe, a state of affairs that has rapidly been gaining momentum from the 1970s onwards.

Revisiting history, reconstructing Europe

Harvey (1989) flags the twin forces of modernity – transience and change – in relation to his assertion that the 1970s constitute a critical moment in the transition from modernity to postmodernity. He asserts that this transition is marked by intensified time–space compression, arguably the most prominent contextualizing feature in relation to the patchy changes bound up with globalization. Coupland's (2003) discussion of global processes – community interdependence, commodification, compression of time and space and disembedding – can be drawn on to situate the 2007 ECC materials in the broader sociopolitical context as well as to understand the conditions shaping their production. Increasing community interdependence (between regions and beyond) has facilitated the commodification of cultural and linguistic diversity, which is 'packaged and sold' as part of the 2007 ECC programme. Furthermore, compression of time and space allows for the disembedding of nationalist discourses so that they may be cast as post-nationalist in these materials. Although the construction of 'Europeanness' is not directly comparable with that of nationhood, the discursive models and strategies drawn on are not wholly dissimilar. Present-day discourses draw on pre-existing ones, albeit in innovative ways that do not constitute precise repetitions of former discourses, not least because the conditions in which discourses are produced and received do not remain static. Moreover, the common saying that 'history repeats itself' is perhaps more productively cast as 'revisiting history', especially because it is social actors who narrate histories (cf. White 1981; Carl and Stevenson, this volume).

It has been argued that certain individuals are experiencing a heightened sense of identity and search for belonging as a reaction against major transformations affecting their daily lives; there is a perceived need for a well-defined sense of place as a counterweight to change. Cultural and social geographers have pointed out that identity and a sense of place are frequently bound up with one another (Rose 1995). Debates over essentialist and constructivist approaches to senses of place (Feld and Basso 1996b) and to ethnic and national identity (May 2001) have been responded to most sensibly with calls for a middle ground between the two positions. Although all forms of identity are malleable to a certain degree and operate in similar ways, ethnicity is characterized by mutual perceptions of 'cultural stuff', including shared perceptions of a territory of origin or an ancestral language passed down from generation to generation (Jenkins 1997). References to ethnicity and common origins – including linguistic origins – proliferate in 2007 ECC materials, suggesting that it may be the role of the state rather than identification with ethnicity and nationhood that is under increasing pressure in relation to the consolidation of the EU and the processes of globalization. As Gal (2006) points out, the Herderian link between shared language and culture remains deeply entrenched; it informs the EU discourse of unity in diversity – together with the 'integrative geography' of Europe – that is omnipresent in 2007 ECC materials.

According to Sassatelli (2002: 436), 'the ECC is a salient example of the attempts at awakening a European consciousness by diffusing its symbols, while respecting the contents of national and local cultures'. With Luxembourg and the entire Grande Région together with the partner city of Sibiu, Romania 'to the east' hosting the 2007 ECC, multiple representations and related activities constitute further examples of this phenomenon. Discourses in the mainstream Luxembourgish press, together with officially sanctioned visual displays – prominent in multiple sites in 2007, in particular Luxembourg city – work towards constructing a sense of consensus about the 2007 ECC. However, protest stickers against the 2007 ECC depicting pornographic images of the blue stag were prominent in Luxembourg city in spring 2007, which resonated with criticisms of the 2007 ECC in general conversation and in the columns of satirical newspapers. This provides yet another example of the lack of consensus concerning who or what the EU represents (cf. Armbruster et al. 2003). Furthermore, many individuals do not identify themselves as EU citizens in spite of the fact that they are officially categorized as such due to their status as passport holders of the various EU member-states.

What is striking in 2007 ECC representations is the implicit discourse of endangerment, which is perhaps best exemplified by the images depicting a 'warning' road sign bearing the blue stag. In this light, seemingly paradoxical representations no longer appear so paradoxical. The choice to foreground Germanic language varieties spoken by Transylvanian Saxons when there are fewer than 50,000 speakers in Transylvania (Rein 1997: 1471) may be regarded as an attempt to cast these varieties as endangered and in need of rescue. Informing the 2007 ECC materials as well as the overarching discourse of unity in diversity are the same essentialist biological and ecological metaphors underpinning language endangerment movements (cf. Heller and Duchêne 2007). Transylvanian Saxon language varieties, linguistic diversity, unity in diversity and perhaps even EU citizens themselves may *potentially* be perceived as in need of protection. If the blue stag is meant to be indexical of the mobile EU citizen, then the reference to 'without borders' most likely indexes the integration of fractal Europe. It remains the task of future research to continue to unpack these discourses and to expose the stakes bound up with them, not least how they affect the lives of real people in a changing Europe.

Acknowledgements

I would like to thank everyone at the Centre for Transnational Studies Research Seminar (November 2007) and the conference in Southampton (July 2007) who raised thought-provoking questions that led to me to reflect further on many aspects of this chapter.

I am also grateful to alta4 Geoinformatik AG (Trier) for their kind permission to reproduce Figure 12.1 and to Agnès Prüm for her assistance with formatting the image for this chapter. I remain fully responsible for any errors or shortcomings.

Notes

1. Five of the nine 2000 ECC host cities are in EU member-states: Avignon (France), Bologna (Italy), Brussels (Belgium), Santiago de Compostela (Spain) and Helsinki (Finland). In addition, two cities in European states outside the EU were selected – Bergen (Norway) and Reykjavik (Iceland) – as well as two cities that were at the time in EU candidate countries – Krakow (Poland) and Prague (Czech Republic). See Sassatelli (2002) for detailed discussion of the 2000 ECC.
2. Although scholars are in broad agreement that it is productive to differentiate theoretically between 'space' and 'place', they go about this in different ways. In this chapter, I follow Blommaert (2005: 222), who states that '[s]pace can be filled with all kinds of social, cultural, epistemic, and affective attributes. It then becomes "place", a particular space on which senses of belonging, property rights, and authority can be projected' (cf. Scollon and Scollon 2003).
3. Because these settlers did not originate (in large part) from Saxony, the denotation 'Transylvanian Saxons' may seem confusing; however, it is derived from the name attributed to speakers of Germanic language varieties who had settled previously in the medieval Kingdom of Hungary.
4. English translations of excerpts (1), (2), (4) and (5) are my own. Unlike many other 2007 ECC materials produced in the Grande Région, including the official website and programme, the brochure from which excerpts

(1), (4) and (5) originate was published in French and German with no English translations, probably due to spatial constraints. 2007 ECC materials designed in Romania were commonly published in Romanian and German with English translations.

5. On official EU websites, the marginalization of Romania is underlined by the fact that it is not always visibly present in cartographical representations, that is during earlier stages of EU consolidation.

References

Anderson, B. ([1983] 1991) *Imagined Communities: Reflections on the Origin and Spread of Nationalism* (London: Verso).

Armbruster, H., Rollo, C. and Meinhof, U. H. (2003) 'Imagining Europe: everyday narratives in European border communities', *Journal of Ethnic and Migration Studies* 29(5), 885–99.

Baár, M. and Ritivoi, A. D. (2006) 'The Tranyslvanian Babel: negotiating national identity through language in a disputed territory', *Language and Communication* 26(3/4), 203–17.

Blommaert, J. (2005) *Discourse: A Critical Introduction* (Cambridge: Cambridge University Press).

Blommaert, J. and Verschueren, J. (1992) 'The role of language in European nationalist ideologies', *Pragmatics* 2(3), 355–75.

Boia, L. ([2001] 2006) *Romania: Borderland of Europe*, trans. James Christian Brown (London: Reaktion Books).

Brubaker, R., Feischmidt, M., Fox, J. and Grancea, L. (2006) *Nationalist Politics and Everyday Ethnicity in a Transylvanian Town* (Princeton, NJ: Princeton University Press).

Caliendo, G. (2007) 'Communication and identity values in EU discourse', conference paper presented at Language, Discourse and Identity in Central Europe (University of Southampton).

Coupland, N. (2003) 'Introduction: sociolinguistics and globalisation', *Journal of Sociolinguistics* 7(4), 465–73.

Davies, W.V. and Langer, N. (2006) *The Making of Bad Language: Lay Linguistic Stigmatisations in German: Past and Present* (Frankfurt/Main: Peter Lang).

Delanty, G. and Rumford, C. (2005) *Rethinking Europe: Social Theory and the Implications of Europeanization* (London: Routledge).

Dietz, B. (2000) 'German and Jewish migration from the former Soviet Union to Germany: background, trends and implications', *Journal of Ethnic and Migration Studies* 26(4), 635–52.

Duchêne, A. and Heller, M. (eds) (2007) *Discourses of Endangerment: Ideology and Interest in the Defence of Languages* (London: Continuum).

Elspaß S., Langer, N., Scharloth, J. and Vandenbussche, W. (eds) (2007) *Germanic Language Histories 'from Below' (1700–2000)* (Berlin: Walter de Gruyter).

Featherstone, M. and Lash, S. (eds) (1999) *Spaces of Culture: City, Nation, World* (London: Sage).

Fehlen, F. (2007) 'Luxemburg und Siebenbürgen 2007 (STADE Working Paper)', http://wwwen.uni.lu/recherche/flshase/stade_1993_2007/publications. Accessed 1 July 2008.

Feld, S. and Basso, K. H. (eds) (1996a) *Senses of Place* (Santa Fe, NM: School of American Research Press).

Feld, S. and Basso, K. H. (1996b) 'Introduction', in Feld and Basso (1996a), 3–11.

Gal, S. (2006) 'Migration, minorities and multilingualism: language ideologies in Europe', in Mar-Molinero and Stevenson (2006), 13–27.

Gee, J. P. ([1999] 2005) *An Introduction to Discourse Analysis: Theory and Method* (London: Routledge).

Goebl, H., Nelde, P. H., Stary, Z. and Wölck, W. (eds) (1997) *Kontaktlinguistik: Ein internationales Handbuch zeitgenössischer Forschung (2. Halbband)* (Berlin: Walter de Gruyter).

Harvey, D. (1989) *The Condition of Postmodernity* (Oxford: Basil Blackwell).

Heller, M. and Duchêne, A. (2007) 'Discourses of endangerment: sociolinguistics, globalization and social order', in Duchêne and Heller (2007), 1–13.

Hermes, M. (2002) 'Gastfreundlich, geschichtsträchtig und ein bisschen luxemburgisch…', *Luxemburger Wort*, 31 July, p. 16.

Hobsbawm, E. and Ranger, T. (eds) (1983) *The Invention of Tradition* (Cambridge: Cambridge University Press).

Hoffmann, J-P. (1996) 'Beyond the boundaries: Lëtzebuergesch outside the Grand Duchy', in Newton (1996), 157–79.

Horner, K. (2005) 'Reimagining the nation: discourses of language purism in Luxembourg', in Langer and Davies (2005), 166–85.

Horner, K. (2007) 'Language and Luxembourgish national identity: ideologies of hybridity and purity in the past and present', in Elspaß, Langer, Scharloth and Vandenbussche (2007), 363–78.

Irvine, J.T. and Gal, S. (2000) 'Language ideology and linguistic differentiation', in Kroskrity (2000), 35–83.

Jenkins, R. (1997) *Rethinking Ethnicity: Arguments and Explorations* (London: Sage).

Johnstone, B. (2002) *Discourse Analysis* (Oxford: Blackwell).

Kroskrity, P.V. (ed.) (2000) *Regimes of Language: Ideologies, Polities, and Identities* (Santa Fe, NM: School of American Research Press).

Langer, N. and Davies, W. V. (eds) (2005) *Linguistic Purism in the Germanic Languages* (Berlin: Walter de Gruyter).

Liotta, P.H. (2005) 'Imagining Europe: symbolic geography and the future', *Mediterranean Quarterly* 16(3), 67–85.

Luxembourg et grande région capitale européenne de la culture (LGRCEC) (2007a) ASBL (ed.) 'Sibiu: Building bridges in an expanding Europe', http://www.luxembourg2007.org/GB/sibiu.php. Accessed 1 November 2007.

Luxembourg et grande région capitale européenne de la culture (LGRCEC) (2007b) ASBL (ed.) *Luxembourg et grande région capitale européenne de la culture 2007: Programme officiel* (Luxembourg: Imprimerie Centrale, Fournisseur Officiel).

Makoni, S. and Pennycook, A. (eds) (2007a) *Disinventing and Reconstituting Languages* (Clevedon: Multilingual Matters).

Makoni, S. and Pennycook, A. (2007b) 'Disinventing and reconstituting languages', in Makoni and Pennycook (2007a), 1–41.

Mar-Molinero, C. and Stevenson, P. (eds) (2006) *Language Ideologies, Policies and Practices: Language and the Future of Europe* (Basingstoke: Palgrave Macmillan).

Massey, D. and Jess, P. (eds) (1995) *A Place in the World? Places, Cultures and Globalization* (Oxford: Oxford University Press).

260   *Kristine Horner*

May, S. (2001) *Language and Minority Rights: Ethnicity, Nationalism and the Politics of Language* (Harlow: Longman).

Mitchell, W. J. T. (ed.) (1981) *On Narrative* (Chicago: University of Chicago Press).

Mummert, S. (1995) 'Sprachpflege bei den Siebenbürger Sachsen', in *Muttersprache* 105(1), 31–54.

Newton, G. (ed.) (1996) *Luxembourg and Lëtzebuergesch: Language and Communication at the Crossroads of Europe* (Oxford: Clarendon Press).

Pavlenko, A. and Blackledge, A. (eds) (2004a) *Negotiation of Identities in Multilingual Contexts* (Clevedon: Multilingual Matters).

Pavlenko, A. and Blackledge, A. (2004b) 'Introduction: new theoretical approaches to the study of negotiation of identities in multilingual contexts', in Pavlenko and Blackledge (2004a), 1–33.

Rein, K. (1997) 'Rumänisch-Deutsch', in Goebl et al. (1997), 1470–7.

Rose, G. (1995) 'Place and identity: a sense of place', in Massey and Jess (1995), 87–132.

Sassatelli, M. (2002) 'Imagined Europe: the shaping of a European cultural identity through EU cultural policy', *European Journal of Social Theory* 5(4), 435–51.

Scollon, R. and Scollon, S. (2003) *Discourses in Place: Language in the Material World* (London: Routledge).

Shapiro, M. J. (1999) 'Triumphalist geographies', in Featherstone and Lash (1999), 159–74.

Stråth, B. (2006) 'Future of Europe', in *Journal of Language and Politics* 5(3), 427–48.

Studio Martial Damblant (2007) *Luxemburg und Grossregion: Kulturhauptstadt Europas* (brochure) (Metz: Studio Martial Damblant).

Weber-Newth, I. (1995) 'Ethnic Germans come "home to the fatherland"', *Debatte: Journal of Contemporary Central and Eastern Europe* 3(1), 126–42.

White, H. (1981) 'The value of narrativity in the representation of reality', in Mitchell (1981), 1–23.

Index

Note: Page numbers in **bold** refer to Tables; those in *italic* refer to Figures